GARFIELD
WHAT LEFTOVERS?

BY JIM DAVIS

Ballantine Books • New York

A Ballantine Books Trade Paperback Original

Copyright © 2021 by PAWS, Inc. All Rights Reserved. "GARFIELD" and the GARFIELD characters are trademarks of PAWS, Inc.
Based on the Garfield® characters created by Jim Davis

Published in the United States by Ballantine Books, an imprint of Random House,
a division of Penguin Random House LLC, New York.

BALLANTINE and the HOUSE colophon are registered trademarks of Penguin Random House LLC.

NICKELODEON is a Trademark of Viacom International, Inc.

All of the comics in this work have been previously published.

ISBN 978-0-593-15644-5
Ebook ISBN 978-0-593-15645-2

Printed in China on acid-free paper

randomhousebooks.com

9 8 7 6 5 4 3 2

GARFIELD'S STRESS-BUSTING TIPS

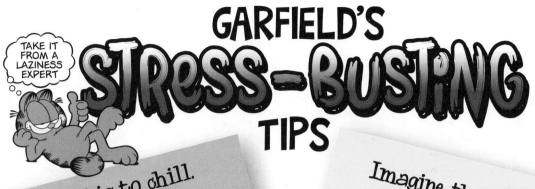

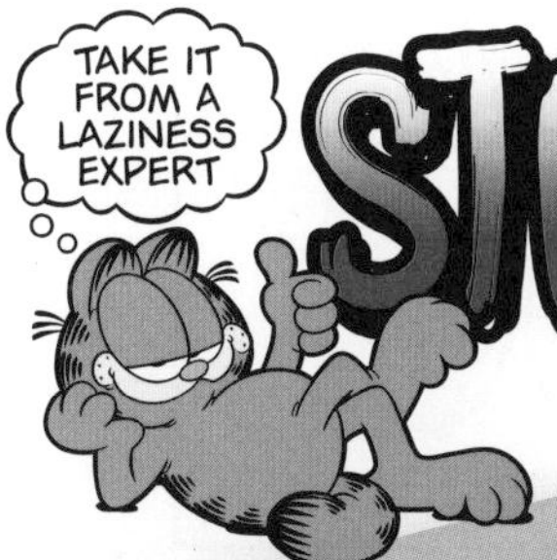
TAKE IT FROM A LAZINESS EXPERT

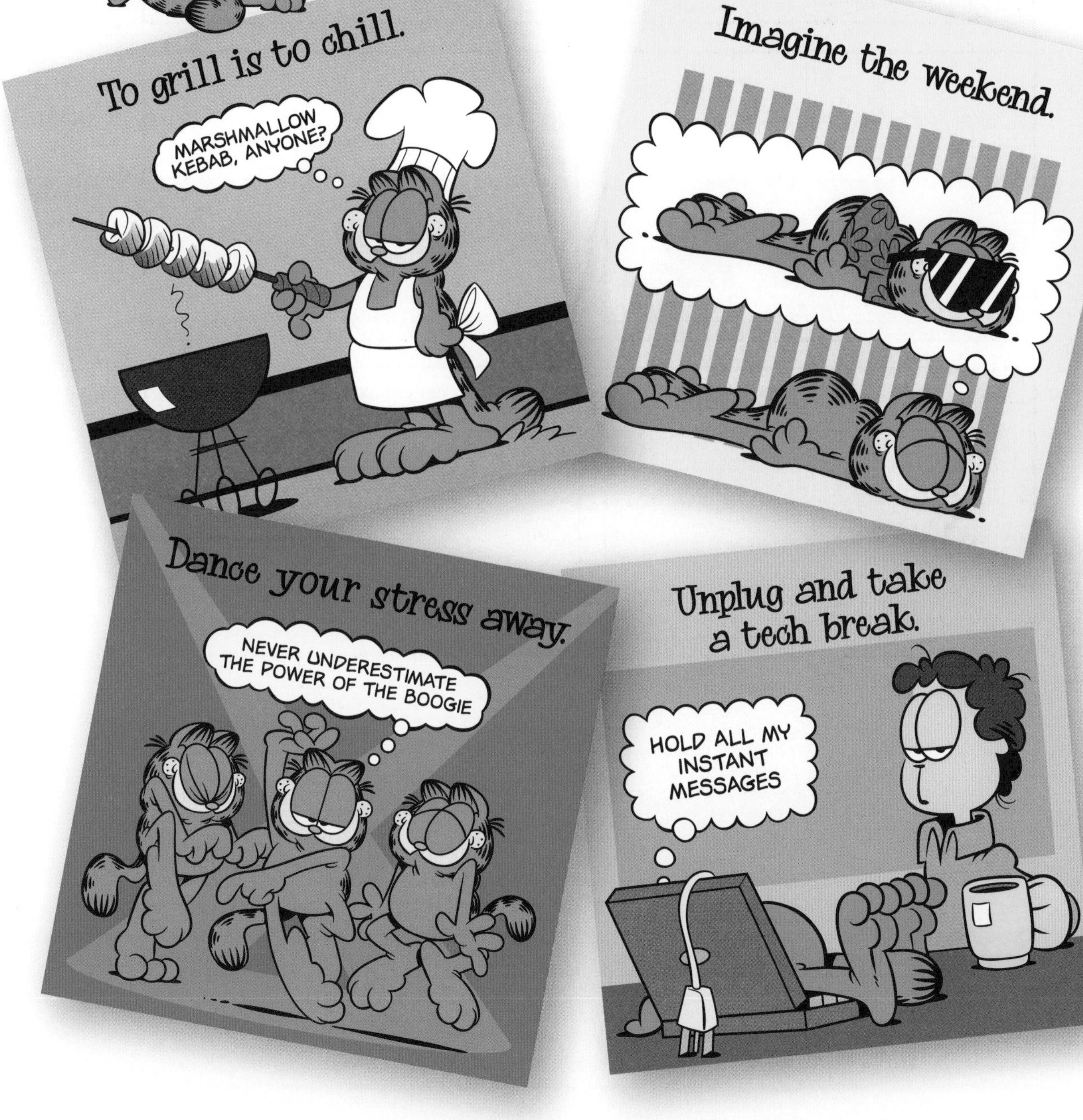
To grill is to chill.
MARSHMALLOW KEBAB, ANYONE?
Imagine the weekend.
Dance your stress away.
NEVER UNDERESTIMATE THE POWER OF THE BOOGIE
Unplug and take a tech break.
HOLD ALL MY INSTANT MESSAGES

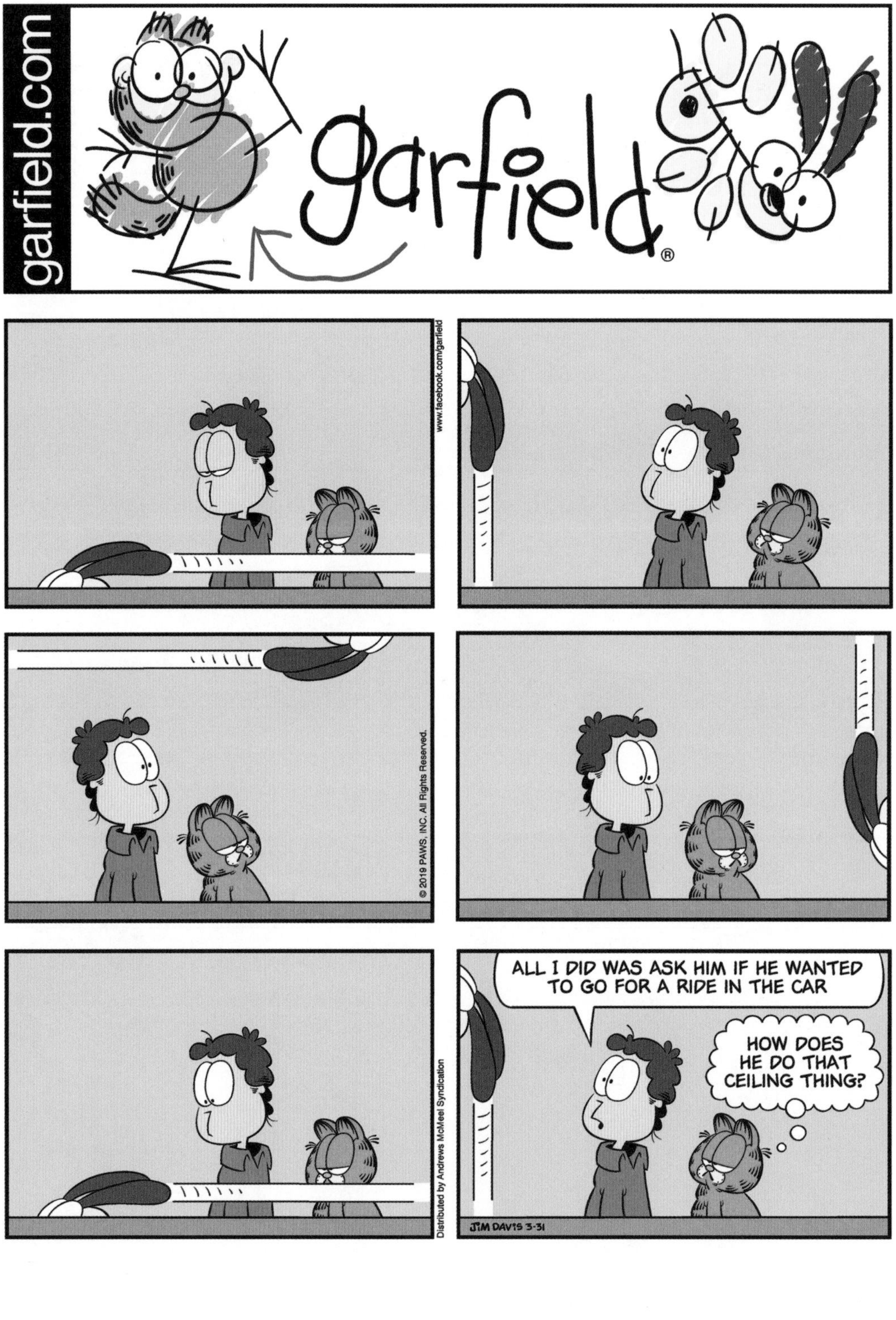
garfield.com
garfield®
www.facebook.com/garfield
© 2019 PAWS, INC. All Rights Reserved.
ALL I DID WAS ASK HIM IF HE WANTED TO GO FOR A RIDE IN THE CAR
HOW DOES HE DO THAT CEILING THING?
Distributed by Andrews McMeel Syndication
JIM DAVIS 3-31

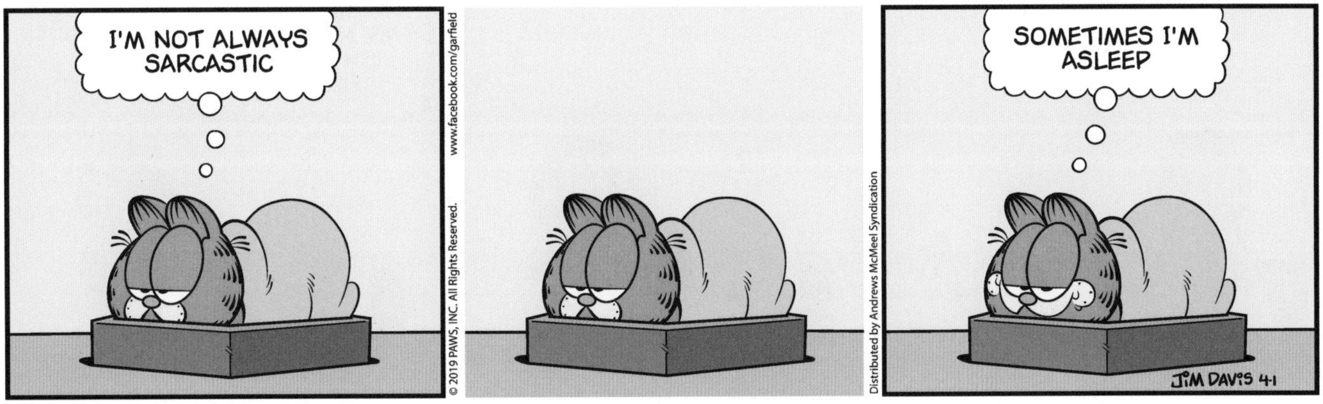
I'M NOT ALWAYS SARCASTIC
SOMETIMES I'M ASLEEP
JIM DAVIS 4-1

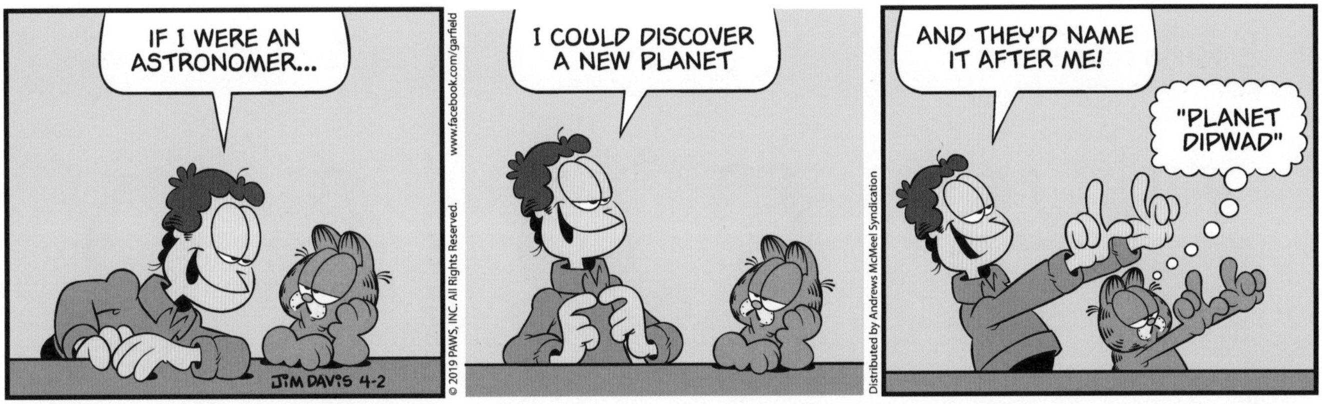
IF I WERE AN ASTRONOMER...
JIM DAVIS 4-2
I COULD DISCOVER A NEW PLANET
AND THEY'D NAME IT AFTER ME!
"PLANET DIPWAD"

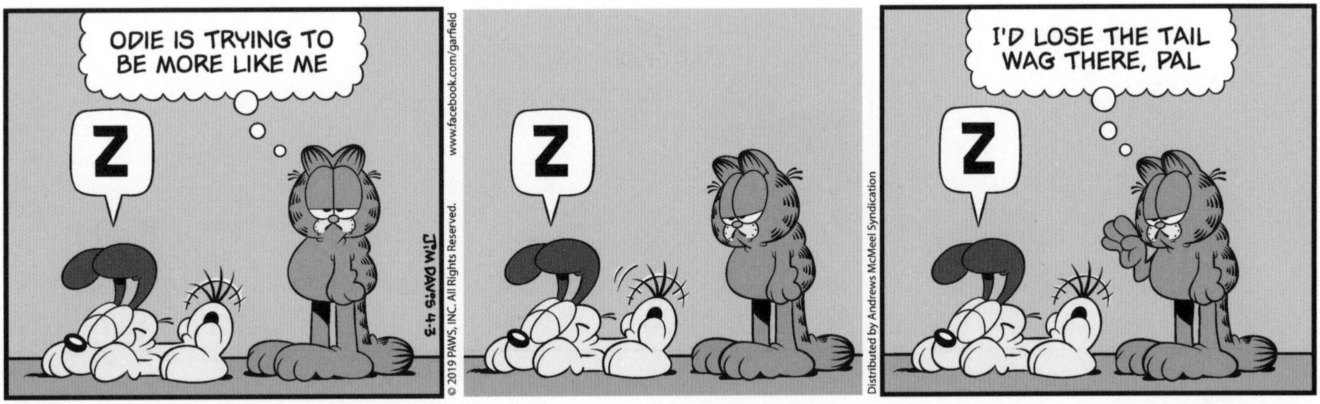
ODIE IS TRYING TO BE MORE LIKE ME
Z
JIM DAVIS 4-3
Z
Z
I'D LOSE THE TAIL WAG THERE, PAL

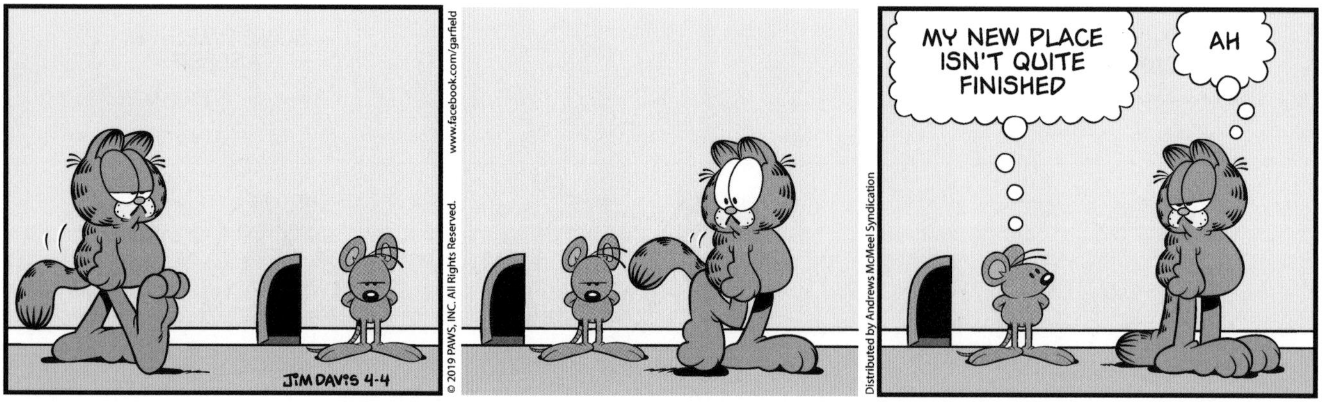
JIM DAVIS 4-4
MY NEW PLACE ISN'T QUITE FINISHED
AH

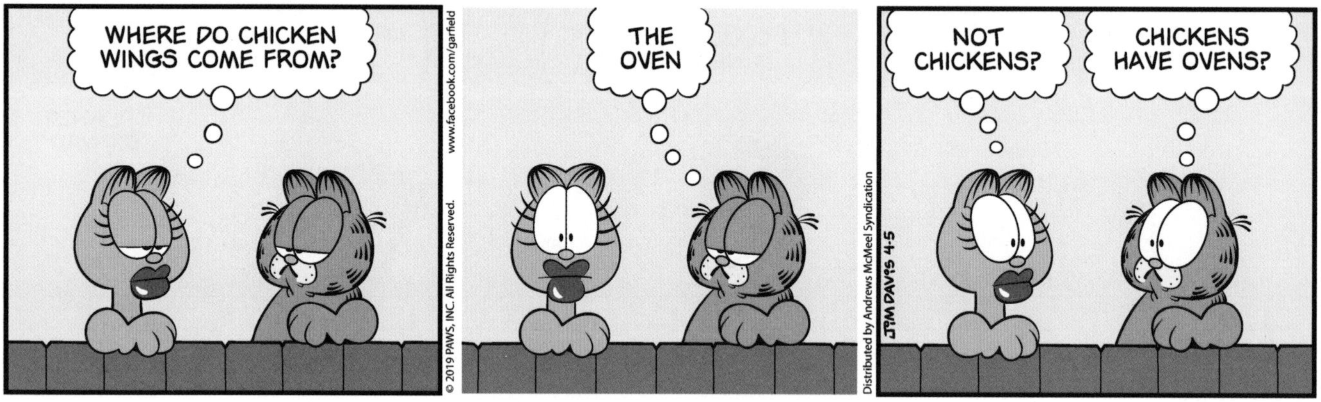
WHERE DO CHICKEN WINGS COME FROM?
THE OVEN
JIM DAVIS 4-5
NOT CHICKENS?
CHICKENS HAVE OVENS?

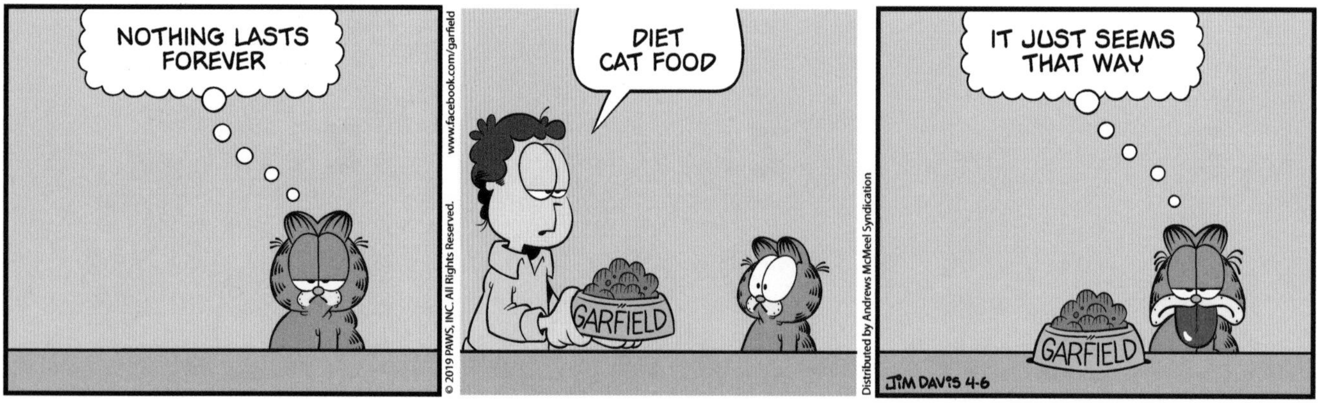
NOTHING LASTS FOREVER
DIET CAT FOOD
GARFIELD
IT JUST SEEMS THAT WAY
GARFIELD
JIM DAVIS 4-6

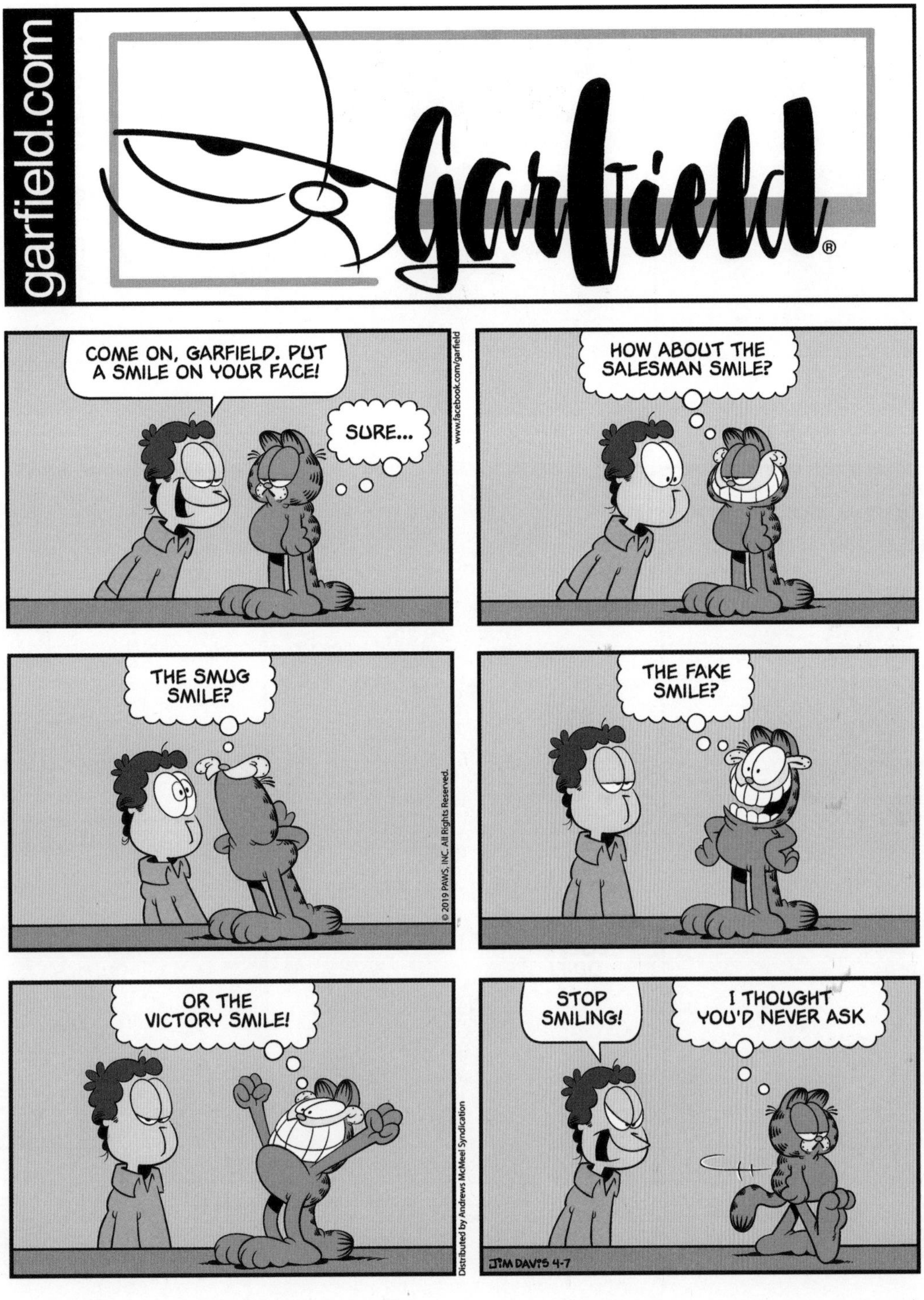
garfield.com
Garfield®
COME ON, GARFIELD. PUT A SMILE ON YOUR FACE!
SURE...
www.facebook.com/garfield
HOW ABOUT THE SALESMAN SMILE?
THE SMUG SMILE?
© 2019 PAWS, INC. All Rights Reserved.
THE FAKE SMILE?
OR THE VICTORY SMILE!
Distributed by Andrews McMeel Syndication
STOP SMILING!
I THOUGHT YOU'D NEVER ASK
JIM DAVIS 4-7

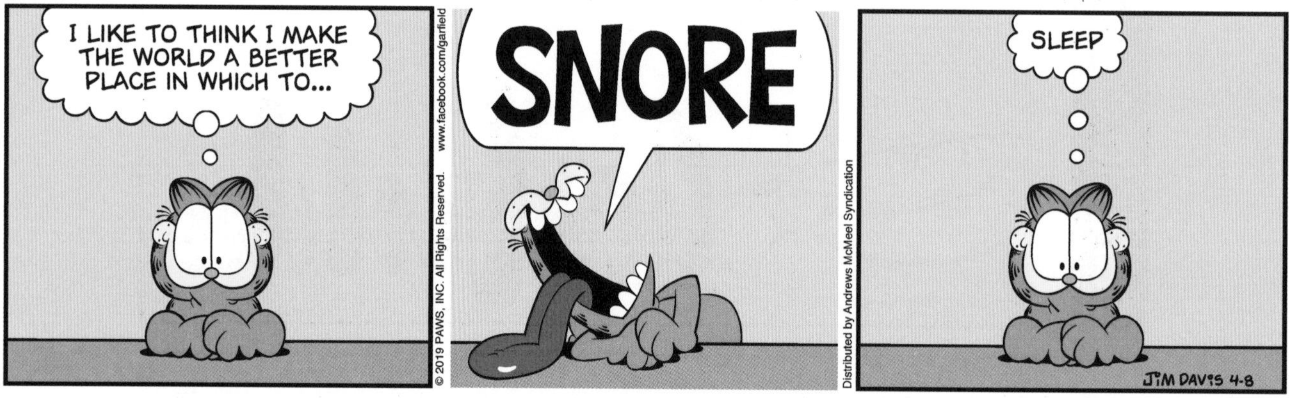
I LIKE TO THINK I MAKE THE WORLD A BETTER PLACE IN WHICH TO...
SNORE
SLEEP
JIM DAVIS 4-8
© 2019 PAWS, INC. All Rights Reserved. www.facebook.com/garfield
Distributed by Andrews McMeel Syndication

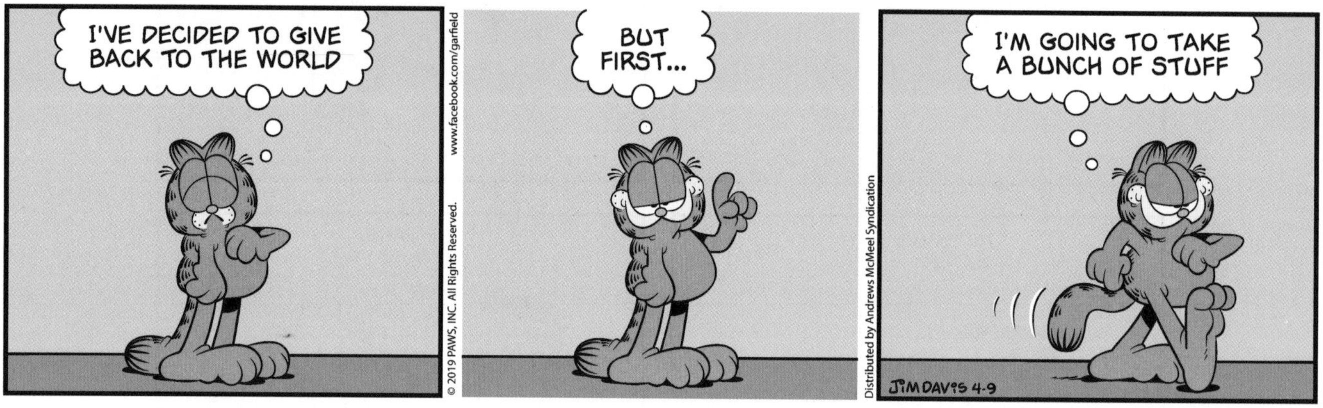
I'VE DECIDED TO GIVE BACK TO THE WORLD
BUT FIRST...
I'M GOING TO TAKE A BUNCH OF STUFF
JIM DAVIS 4-9
© 2019 PAWS, INC. All Rights Reserved. www.facebook.com/garfield
Distributed by Andrews McMeel Syndication

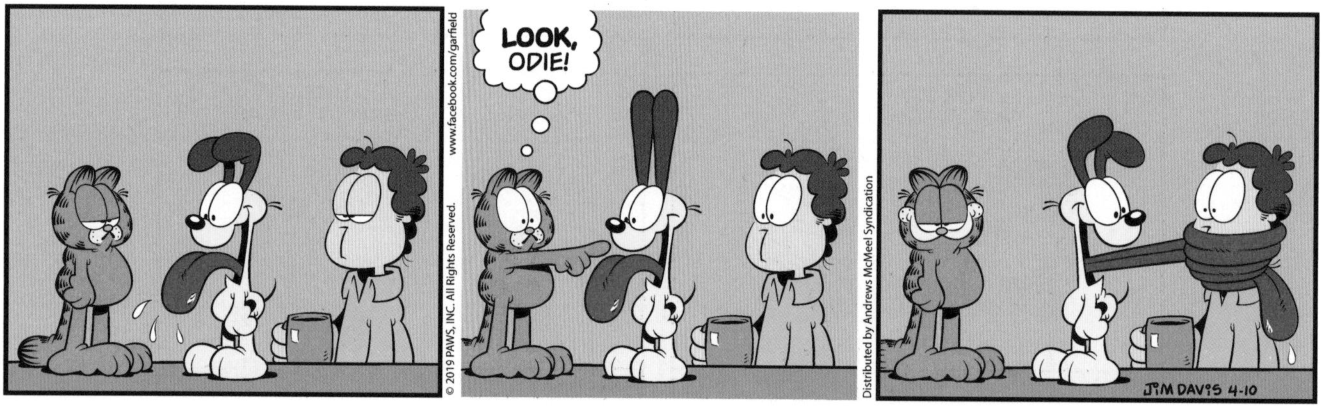
LOOK, ODIE!
JIM DAVIS 4-10
© 2019 PAWS, INC. All Rights Reserved. www.facebook.com/garfield
Distributed by Andrews McMeel Syndication

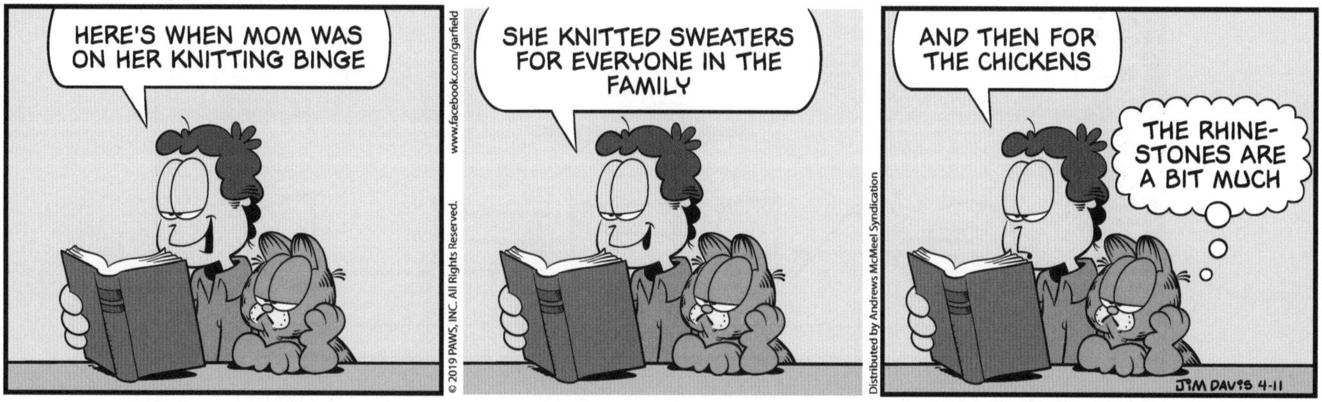
HERE'S WHEN MOM WAS ON HER KNITTING BINGE
© 2019 PAWS, INC. All Rights Reserved. www.facebook.com/garfield
SHE KNITTED SWEATERS FOR EVERYONE IN THE FAMILY
Distributed by Andrews McMeel Syndication
AND THEN FOR THE CHICKENS
THE RHINE-STONES ARE A BIT MUCH
JIM DAVIS 4-11

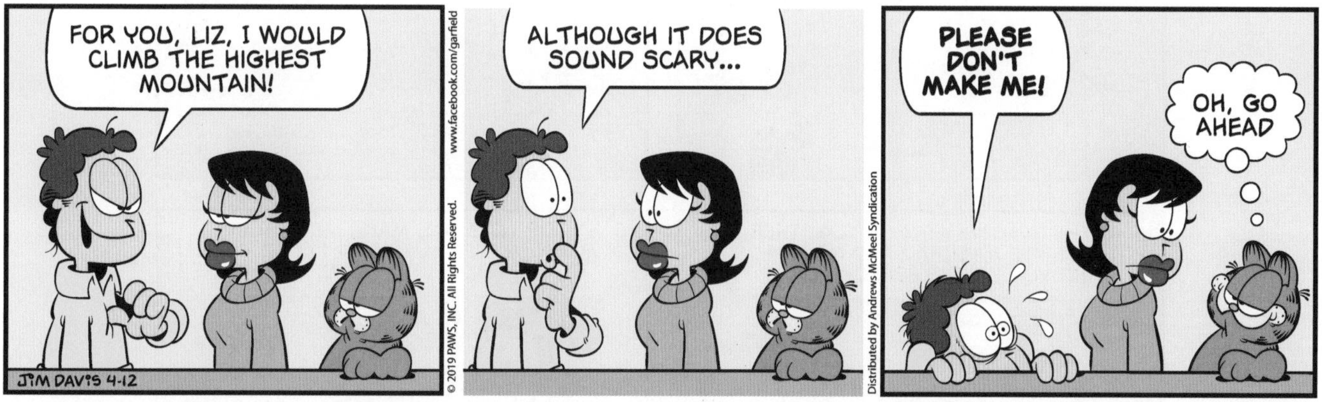
FOR YOU, LIZ, I WOULD CLIMB THE HIGHEST MOUNTAIN!
JIM DAVIS 4-12
© 2019 PAWS, INC. All Rights Reserved. www.facebook.com/garfield
ALTHOUGH IT DOES SOUND SCARY...
Distributed by Andrews McMeel Syndication
PLEASE DON'T MAKE ME!
OH, GO AHEAD

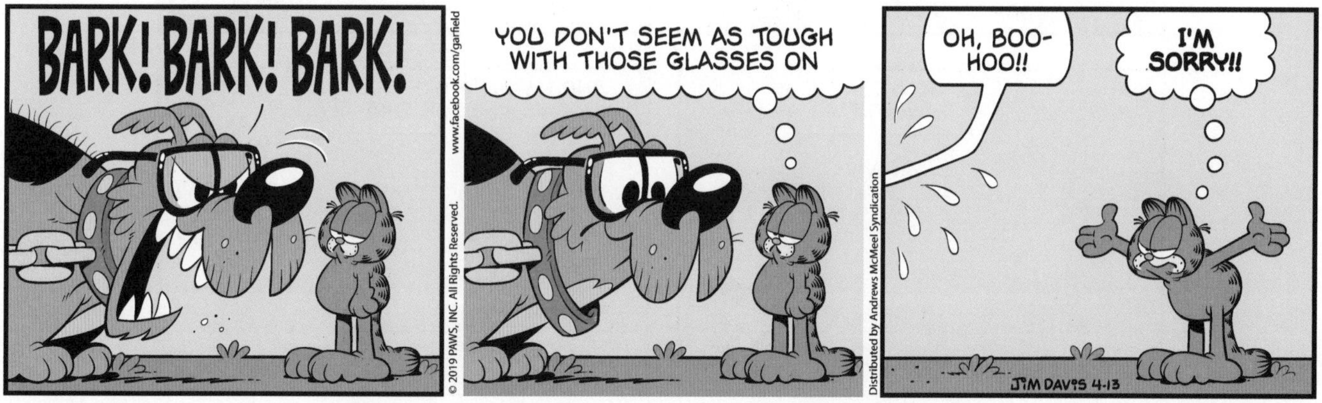
BARK! BARK! BARK!
© 2019 PAWS, INC. All Rights Reserved. www.facebook.com/garfield
YOU DON'T SEEM AS TOUGH WITH THOSE GLASSES ON
Distributed by Andrews McMeel Syndication
OH, BOO-HOO!!
I'M SORRY!!
JIM DAVIS 4-13

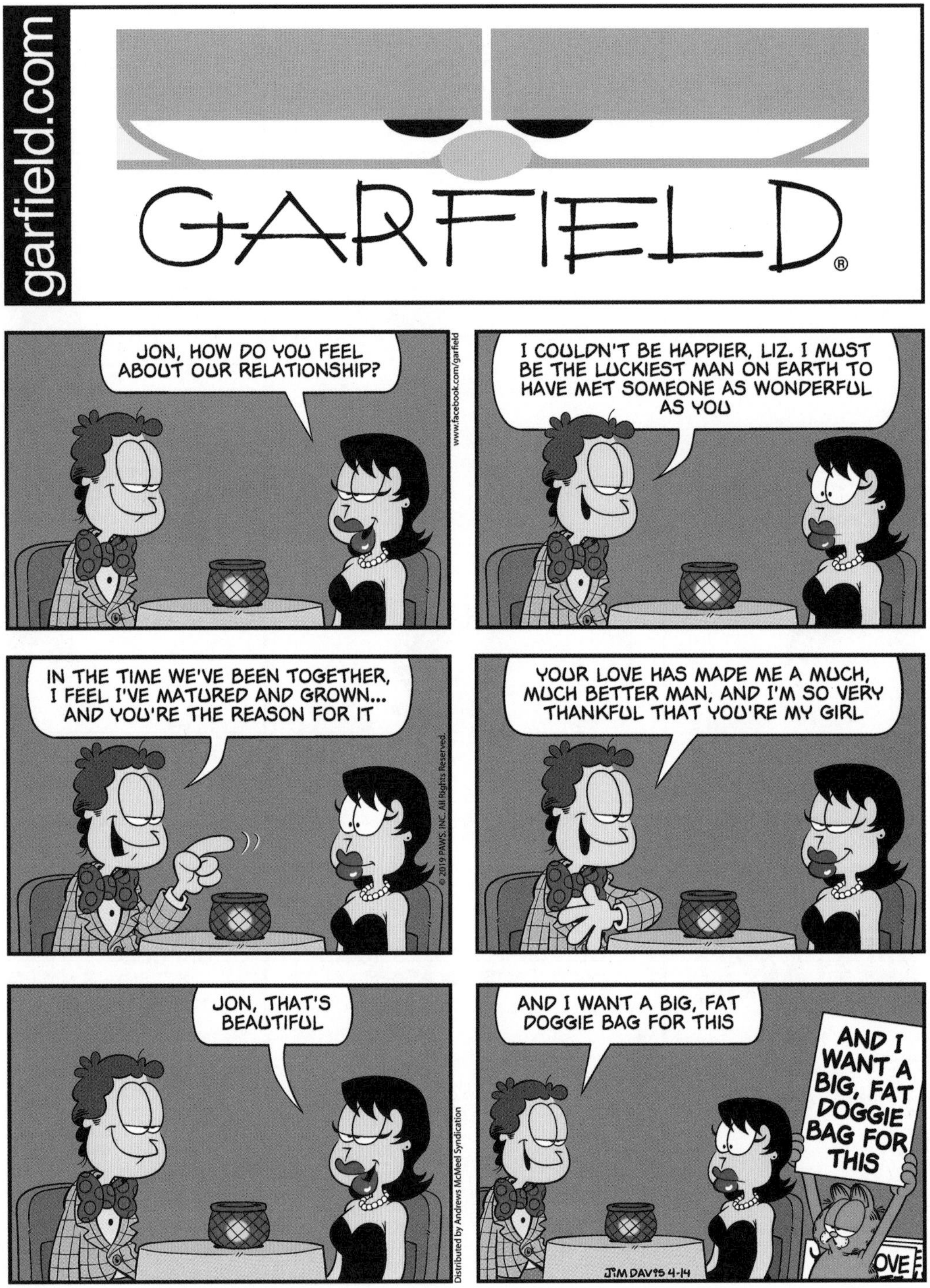
garfield.com
GARFIELD
JON, HOW DO YOU FEEL ABOUT OUR RELATIONSHIP?
www.facebook.com/garfield
I COULDN'T BE HAPPIER, LIZ. I MUST BE THE LUCKIEST MAN ON EARTH TO HAVE MET SOMEONE AS WONDERFUL AS YOU
IN THE TIME WE'VE BEEN TOGETHER, I FEEL I'VE MATURED AND GROWN... AND YOU'RE THE REASON FOR IT
© 2019 PAWS, INC. All Rights Reserved.
YOUR LOVE HAS MADE ME A MUCH, MUCH BETTER MAN, AND I'M SO VERY THANKFUL THAT YOU'RE MY GIRL
JON, THAT'S BEAUTIFUL
Distributed by Andrews McMeel Syndication
AND I WANT A BIG, FAT DOGGIE BAG FOR THIS
AND I WANT A BIG, FAT DOGGIE BAG FOR THIS
JIM DAVIS 4-14

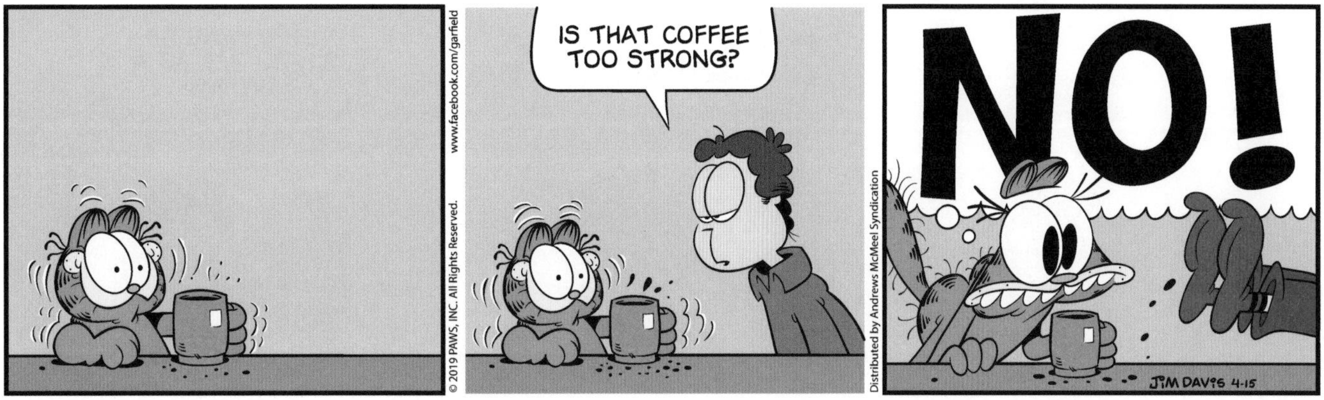
IS THAT COFFEE TOO STRONG?
NO!
JIM DAVIS 4-15
© 2019 PAWS, INC. All Rights Reserved. www.facebook.com/garfield
Distributed by Andrews McMeel Syndication

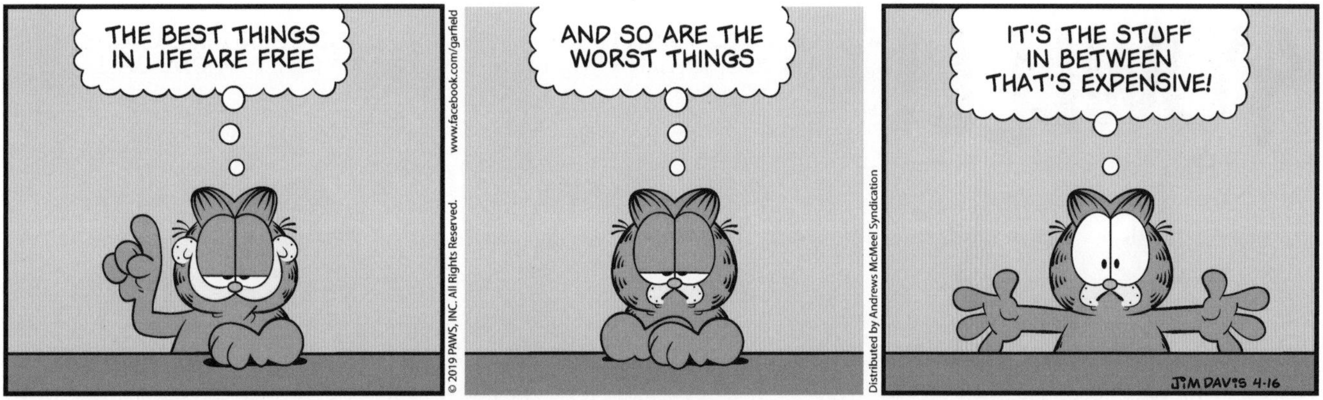
THE BEST THINGS IN LIFE ARE FREE
AND SO ARE THE WORST THINGS
IT'S THE STUFF IN BETWEEN THAT'S EXPENSIVE!
JIM DAVIS 4-16
© 2019 PAWS, INC. All Rights Reserved. www.facebook.com/garfield
Distributed by Andrews McMeel Syndication

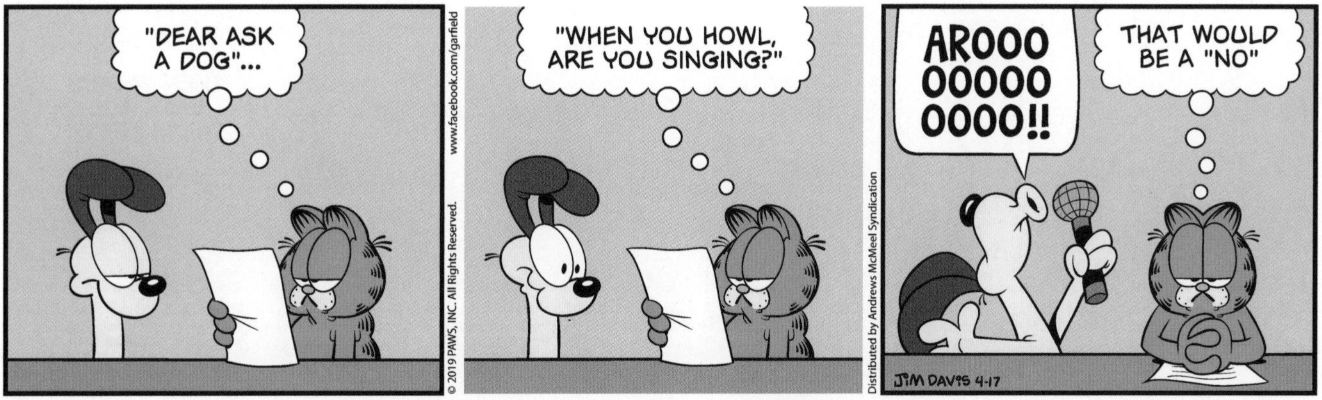
"DEAR ASK A DOG"...
"WHEN YOU HOWL, ARE YOU SINGING?"
AROOO OOOOO OOOO!!
THAT WOULD BE A "NO"
JIM DAVIS 4-17
© 2019 PAWS, INC. All Rights Reserved. www.facebook.com/garfield
Distributed by Andrews McMeel Syndication

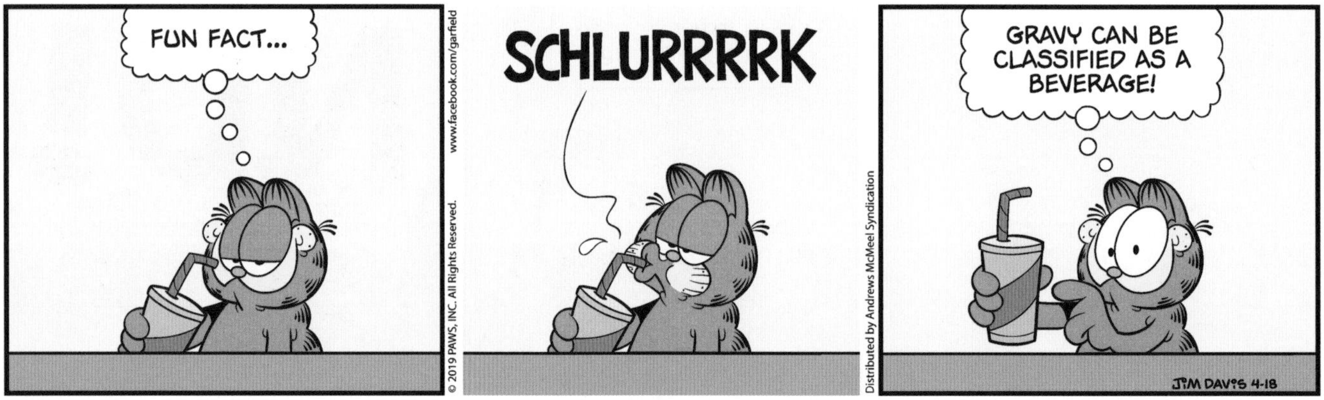
FUN FACT...
SCHLURRRRK
GRAVY CAN BE CLASSIFIED AS A BEVERAGE!
JIM DAVIS 4-18
© 2019 PAWS, INC. All Rights Reserved. www.facebook.com/garfield
Distributed by Andrews McMeel Syndication

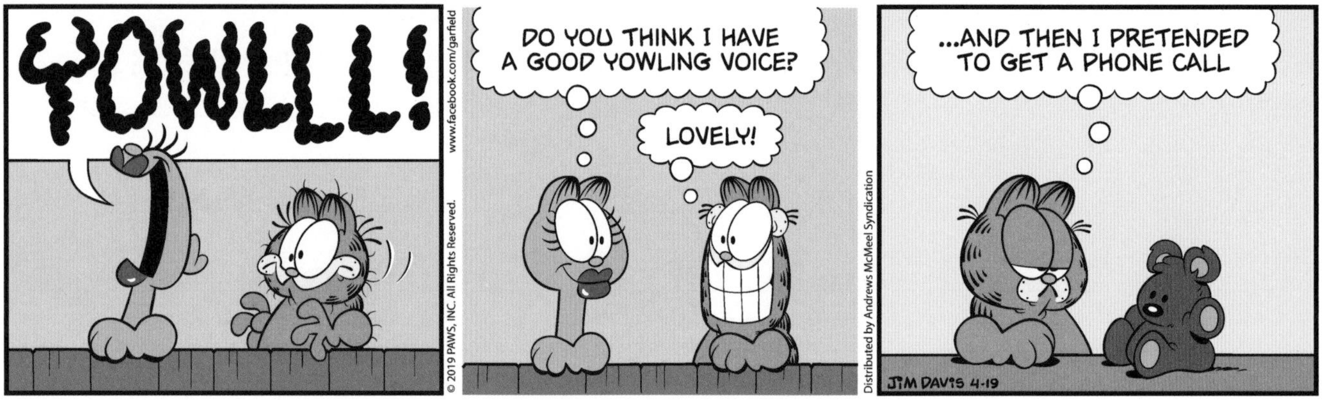
YOWLLL!
DO YOU THINK I HAVE A GOOD YOWLING VOICE?
LOVELY!
...AND THEN I PRETENDED TO GET A PHONE CALL
JIM DAVIS 4-19
© 2019 PAWS, INC. All Rights Reserved. www.facebook.com/garfield
Distributed by Andrews McMeel Syndication

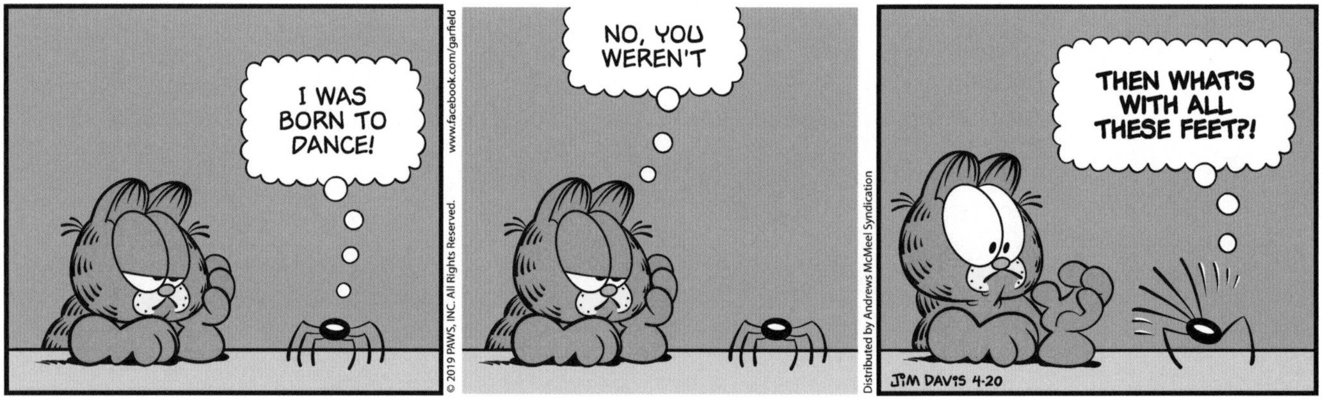
I WAS BORN TO DANCE!
NO, YOU WEREN'T
THEN WHAT'S WITH ALL THESE FEET?!
JIM DAVIS 4-20
© 2019 PAWS, INC. All Rights Reserved. www.facebook.com/garfield
Distributed by Andrews McMeel Syndication

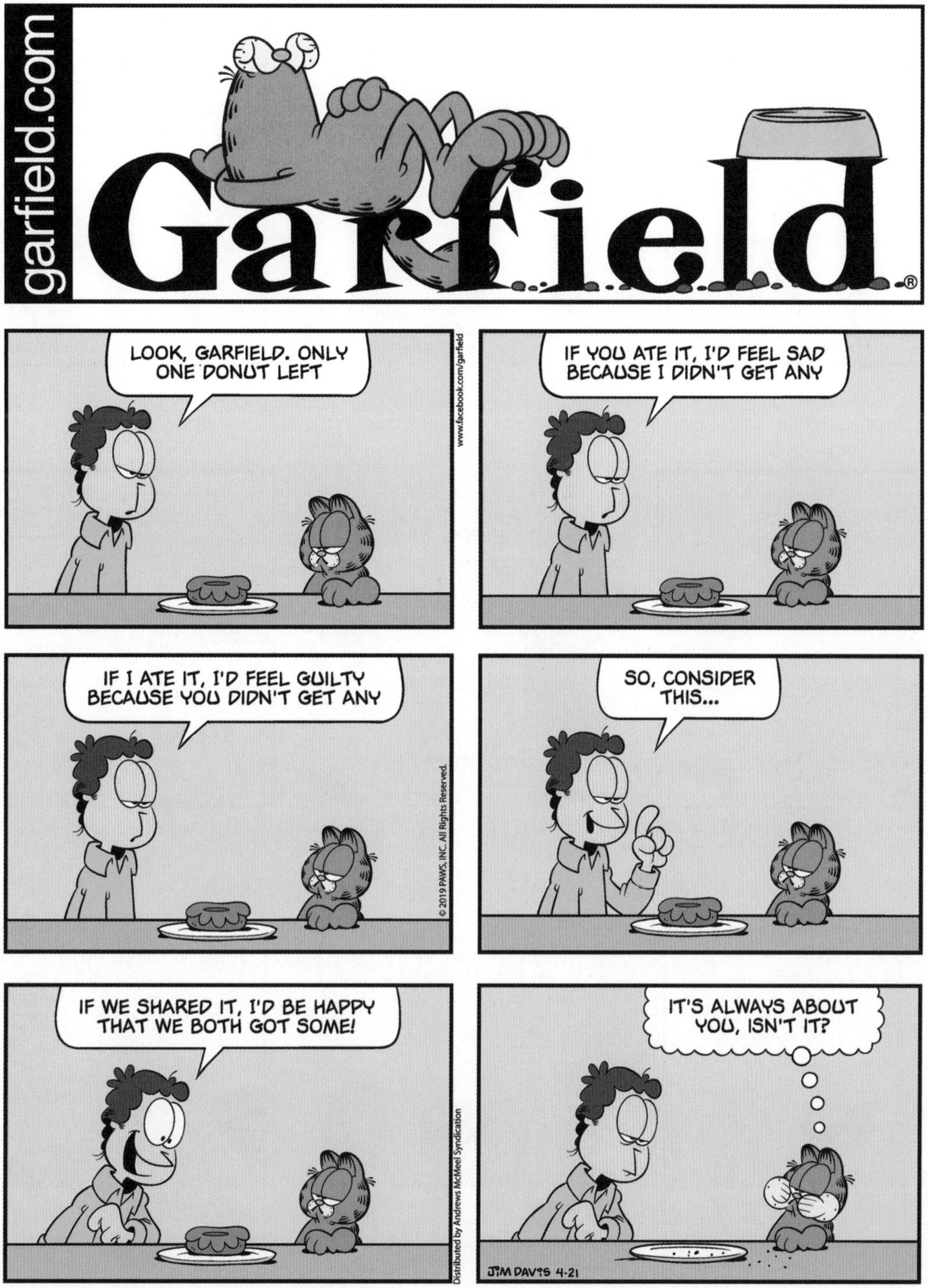
garfield.com
Garfield
LOOK, GARFIELD. ONLY ONE DONUT LEFT
IF YOU ATE IT, I'D FEEL SAD BECAUSE I DIDN'T GET ANY
IF I ATE IT, I'D FEEL GUILTY BECAUSE YOU DIDN'T GET ANY
SO, CONSIDER THIS...
IF WE SHARED IT, I'D BE HAPPY THAT WE BOTH GOT SOME!
IT'S ALWAYS ABOUT YOU, ISN'T IT?
JIM DAVIS 4-21
www.facebook.com/garfield
© 2019 PAWS, INC. All Rights Reserved.
Distributed by Andrews McMeel Syndication

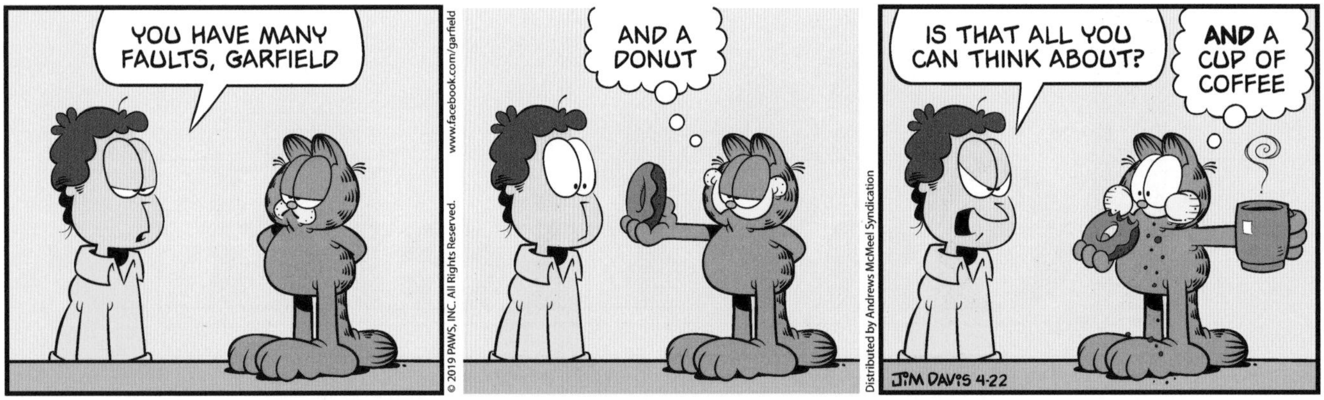
YOU HAVE MANY FAULTS, GARFIELD
AND A DONUT
IS THAT ALL YOU CAN THINK ABOUT?
AND A CUP OF COFFEE
JIM DAVIS 4-22
© 2019 PAWS, INC. All Rights Reserved. www.facebook.com/garfield
Distributed by Andrews McMeel Syndication

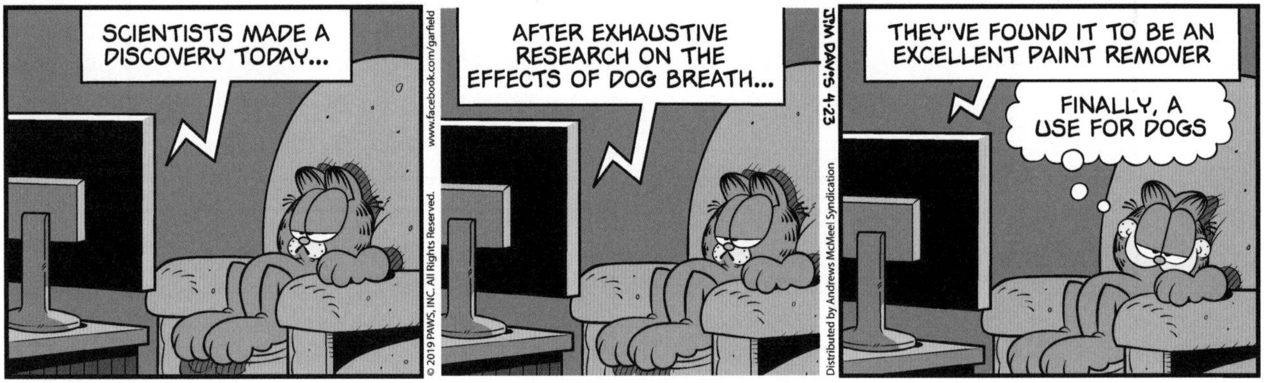
SCIENTISTS MADE A DISCOVERY TODAY...
AFTER EXHAUSTIVE RESEARCH ON THE EFFECTS OF DOG BREATH...
THEY'VE FOUND IT TO BE AN EXCELLENT PAINT REMOVER
FINALLY, A USE FOR DOGS
JIM DAVIS 4-23
© 2019 PAWS, INC. All Rights Reserved. www.facebook.com/garfield
Distributed by Andrews McMeel Syndication

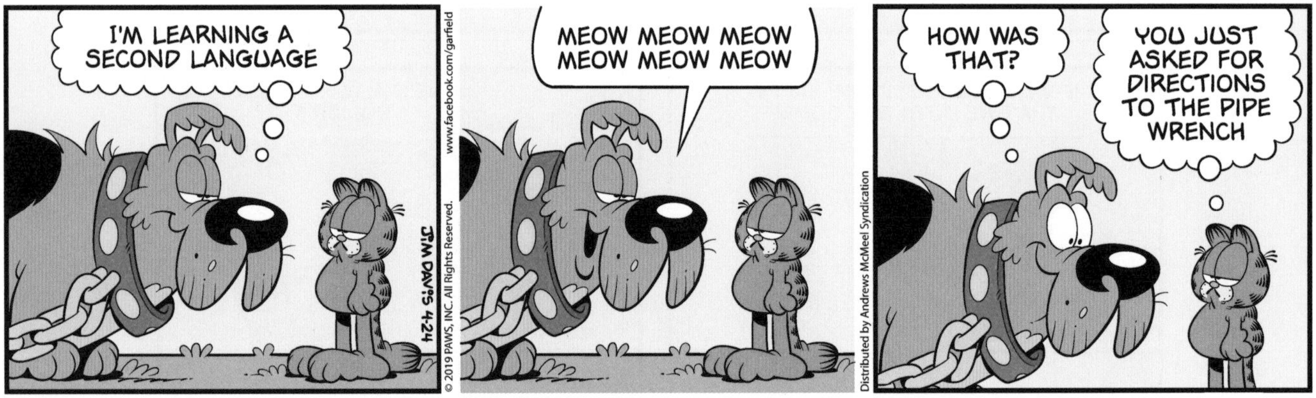
I'M LEARNING A SECOND LANGUAGE
MEOW MEOW MEOW MEOW MEOW MEOW
HOW WAS THAT?
YOU JUST ASKED FOR DIRECTIONS TO THE PIPE WRENCH
JIM DAVIS 4-24
© 2019 PAWS, INC. All Rights Reserved. www.facebook.com/garfield
Distributed by Andrews McMeel Syndication

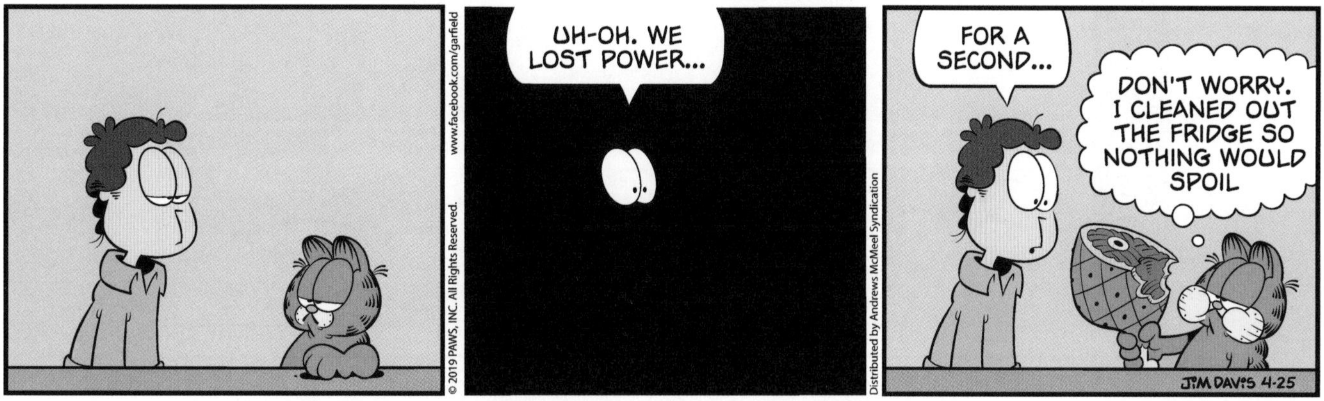
UH-OH. WE LOST POWER...
FOR A SECOND...
DON'T WORRY. I CLEANED OUT THE FRIDGE SO NOTHING WOULD SPOIL
© 2019 PAWS, INC. All Rights Reserved.
www.facebook.com/garfield
Distributed by Andrews McMeel Syndication
JIM DAVIS 4-25

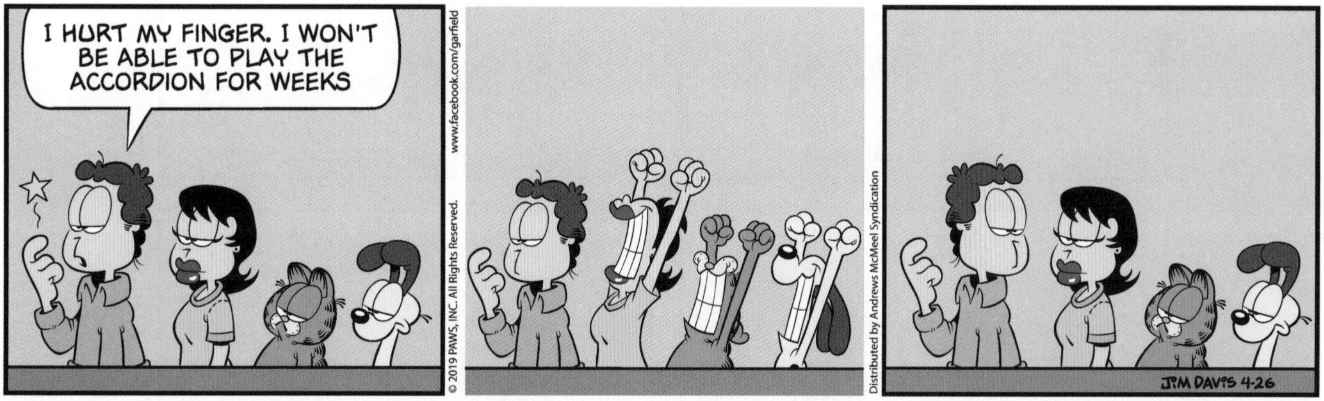
I HURT MY FINGER. I WON'T BE ABLE TO PLAY THE ACCORDION FOR WEEKS
© 2019 PAWS, INC. All Rights Reserved.
www.facebook.com/garfield
Distributed by Andrews McMeel Syndication
JIM DAVIS 4-26

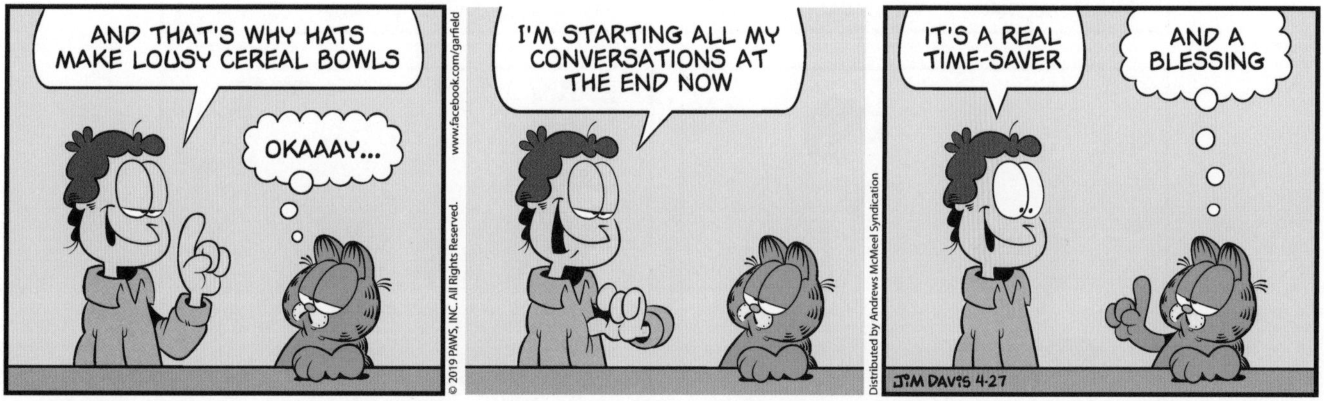
AND THAT'S WHY HATS MAKE LOUSY CEREAL BOWLS
OKAAAY...
I'M STARTING ALL MY CONVERSATIONS AT THE END NOW
IT'S A REAL TIME-SAVER
AND A BLESSING
© 2019 PAWS, INC. All Rights Reserved.
www.facebook.com/garfield
Distributed by Andrews McMeel Syndication
JIM DAVIS 4-27

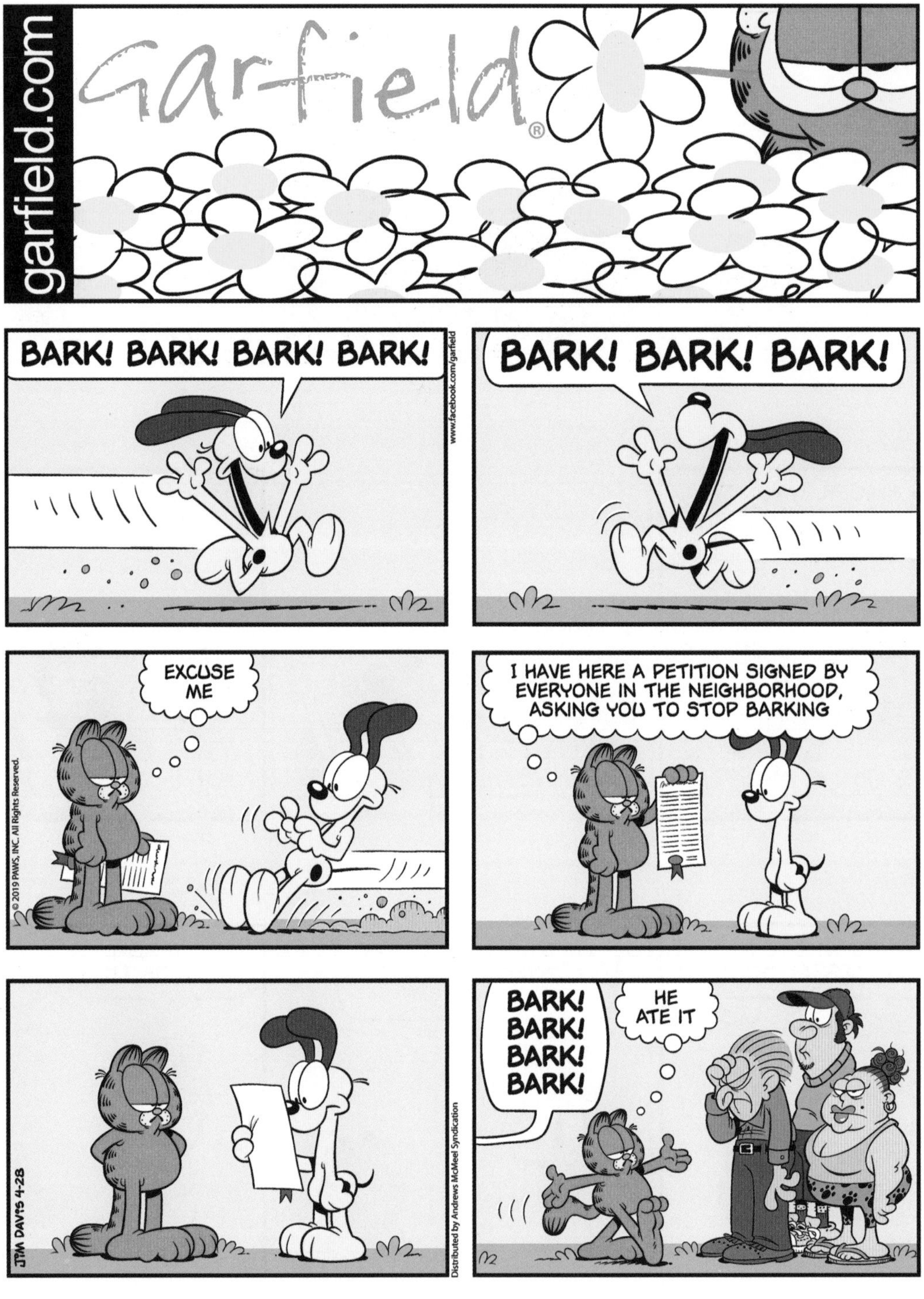
garfield.com
Garfield®
BARK! BARK! BARK! BARK!
www.facebook.com/garfield
BARK! BARK! BARK!
EXCUSE ME
© 2019 PAWS, INC. All Rights Reserved.
I HAVE HERE A PETITION SIGNED BY EVERYONE IN THE NEIGHBORHOOD, ASKING YOU TO STOP BARKING
JIM DAVIS 4-28
Distributed by Andrews McMeel Syndication
BARK! BARK! BARK! BARK!
HE ATE IT

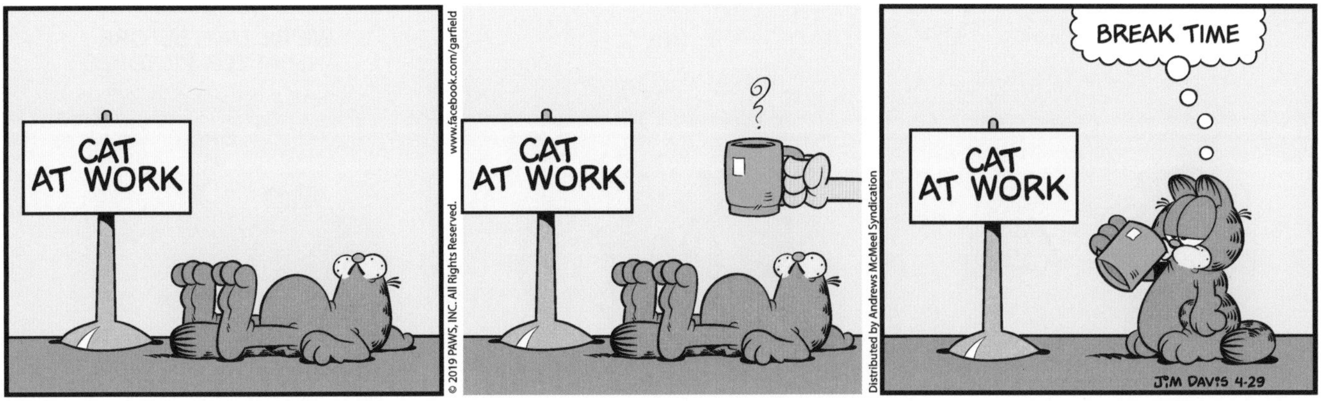
CAT AT WORK
CAT AT WORK
BREAK TIME
CAT AT WORK
© 2019 PAWS, INC. All Rights Reserved. www.facebook.com/garfield
Distributed by Andrews McMeel Syndication
JIM DAVIS 4-29

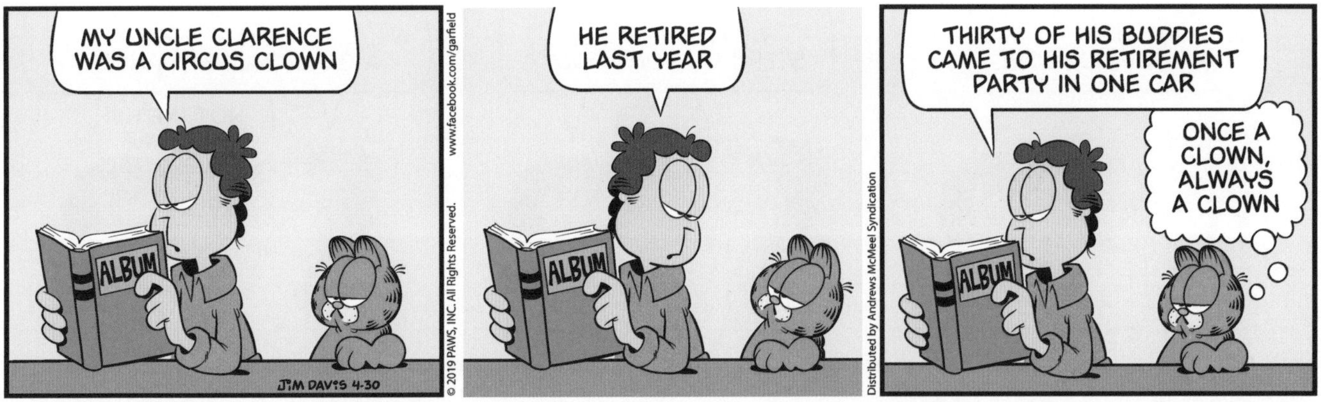
MY UNCLE CLARENCE WAS A CIRCUS CLOWN
ALBUM
JIM DAVIS 4-30
HE RETIRED LAST YEAR
ALBUM
THIRTY OF HIS BUDDIES CAME TO HIS RETIREMENT PARTY IN ONE CAR
ONCE A CLOWN, ALWAYS A CLOWN
ALBUM
© 2019 PAWS, INC. All Rights Reserved. www.facebook.com/garfield
Distributed by Andrews McMeel Syndication

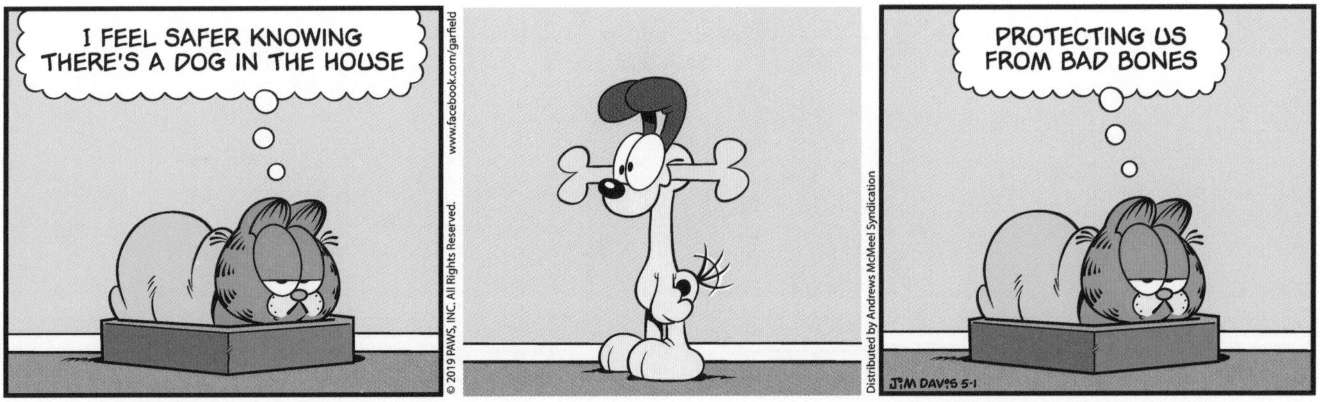
I FEEL SAFER KNOWING THERE'S A DOG IN THE HOUSE
PROTECTING US FROM BAD BONES
© 2019 PAWS, INC. All Rights Reserved. www.facebook.com/garfield
Distributed by Andrews McMeel Syndication
JIM DAVIS 5-1

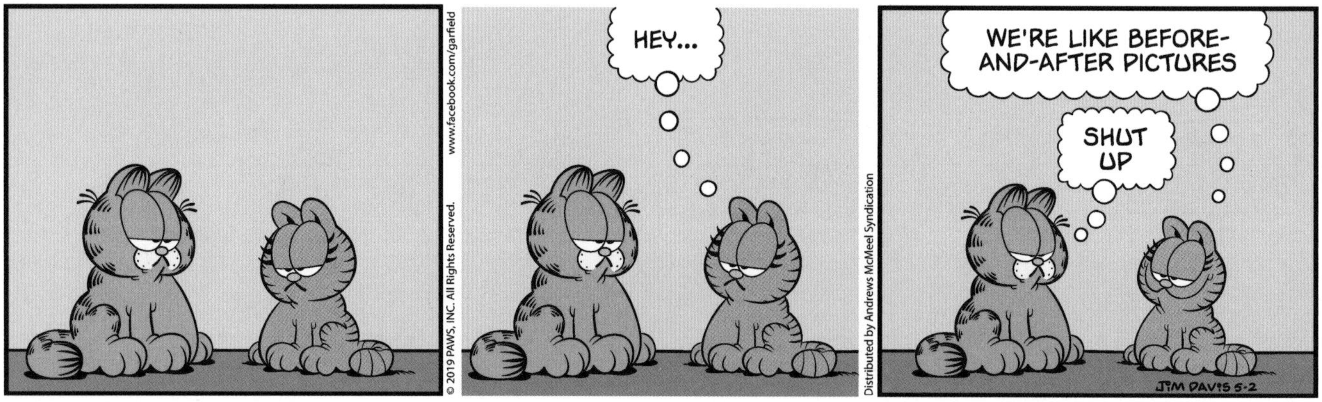
© 2019 PAWS, INC. All Rights Reserved. www.facebook.com/garfield
HEY...
WE'RE LIKE BEFORE-AND-AFTER PICTURES
SHUT UP
Distributed by Andrews McMeel Syndication
JIM DAVIS 5-2

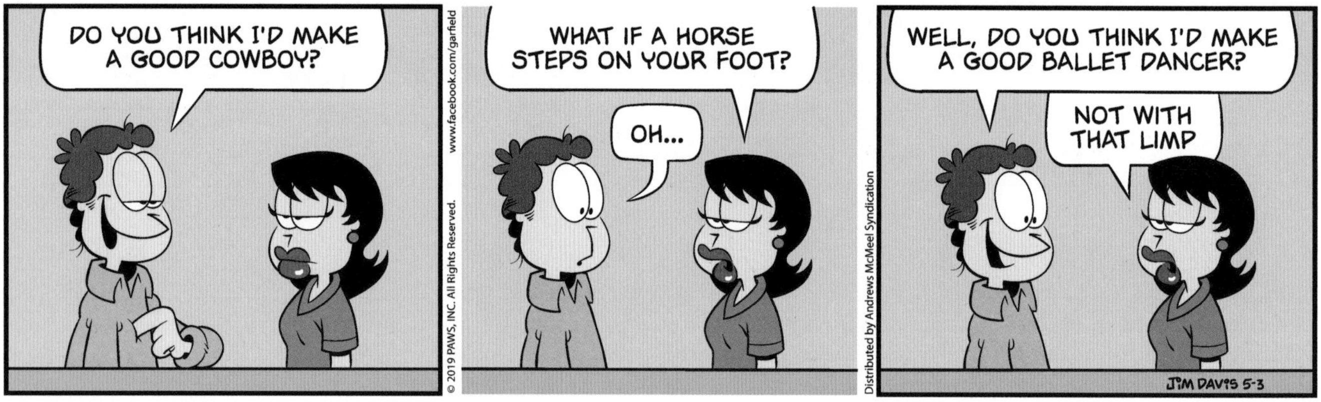
DO YOU THINK I'D MAKE A GOOD COWBOY?
© 2019 PAWS, INC. All Rights Reserved. www.facebook.com/garfield
WHAT IF A HORSE STEPS ON YOUR FOOT?
OH...
WELL, DO YOU THINK I'D MAKE A GOOD BALLET DANCER?
NOT WITH THAT LIMP
Distributed by Andrews McMeel Syndication
JIM DAVIS 5-3

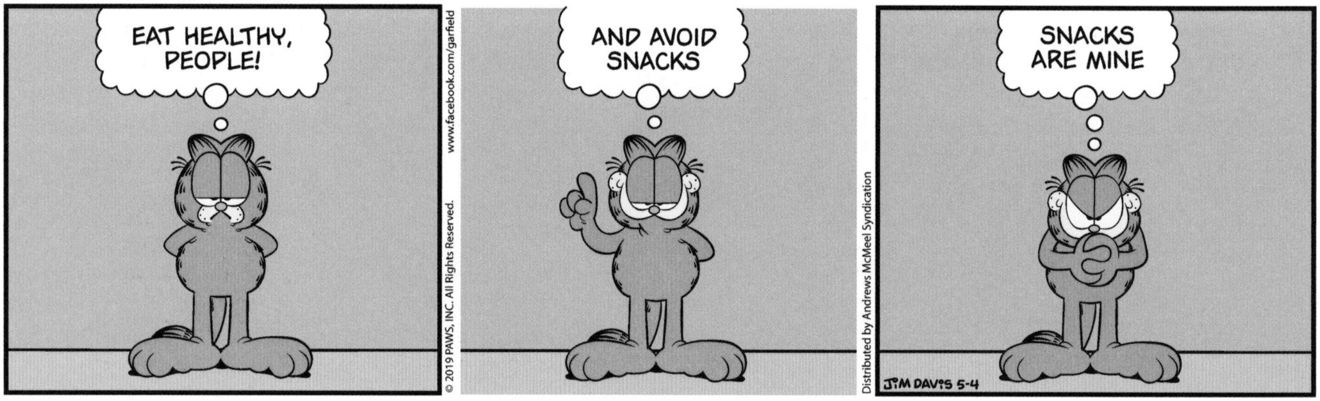
EAT HEALTHY, PEOPLE!
© 2019 PAWS, INC. All Rights Reserved. www.facebook.com/garfield
AND AVOID SNACKS
SNACKS ARE MINE
Distributed by Andrews McMeel Syndication
JIM DAVIS 5-4

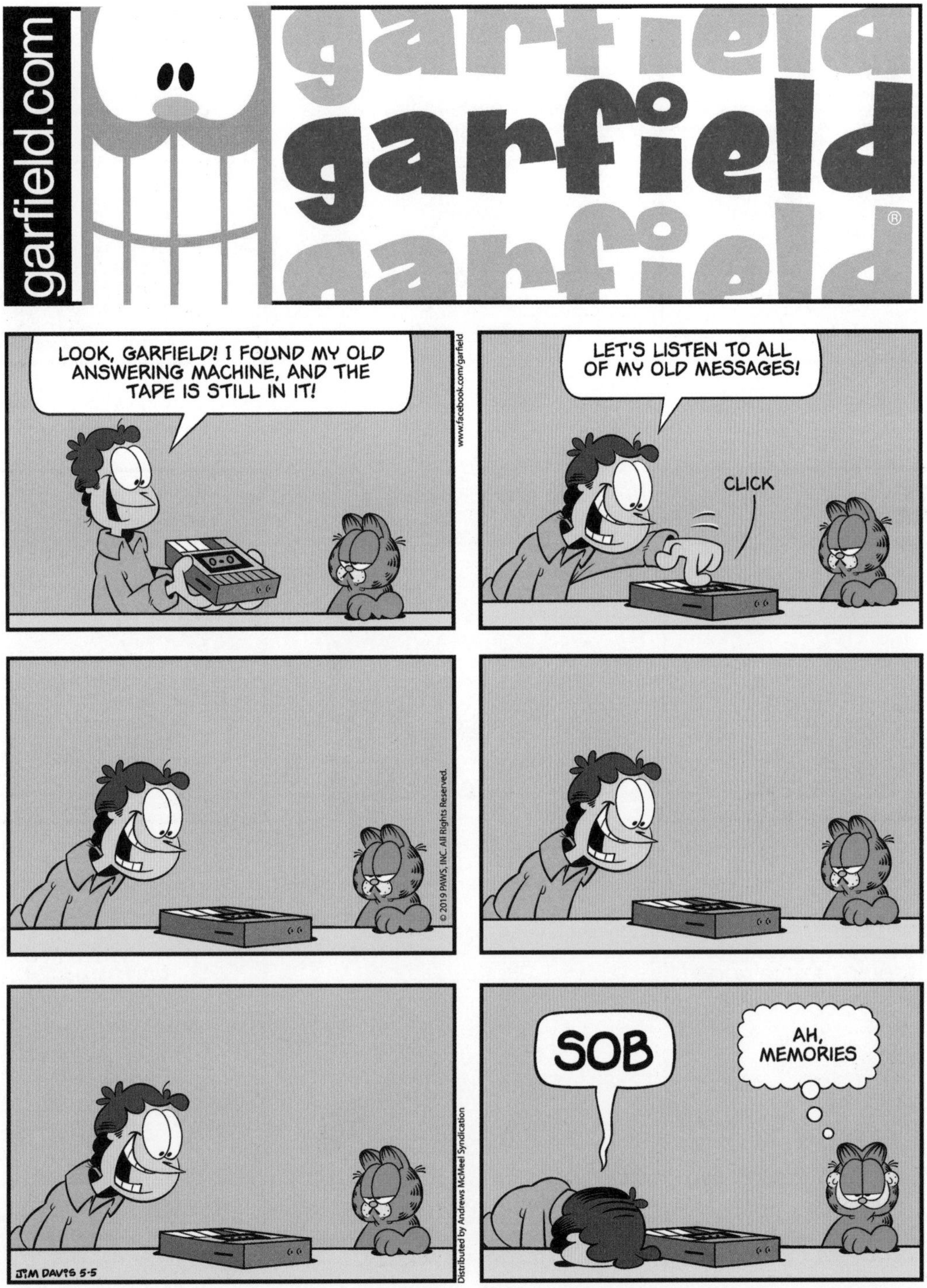
garfield.com
garfield
LOOK, GARFIELD! I FOUND MY OLD ANSWERING MACHINE, AND THE TAPE IS STILL IN IT!
www.facebook.com/garfield
LET'S LISTEN TO ALL OF MY OLD MESSAGES!
CLICK
© 2019 PAWS, INC. All Rights Reserved.
JIM DAVIS 5-5
Distributed by Andrews McMeel Syndication
SOB
AH, MEMORIES

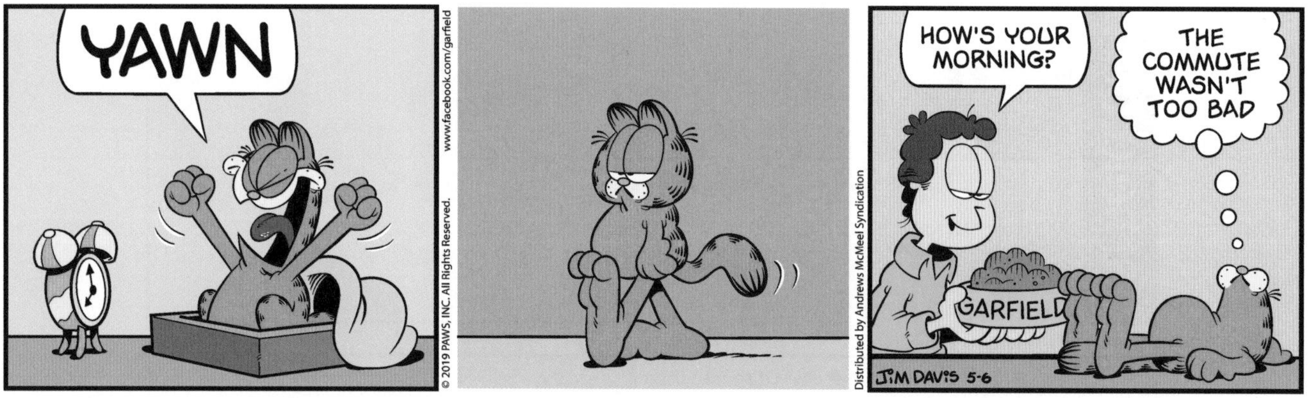
YAWN
© 2019 PAWS, INC. All Rights Reserved.
www.facebook.com/garfield
HOW'S YOUR MORNING?
THE COMMUTE WASN'T TOO BAD
GARFIELD
Distributed by Andrews McMeel Syndication
JIM DAVIS 5-6

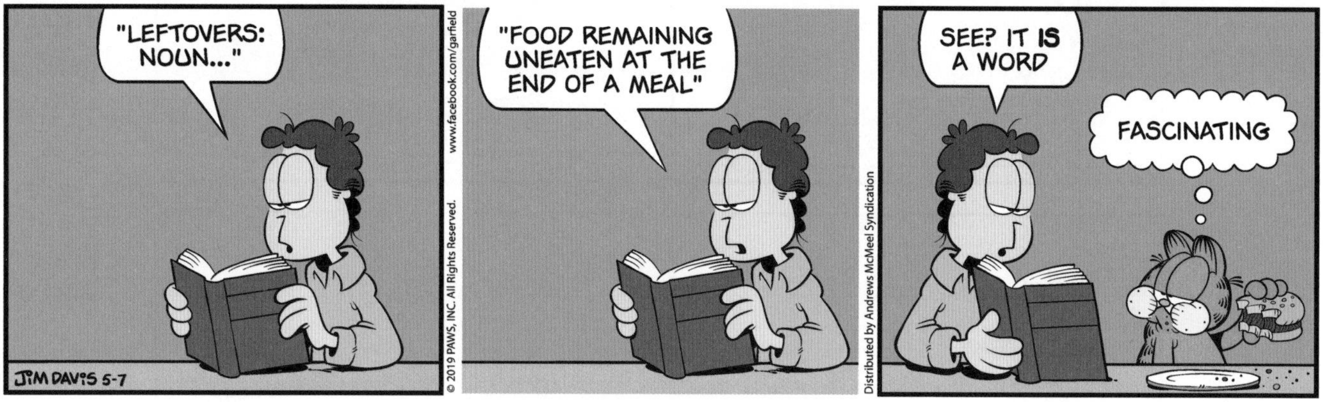
"LEFTOVERS: NOUN..."
JIM DAVIS 5-7
© 2019 PAWS, INC. All Rights Reserved.
www.facebook.com/garfield
"FOOD REMAINING UNEATEN AT THE END OF A MEAL"
SEE? IT **IS** A WORD
FASCINATING
Distributed by Andrews McMeel Syndication

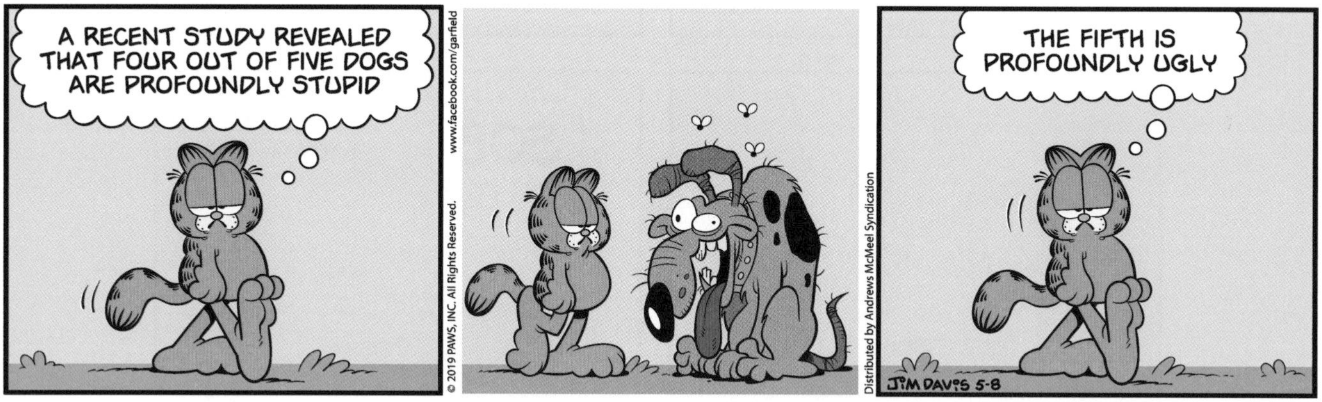
A RECENT STUDY REVEALED THAT FOUR OUT OF FIVE DOGS ARE PROFOUNDLY STUPID
© 2019 PAWS, INC. All Rights Reserved.
www.facebook.com/garfield
THE FIFTH IS PROFOUNDLY UGLY
Distributed by Andrews McMeel Syndication
JIM DAVIS 5-8

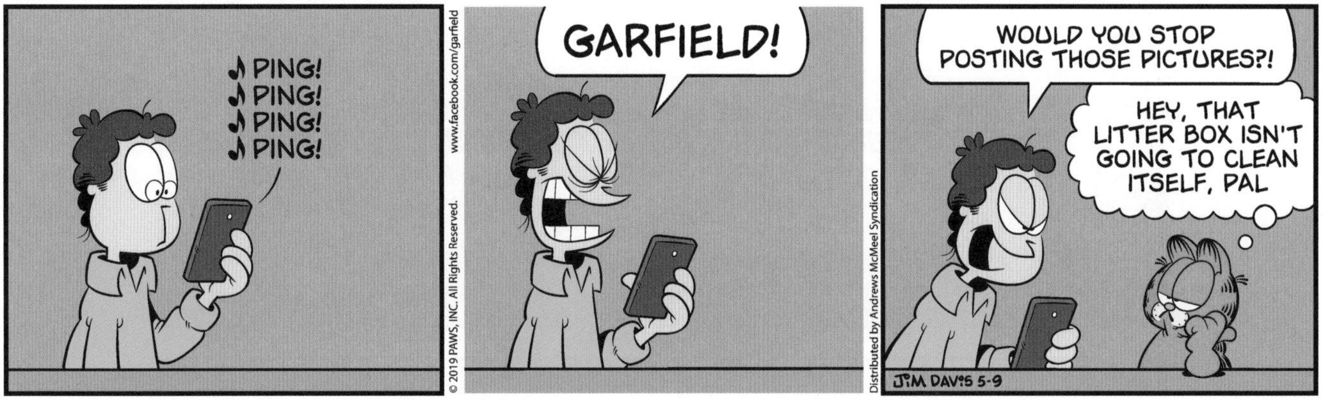
PING!
PING!
PING!
PING!
GARFIELD!
WOULD YOU STOP POSTING THOSE PICTURES?!
HEY, THAT LITTER BOX ISN'T GOING TO CLEAN ITSELF, PAL
© 2019 PAWS, INC. All Rights Reserved. www.facebook.com/garfield
Distributed by Andrews McMeel Syndication
JIM DAVIS 5-9

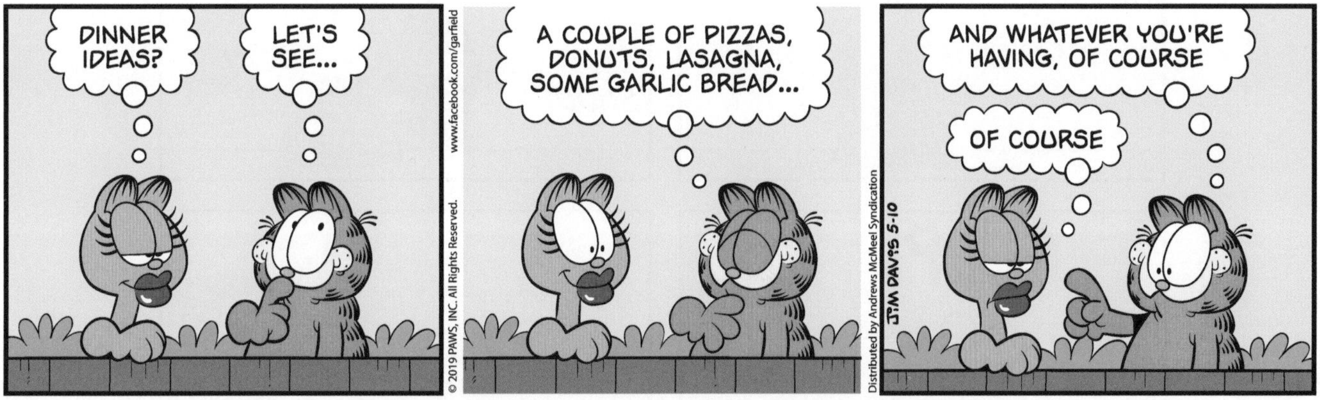
DINNER IDEAS?
LET'S SEE...
A COUPLE OF PIZZAS, DONUTS, LASAGNA, SOME GARLIC BREAD...
AND WHATEVER YOU'RE HAVING, OF COURSE
OF COURSE
© 2019 PAWS, INC. All Rights Reserved. www.facebook.com/garfield
Distributed by Andrews McMeel Syndication
JIM DAVIS 5-10

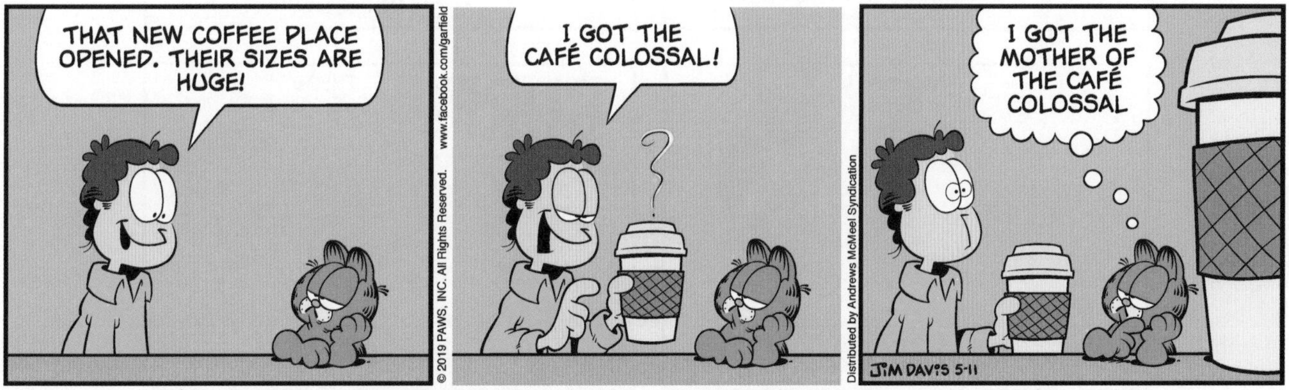
THAT NEW COFFEE PLACE OPENED. THEIR SIZES ARE HUGE!
I GOT THE CAFÉ COLOSSAL!
I GOT THE MOTHER OF THE CAFÉ COLOSSAL
© 2019 PAWS, INC. All Rights Reserved. www.facebook.com/garfield
Distributed by Andrews McMeel Syndication
JIM DAVIS 5-11

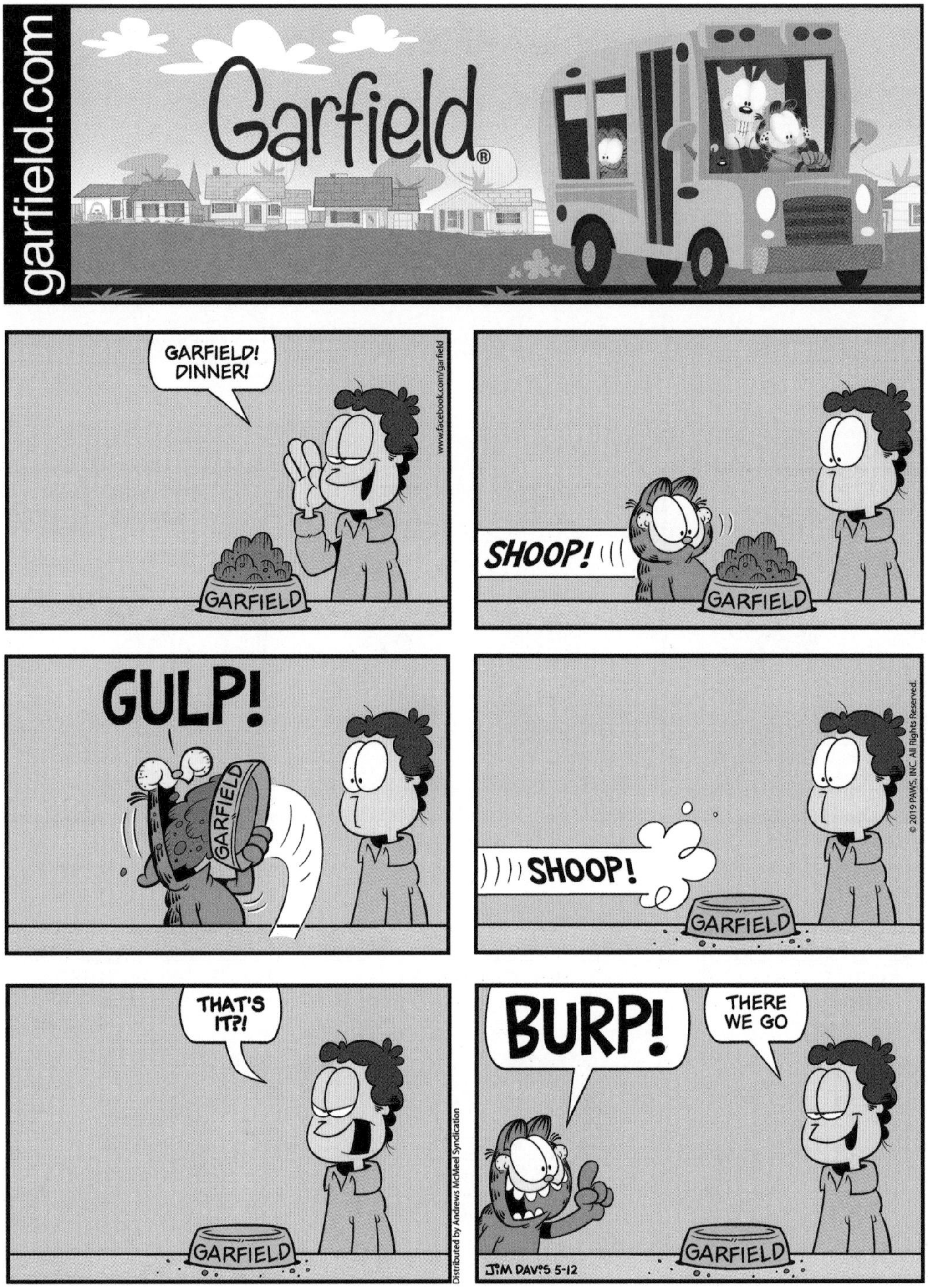

garfield.com
Garfield®
GARFIELD! DINNER!
www.facebook.com/garfield
GARFIELD
SHOOP!
GARFIELD
GULP!
GARFIELD
SHOOP!
GARFIELD
© 2019 PAWS, INC. All Rights Reserved.
THAT'S IT?!
GARFIELD
Distributed by Andrews McMeel Syndication
BURP!
THERE WE GO
GARFIELD
JIM DAVIS 5-12

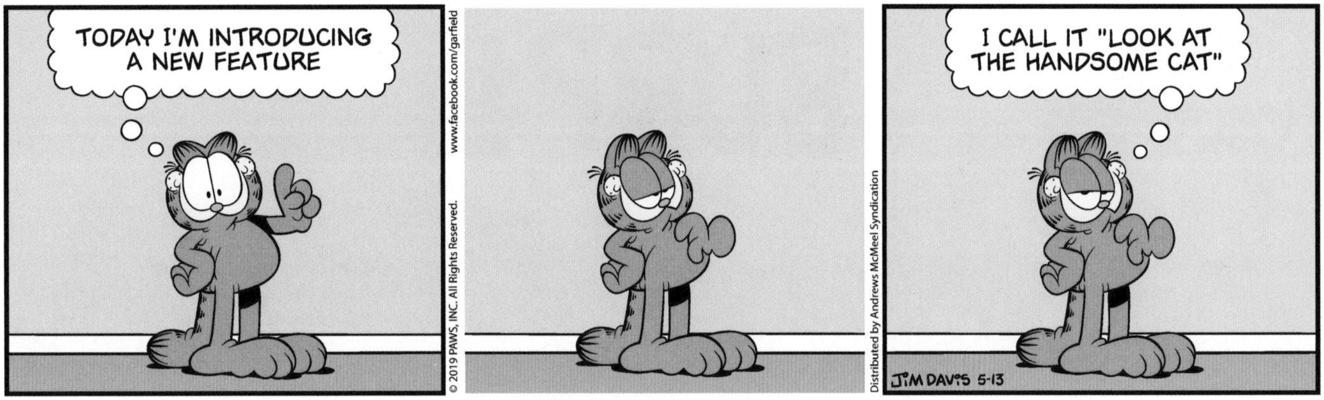
TODAY I'M INTRODUCING A NEW FEATURE
I CALL IT "LOOK AT THE HANDSOME CAT"
JIM DAVIS 5-13

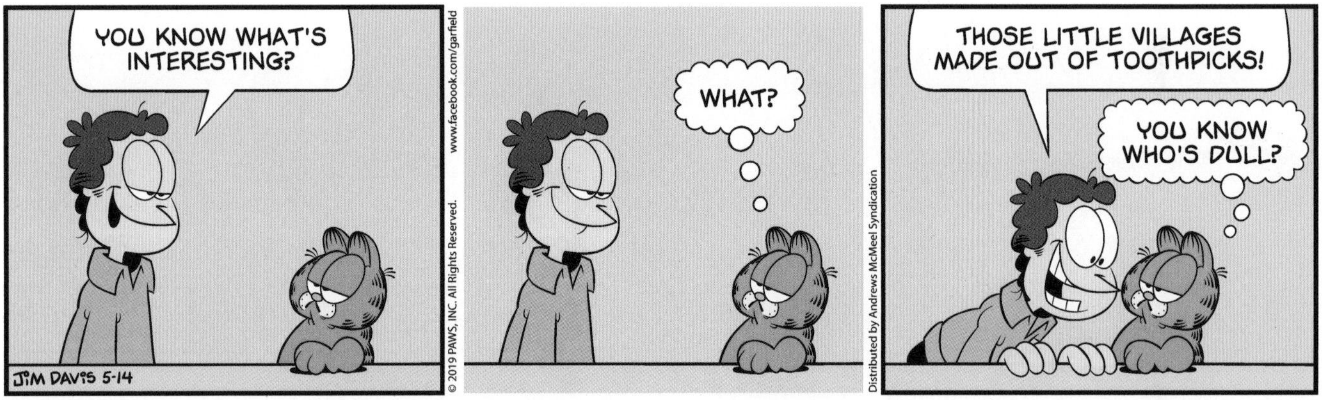
YOU KNOW WHAT'S INTERESTING?
WHAT?
THOSE LITTLE VILLAGES MADE OUT OF TOOTHPICKS!
YOU KNOW WHO'S DULL?
JIM DAVIS 5-14
© 2019 PAWS, INC. All Rights Reserved. www.facebook.com/garfield
Distributed by Andrews McMeel Syndication

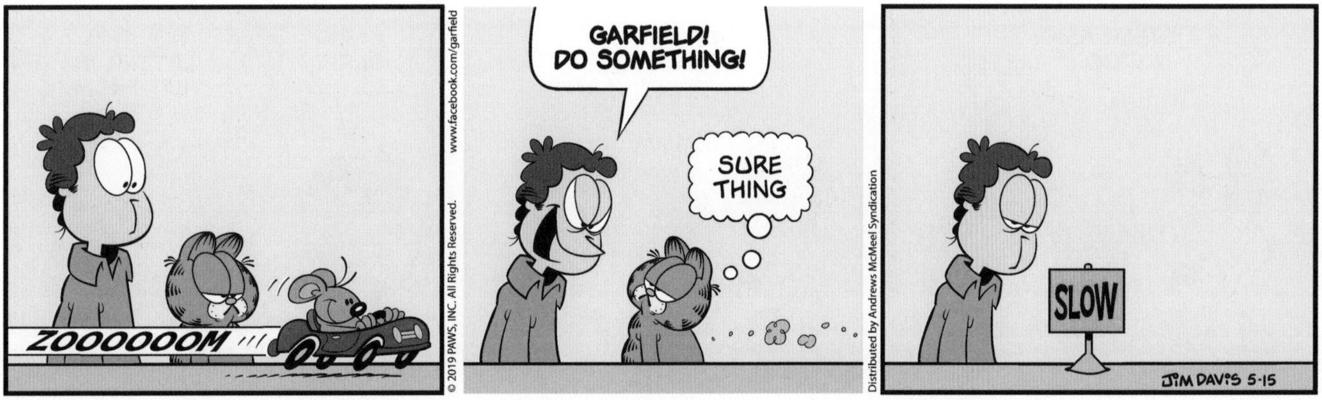
ZOOOOOOM
GARFIELD! DO SOMETHING!
SURE THING
SLOW
JIM DAVIS 5-15
© 2019 PAWS, INC. All Rights Reserved. www.facebook.com/garfield
Distributed by Andrews McMeel Syndication

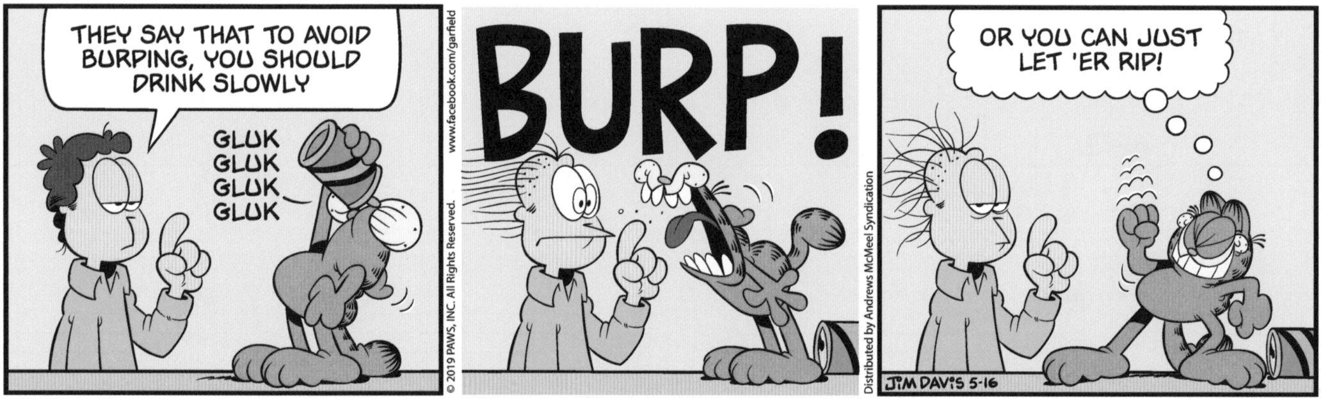
THEY SAY THAT TO AVOID BURPING, YOU SHOULD DRINK SLOWLY
GLUK GLUK GLUK GLUK
BURP!
OR YOU CAN JUST LET 'ER RIP!
JIM DAVIS 5-16
© 2019 PAWS, INC. All Rights Reserved. www.facebook.com/garfield
Distributed by Andrews McMeel Syndication

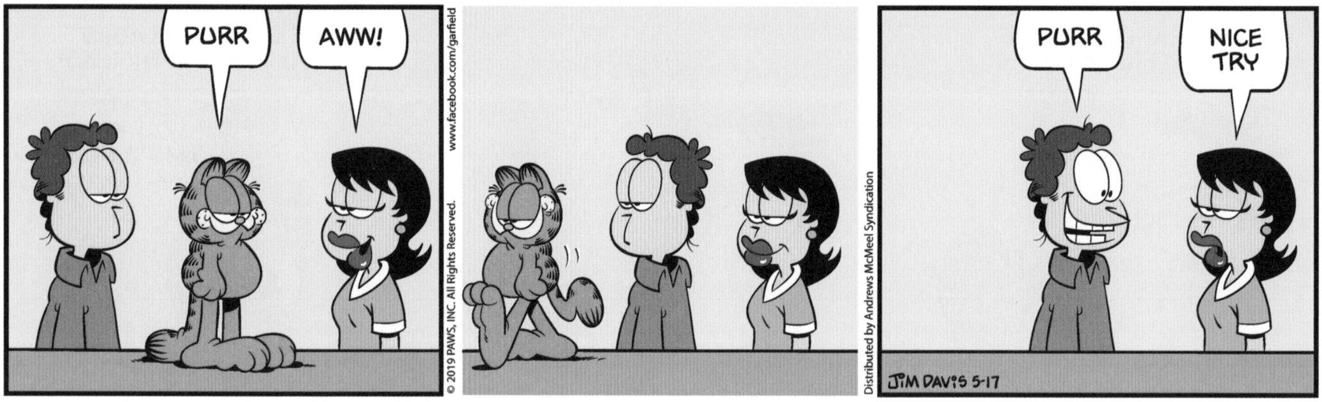
PURR
AWW!
PURR
NICE TRY
JIM DAVIS 5-17
© 2019 PAWS, INC. All Rights Reserved. www.facebook.com/garfield
Distributed by Andrews McMeel Syndication

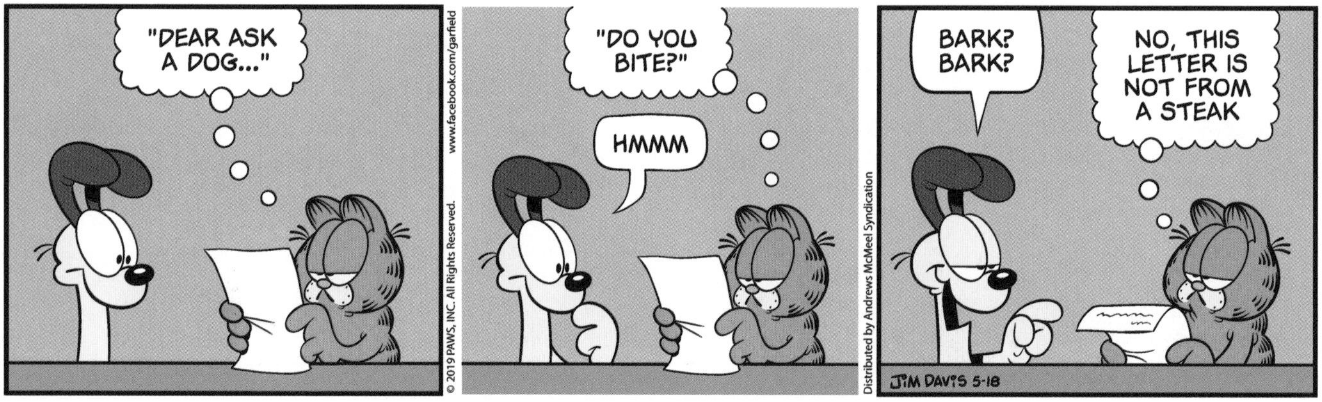
"DEAR ASK A DOG..."
"DO YOU BITE?"
HMMM
BARK? BARK?
NO, THIS LETTER IS NOT FROM A STEAK
JIM DAVIS 5-18
© 2019 PAWS, INC. All Rights Reserved. www.facebook.com/garfield
Distributed by Andrews McMeel Syndication

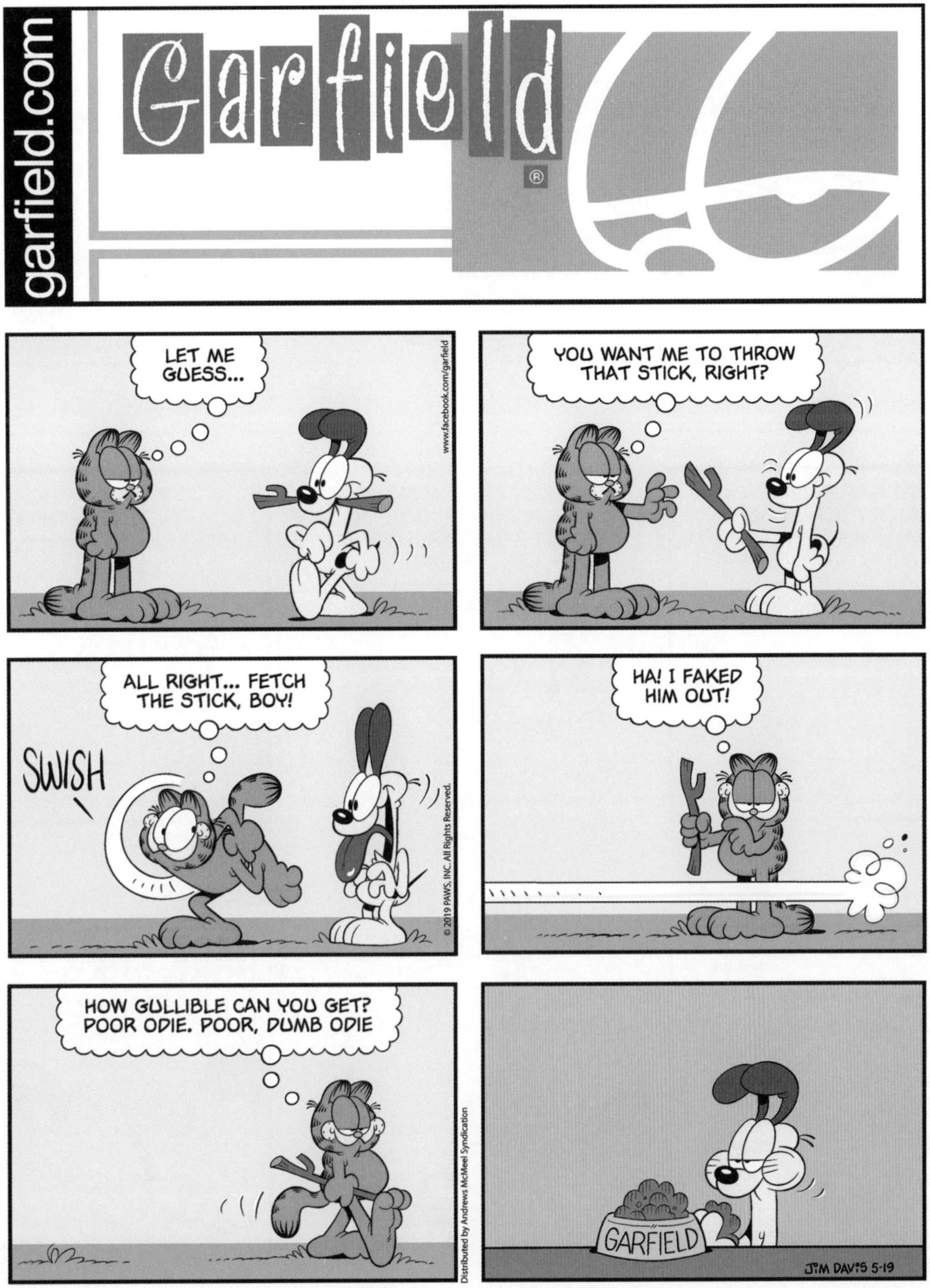
garfield.com
Garfield
LET ME GUESS...
www.facebook.com/garfield
YOU WANT ME TO THROW THAT STICK, RIGHT?
ALL RIGHT... FETCH THE STICK, BOY!
SWISH
© 2019 PAWS, INC. All Rights Reserved.
HA! I FAKED HIM OUT!
HOW GULLIBLE CAN YOU GET? POOR ODIE. POOR, DUMB ODIE
Distributed by Andrews McMeel Syndication
GARFIELD
JIM DAVIS 5-19

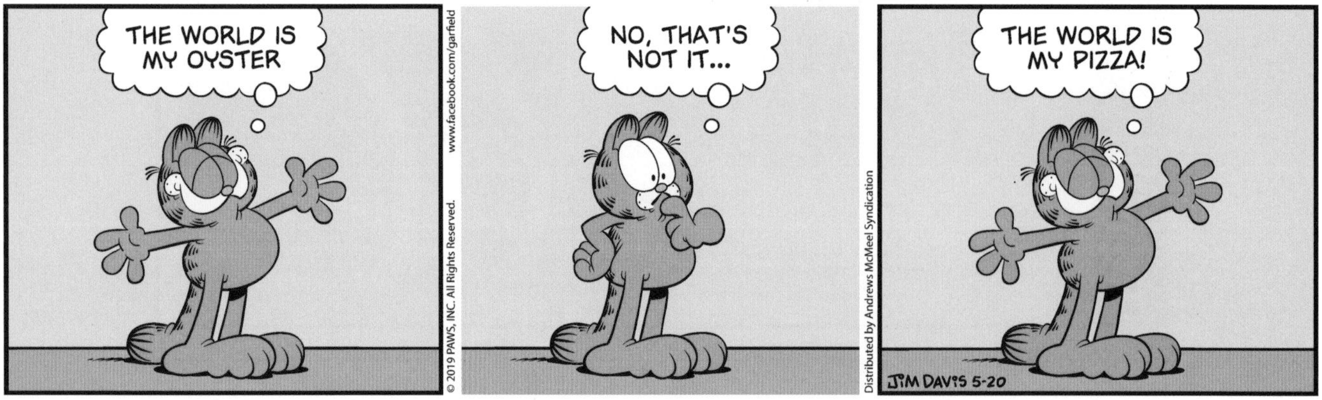
THE WORLD IS MY OYSTER
© 2019 PAWS, INC. All Rights Reserved. www.facebook.com/garfield
NO, THAT'S NOT IT...
Distributed by Andrews McMeel Syndication
THE WORLD IS MY PIZZA!
JIM DAVIS 5-20

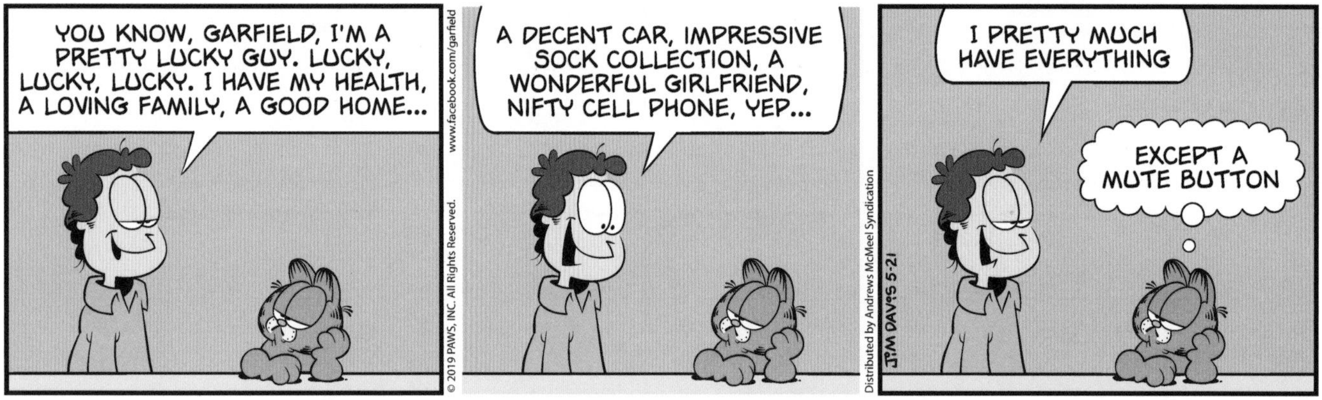
YOU KNOW, GARFIELD, I'M A PRETTY LUCKY GUY. LUCKY, LUCKY, LUCKY. I HAVE MY HEALTH, A LOVING FAMILY, A GOOD HOME...
© 2019 PAWS, INC. All Rights Reserved. www.facebook.com/garfield
A DECENT CAR, IMPRESSIVE SOCK COLLECTION, A WONDERFUL GIRLFRIEND, NIFTY CELL PHONE, YEP...
Distributed by Andrews McMeel Syndication
I PRETTY MUCH HAVE EVERYTHING
EXCEPT A MUTE BUTTON
JIM DAVIS 5-21

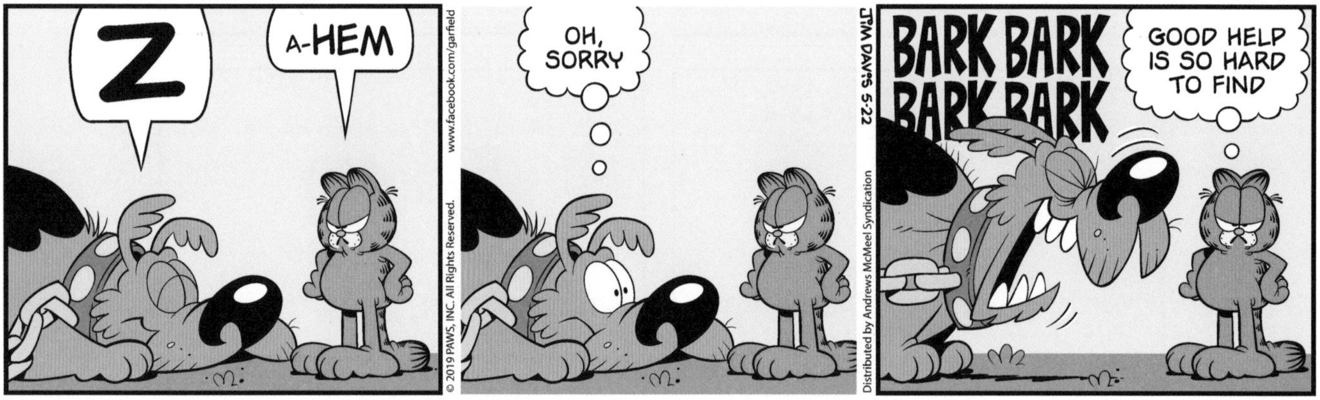
Z
A-HEM
© 2019 PAWS, INC. All Rights Reserved. www.facebook.com/garfield
OH, SORRY
Distributed by Andrews McMeel Syndication
JIM DAVIS 5-22
BARK BARK BARK BARK
GOOD HELP IS SO HARD TO FIND

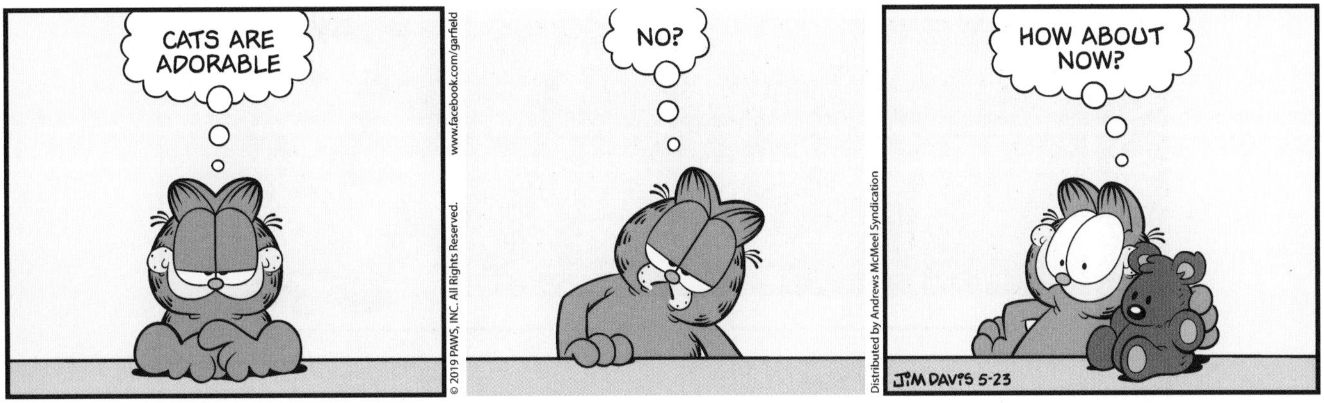
CATS ARE ADORABLE
NO?
HOW ABOUT NOW?
JIM DAVIS 5-23
© 2019 PAWS, INC. All Rights Reserved. www.facebook.com/garfield
Distributed by Andrews McMeel Syndication

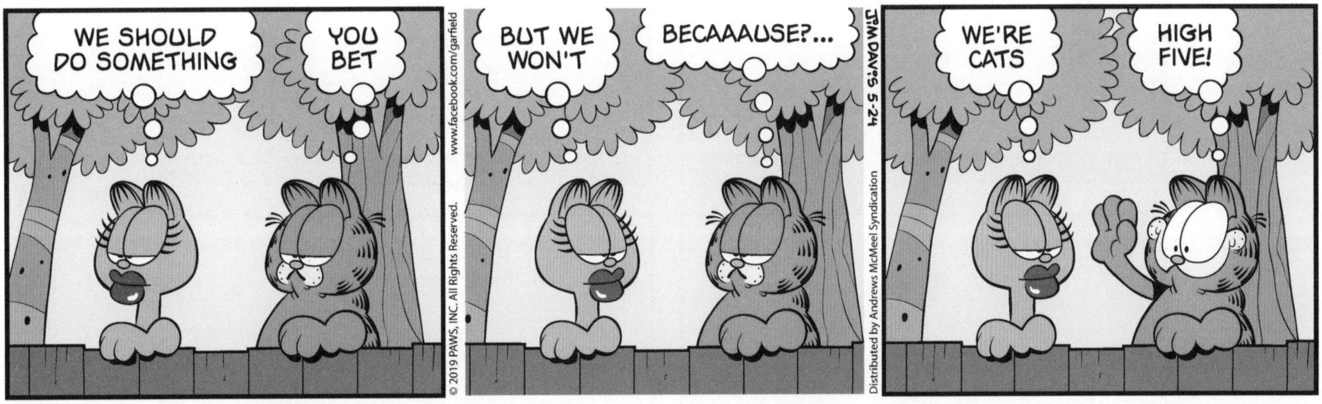
WE SHOULD DO SOMETHING
YOU BET
BUT WE WON'T
BECAAAUSE?...
WE'RE CATS
HIGH FIVE!
JIM DAVIS 5-24
© 2019 PAWS, INC. All Rights Reserved. www.facebook.com/garfield
Distributed by Andrews McMeel Syndication

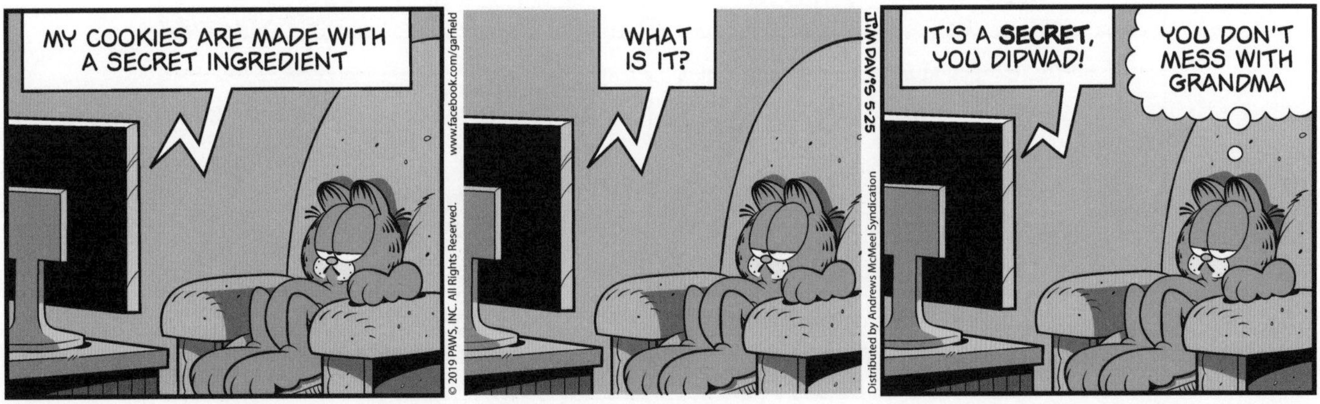
MY COOKIES ARE MADE WITH A SECRET INGREDIENT
WHAT IS IT?
IT'S A **SECRET**, YOU DIPWAD!
YOU DON'T MESS WITH GRANDMA
JIM DAVIS 5-25
© 2019 PAWS, INC. All Rights Reserved. www.facebook.com/garfield
Distributed by Andrews McMeel Syndication

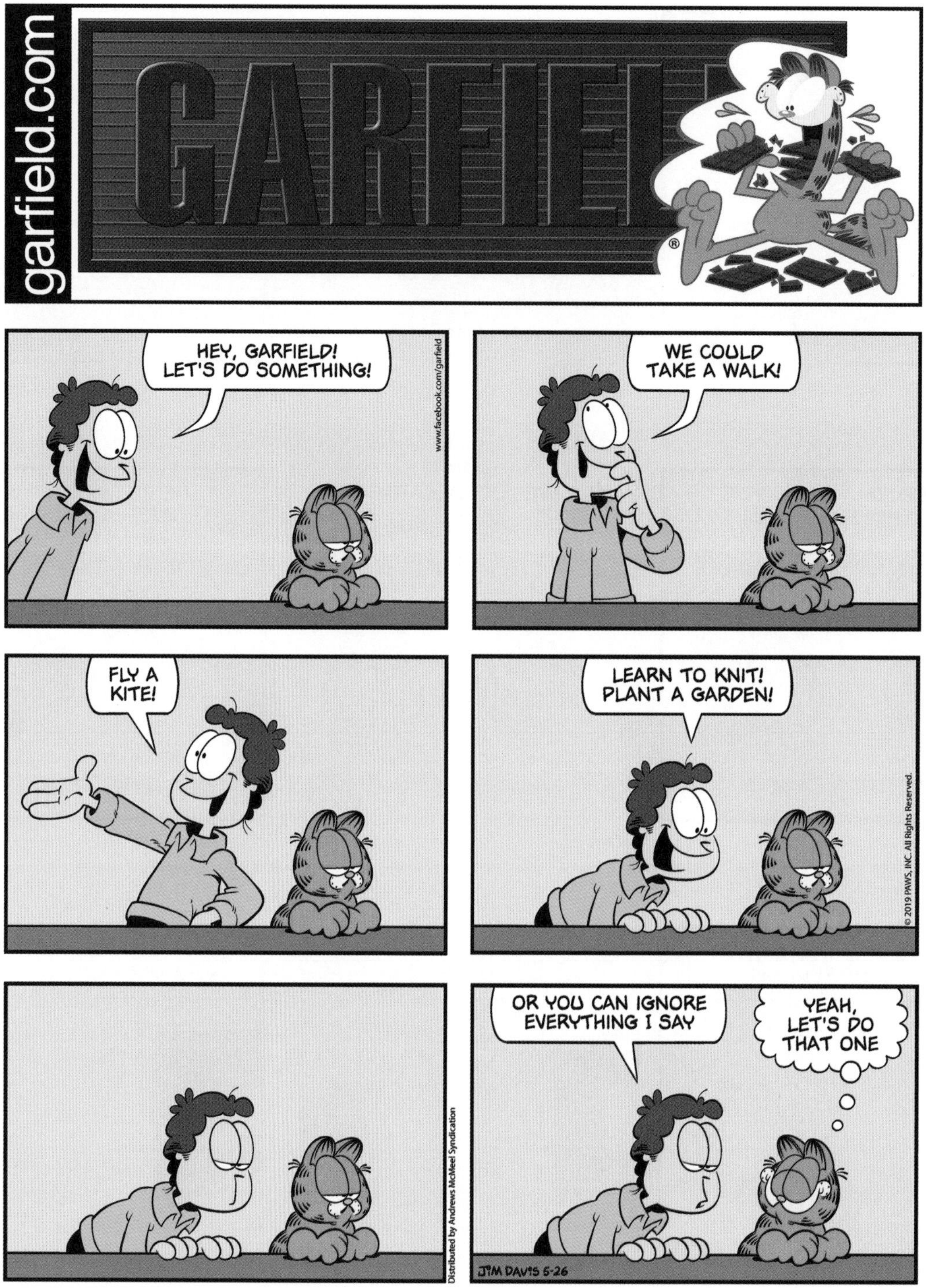
garfield.com
GARFIELD
HEY, GARFIELD! LET'S DO SOMETHING!
www.facebook.com/garfield
WE COULD TAKE A WALK!
FLY A KITE!
LEARN TO KNIT! PLANT A GARDEN!
© 2019 PAWS, INC. All Rights Reserved.
Distributed by Andrews McMeel Syndication
OR YOU CAN IGNORE EVERYTHING I SAY
YEAH, LET'S DO THAT ONE
JIM DAVIS 5-26

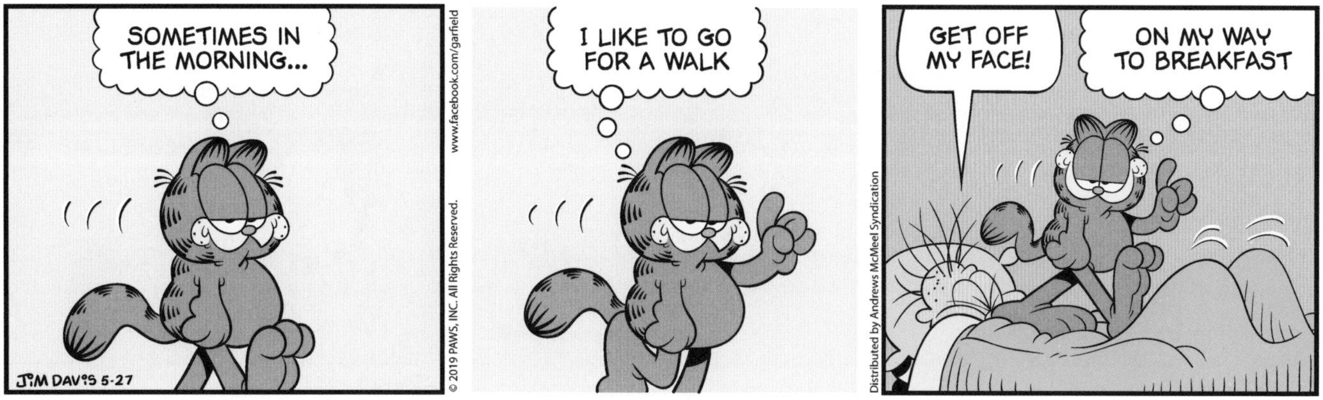
SOMETIMES IN THE MORNING...
I LIKE TO GO FOR A WALK
GET OFF MY FACE!
ON MY WAY TO BREAKFAST
JIM DAVIS 5-27
© 2019 PAWS, INC. All Rights Reserved.
www.facebook.com/garfield
Distributed by Andrews McMeel Syndication

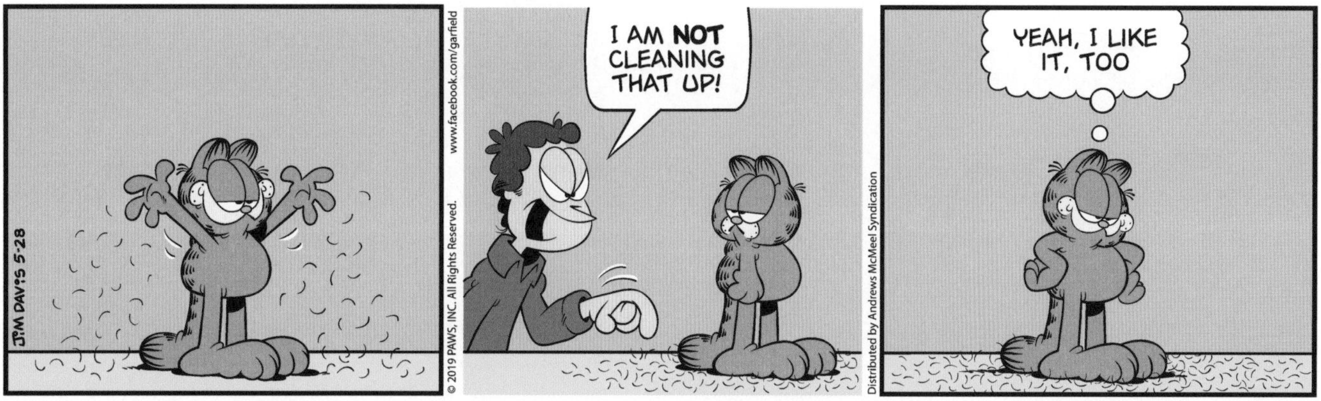
JIM DAVIS 5-28
I AM **NOT** CLEANING THAT UP!
YEAH, I LIKE IT, TOO
© 2019 PAWS, INC. All Rights Reserved.
www.facebook.com/garfield
Distributed by Andrews McMeel Syndication

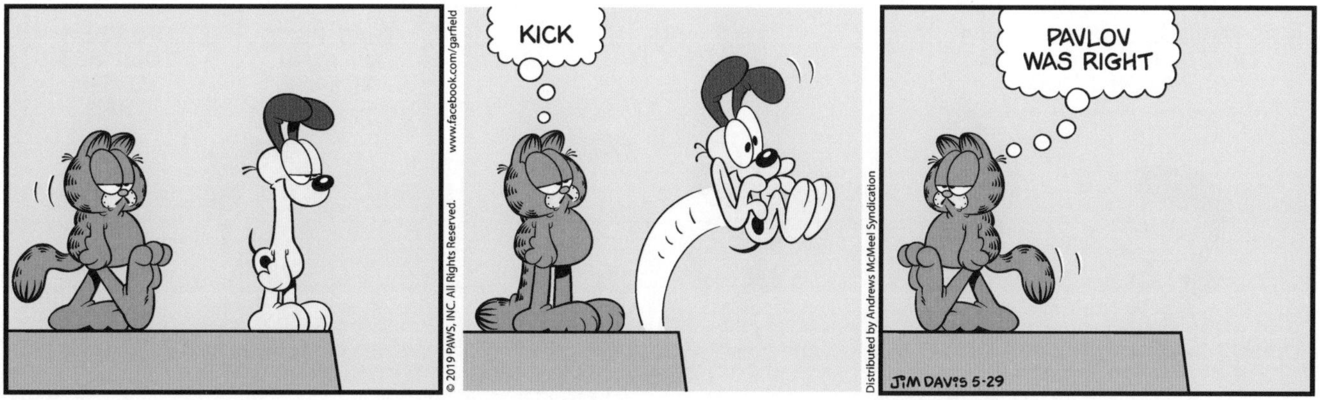
KICK
PAVLOV WAS RIGHT
JIM DAVIS 5-29
© 2019 PAWS, INC. All Rights Reserved.
www.facebook.com/garfield
Distributed by Andrews McMeel Syndication

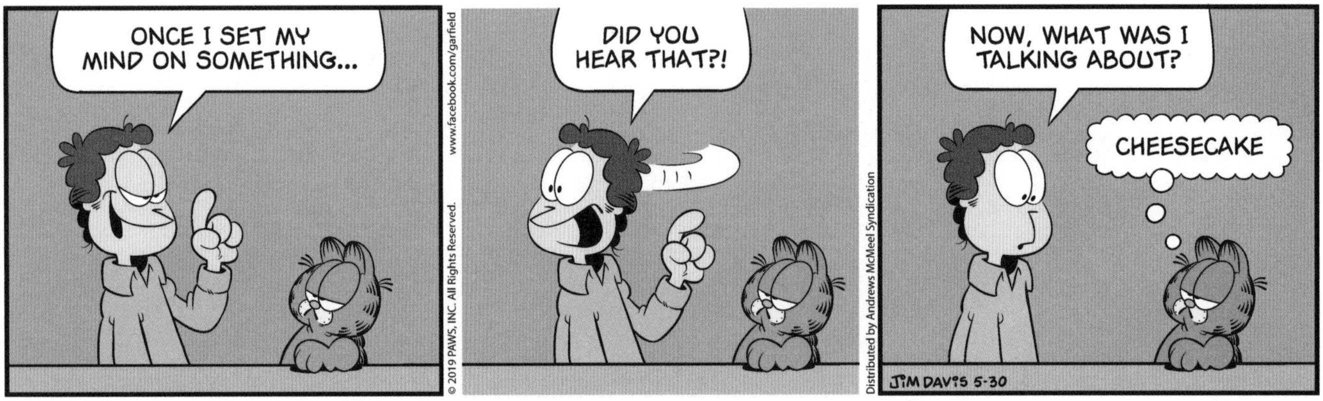
ONCE I SET MY MIND ON SOMETHING...
© 2019 PAWS, INC. All Rights Reserved. www.facebook.com/garfield
DID YOU HEAR THAT?!
Distributed by Andrews McMeel Syndication
NOW, WHAT WAS I TALKING ABOUT?
CHEESECAKE
JIM DAVIS 5-30

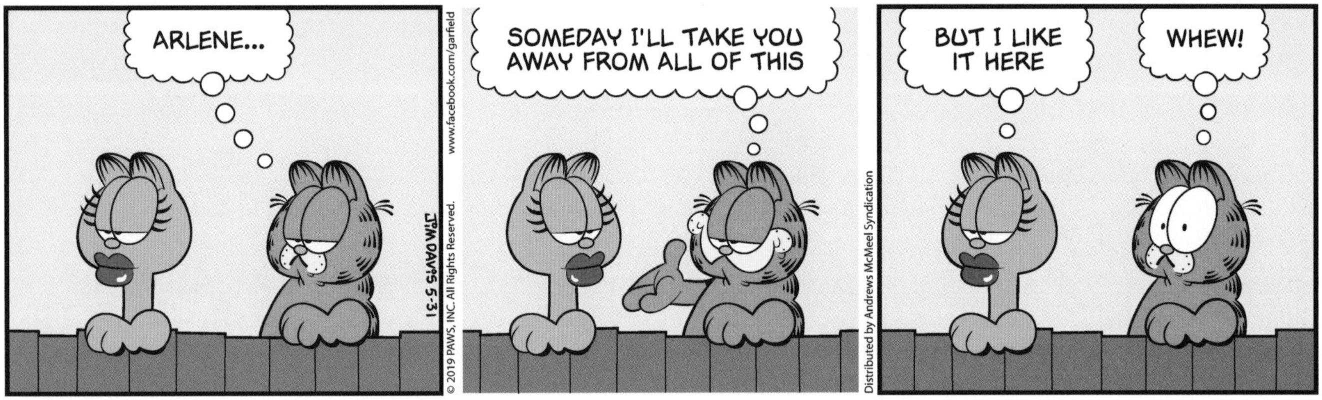
ARLENE...
JIM DAVIS 5-31
© 2019 PAWS, INC. All Rights Reserved. www.facebook.com/garfield
SOMEDAY I'LL TAKE YOU AWAY FROM ALL OF THIS
Distributed by Andrews McMeel Syndication
BUT I LIKE IT HERE
WHEW!

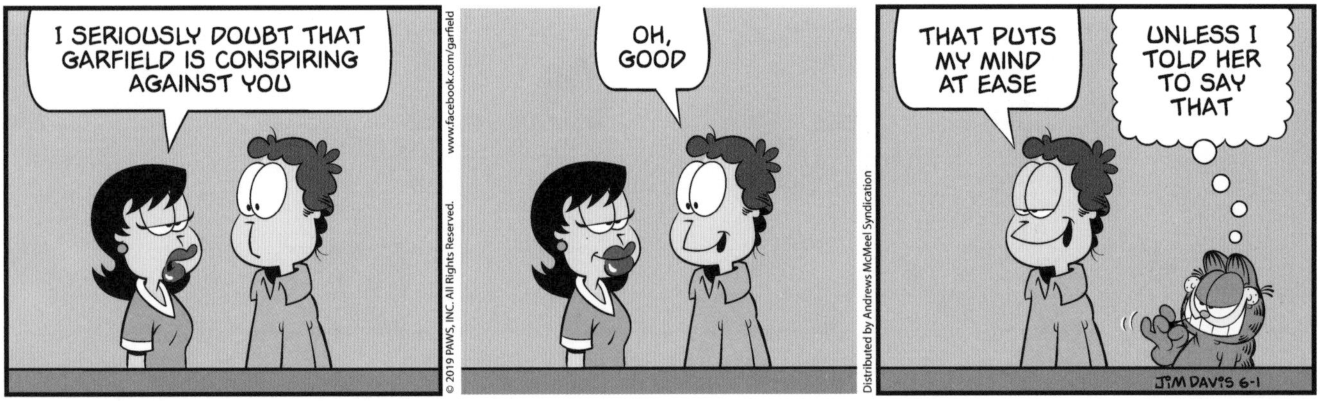
I SERIOUSLY DOUBT THAT GARFIELD IS CONSPIRING AGAINST YOU
© 2019 PAWS, INC. All Rights Reserved. www.facebook.com/garfield
OH, GOOD
Distributed by Andrews McMeel Syndication
THAT PUTS MY MIND AT EASE
UNLESS I TOLD HER TO SAY THAT
JIM DAVIS 6-1

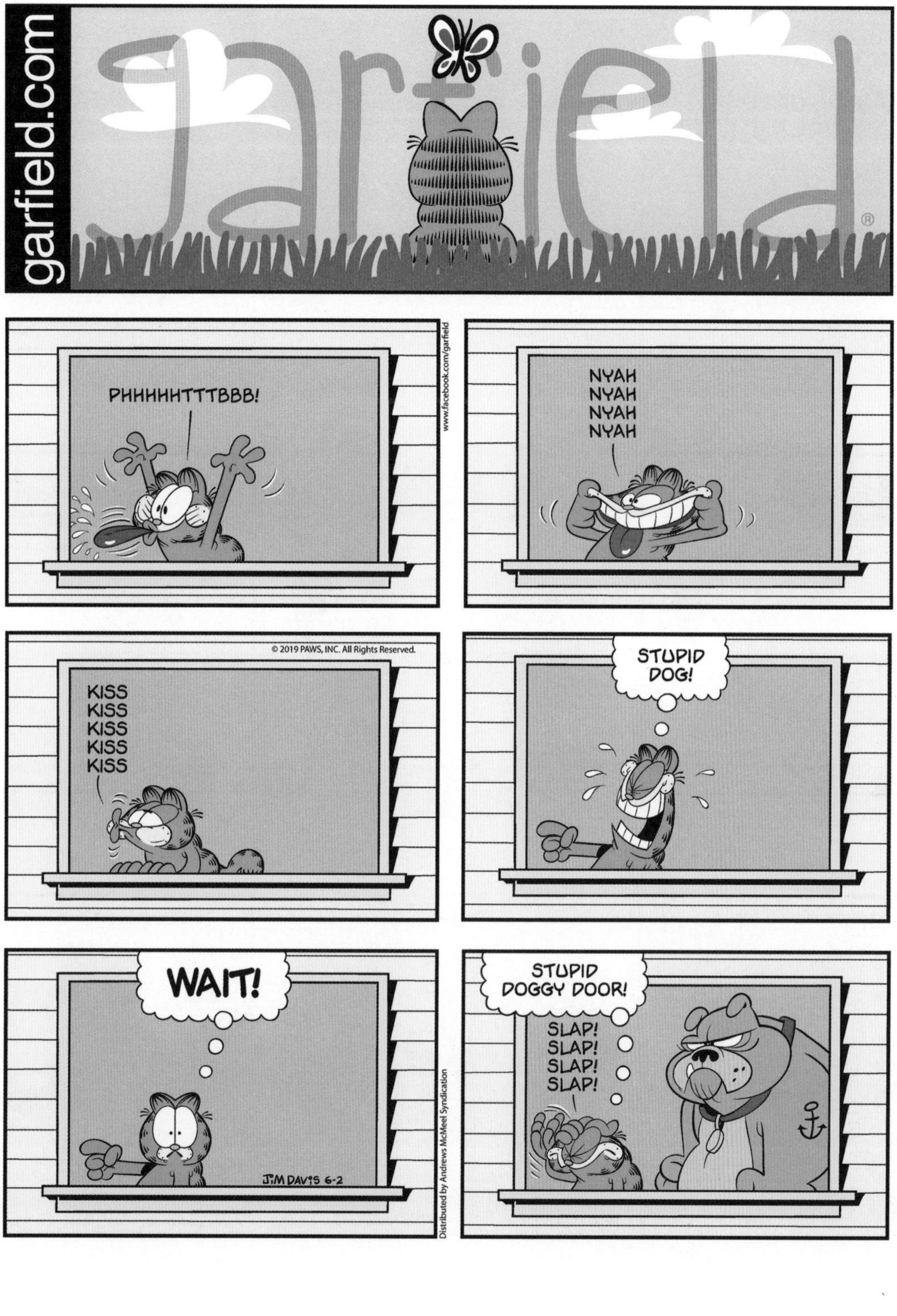
garfield.com
garfield
www.facebook.com/garfield
PHHHHHTTTBBB!
NYAH
NYAH
NYAH
NYAH
© 2019 PAWS, INC. All Rights Reserved.
KISS
KISS
KISS
KISS
KISS
STUPID
DOG!
WAIT!
JIM DAVIS 6-2
Distributed by Andrews McMeel Syndication
STUPID
DOGGY DOOR!
SLAP!
SLAP!
SLAP!
SLAP!

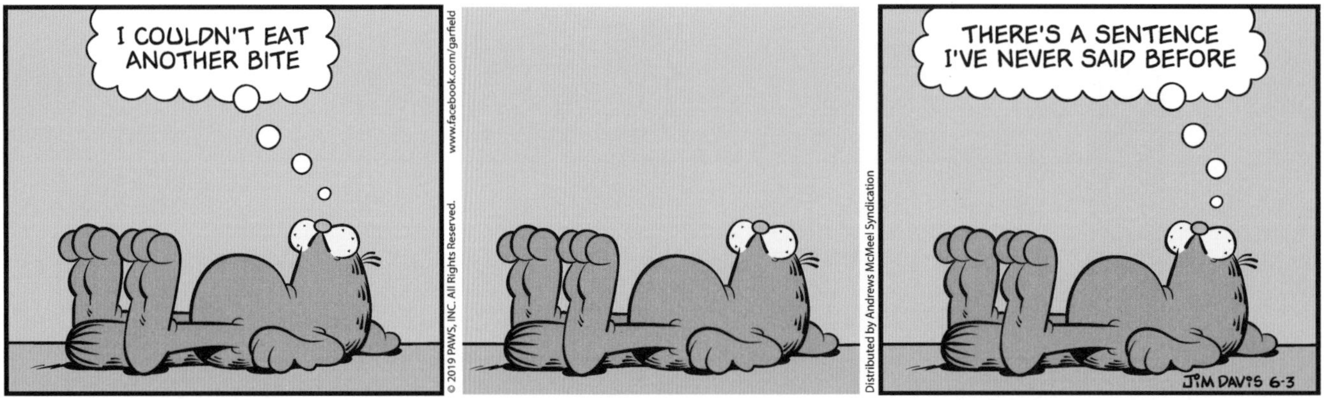
I COULDN'T EAT ANOTHER BITE
THERE'S A SENTENCE I'VE NEVER SAID BEFORE
© 2019 PAWS, INC. All Rights Reserved. www.facebook.com/garfield
Distributed by Andrews McMeel Syndication
JIM DAVIS 6-3

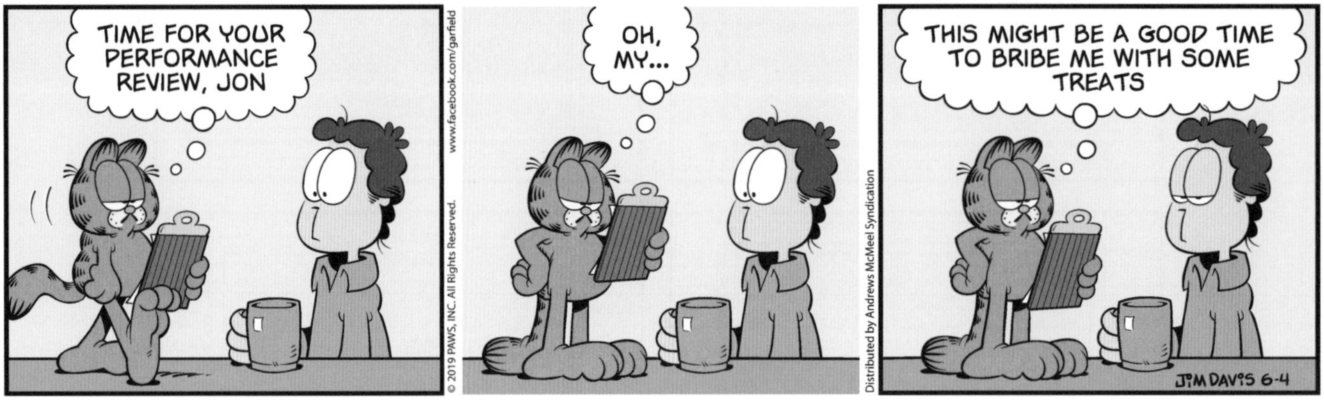
TIME FOR YOUR PERFORMANCE REVIEW, JON
OH, MY...
THIS MIGHT BE A GOOD TIME TO BRIBE ME WITH SOME TREATS
© 2019 PAWS, INC. All Rights Reserved. www.facebook.com/garfield
Distributed by Andrews McMeel Syndication
JIM DAVIS 6-4

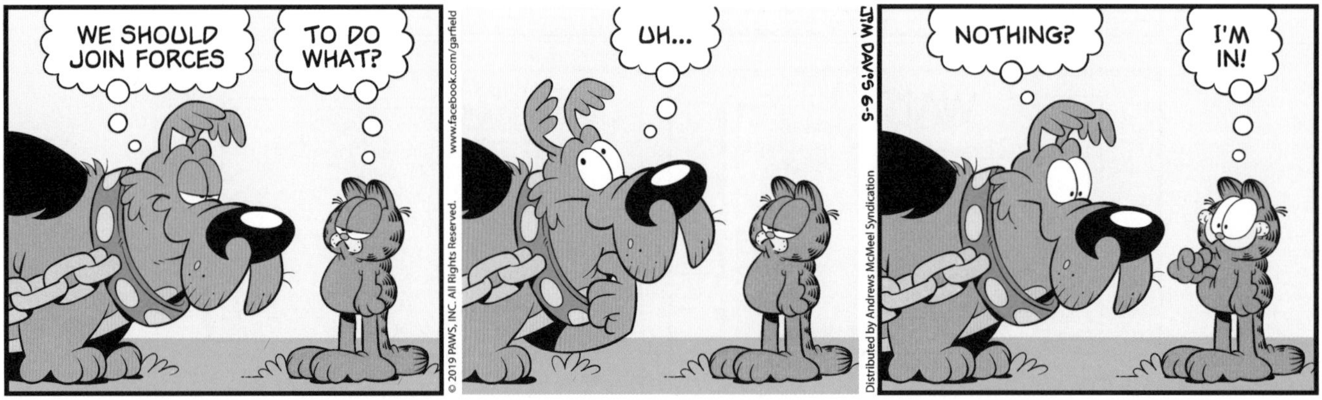
WE SHOULD JOIN FORCES
TO DO WHAT?
UH...
NOTHING?
I'M IN!
© 2019 PAWS, INC. All Rights Reserved. www.facebook.com/garfield
Distributed by Andrews McMeel Syndication
JIM DAVIS 6-5

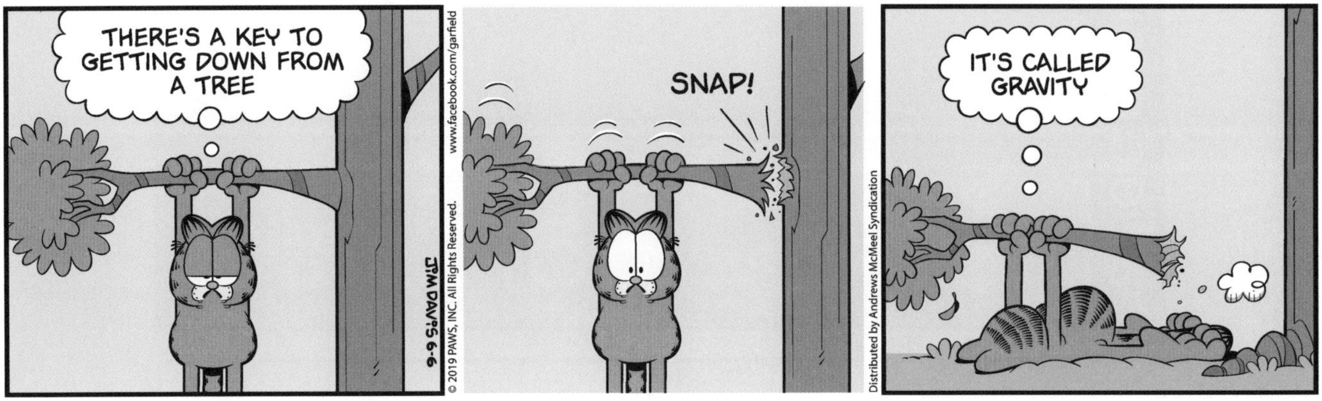
THERE'S A KEY TO GETTING DOWN FROM A TREE
SNAP!
IT'S CALLED GRAVITY
JIM DAVIS 6-6
© 2019 PAWS, INC. All Rights Reserved. www.facebook.com/garfield
Distributed by Andrews McMeel Syndication

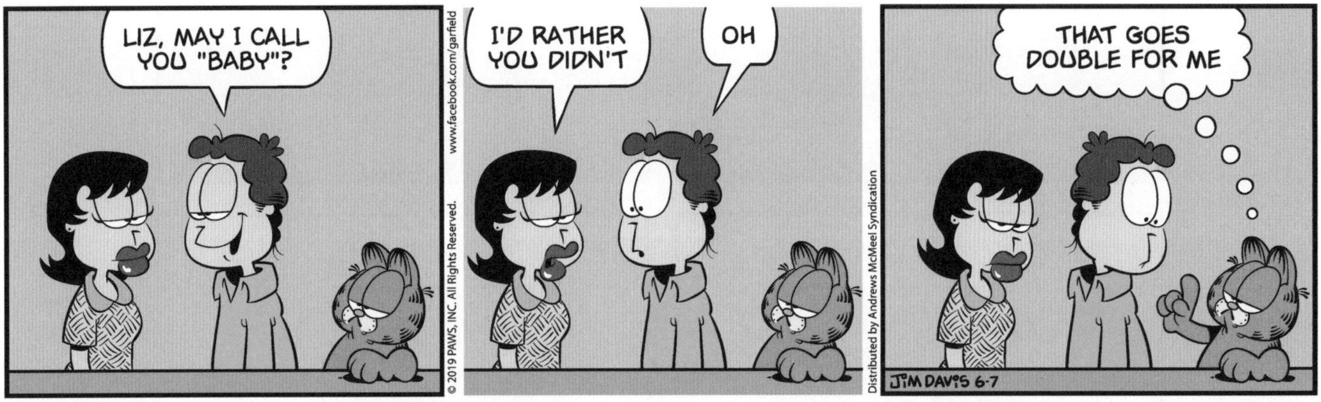
LIZ, MAY I CALL YOU "BABY"?
I'D RATHER YOU DIDN'T
OH
THAT GOES DOUBLE FOR ME
JIM DAVIS 6-7
© 2019 PAWS, INC. All Rights Reserved. www.facebook.com/garfield
Distributed by Andrews McMeel Syndication

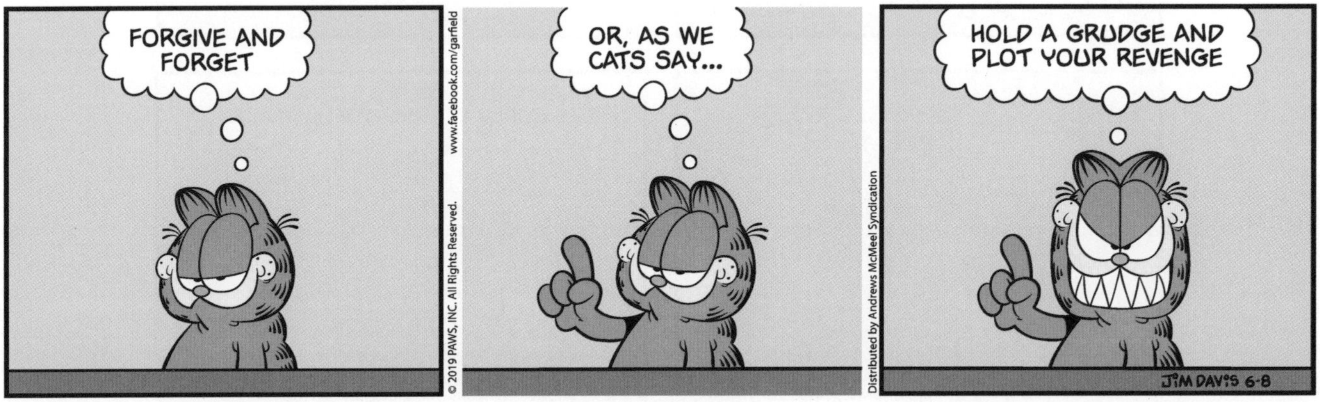
FORGIVE AND FORGET
OR, AS WE CATS SAY...
HOLD A GRUDGE AND PLOT YOUR REVENGE
JIM DAVIS 6-8
© 2019 PAWS, INC. All Rights Reserved. www.facebook.com/garfield
Distributed by Andrews McMeel Syndication

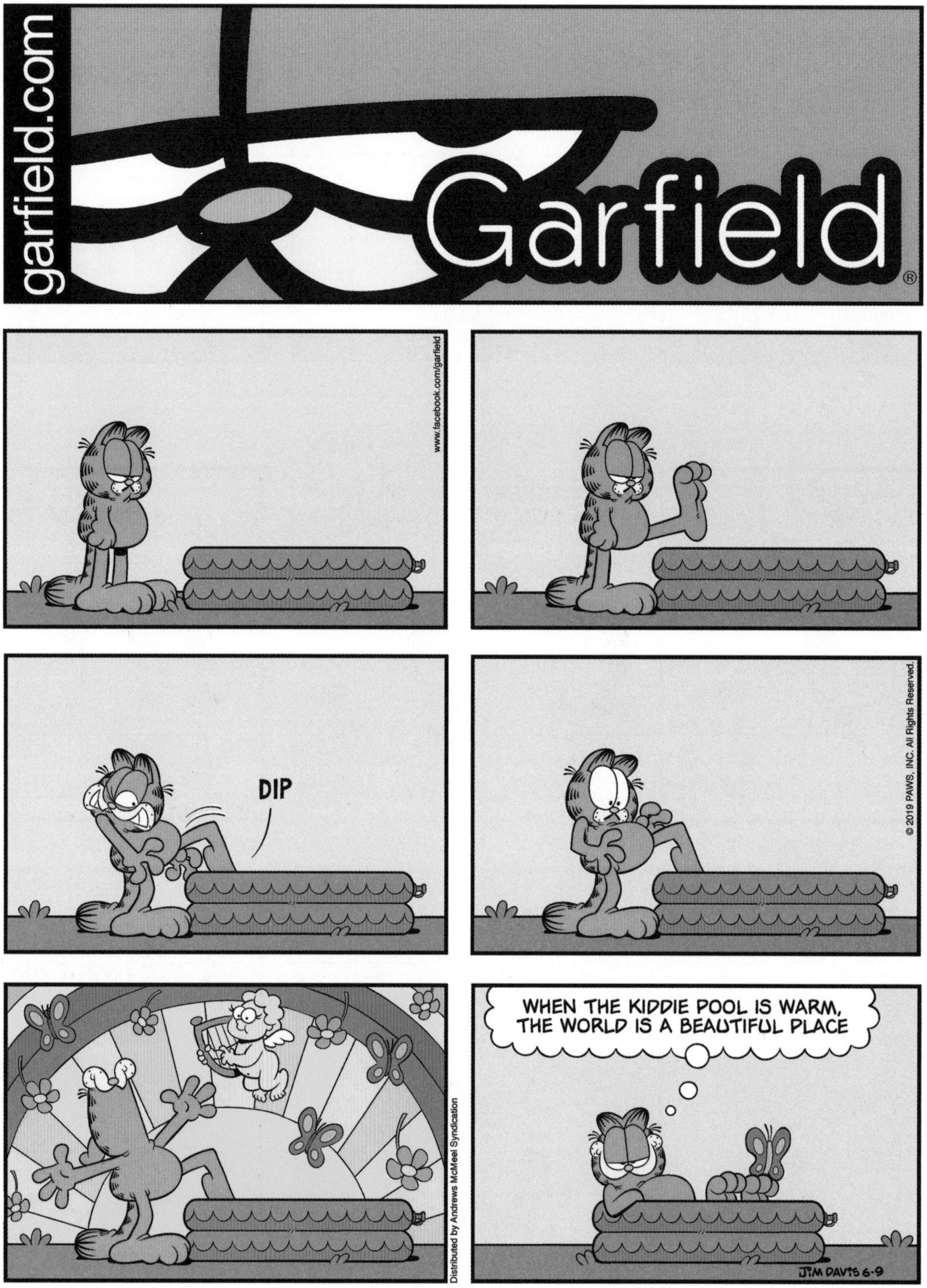
garfield.com
Garfield®
www.facebook.com/garfield
DIP
© 2019 PAWS, INC. All Rights Reserved.
Distributed by Andrews McMeel Syndication
WHEN THE KIDDIE POOL IS WARM, THE WORLD IS A BEAUTIFUL PLACE
JIM DAVIS 6-9

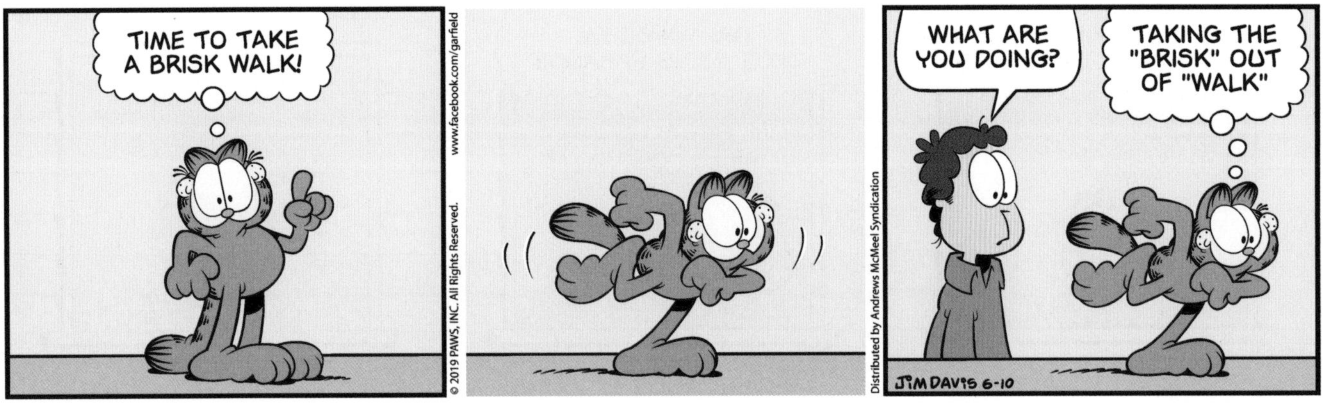
TIME TO TAKE A BRISK WALK!
© 2019 PAWS, INC. All Rights Reserved. www.facebook.com/garfield
Distributed by Andrews McMeel Syndication
WHAT ARE YOU DOING?
TAKING THE "BRISK" OUT OF "WALK"
JIM DAVIS 6-10

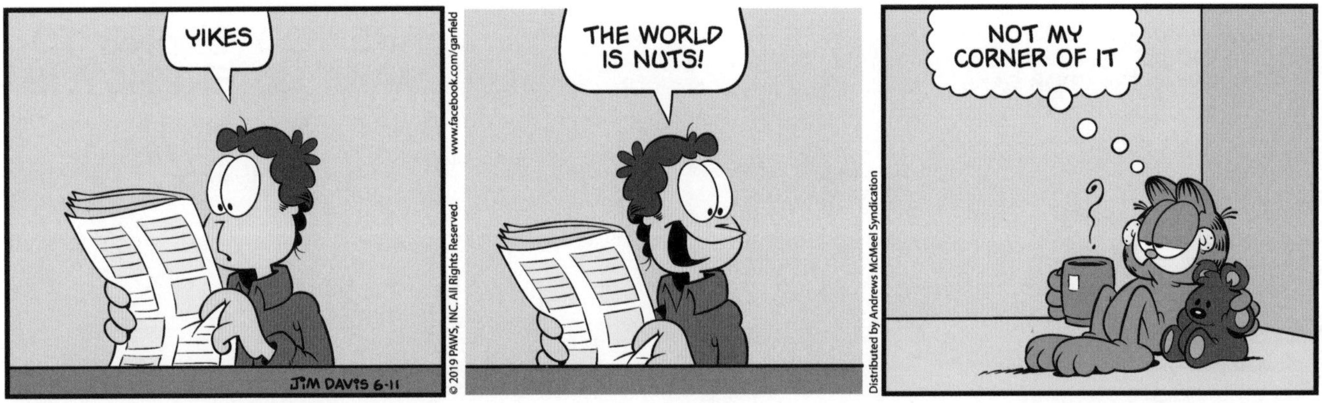
YIKES
JIM DAVIS 6-11
© 2019 PAWS, INC. All Rights Reserved. www.facebook.com/garfield
THE WORLD IS NUTS!
Distributed by Andrews McMeel Syndication
NOT MY CORNER OF IT

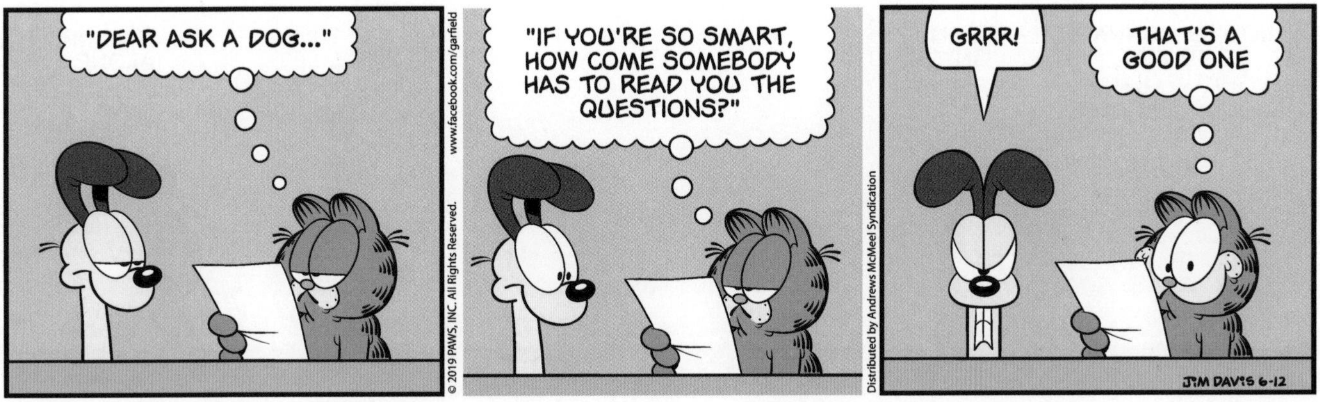
"DEAR ASK A DOG..."
© 2019 PAWS, INC. All Rights Reserved. www.facebook.com/garfield
"IF YOU'RE SO SMART, HOW COME SOMEBODY HAS TO READ YOU THE QUESTIONS?"
Distributed by Andrews McMeel Syndication
GRRR!
THAT'S A GOOD ONE
JIM DAVIS 6-12

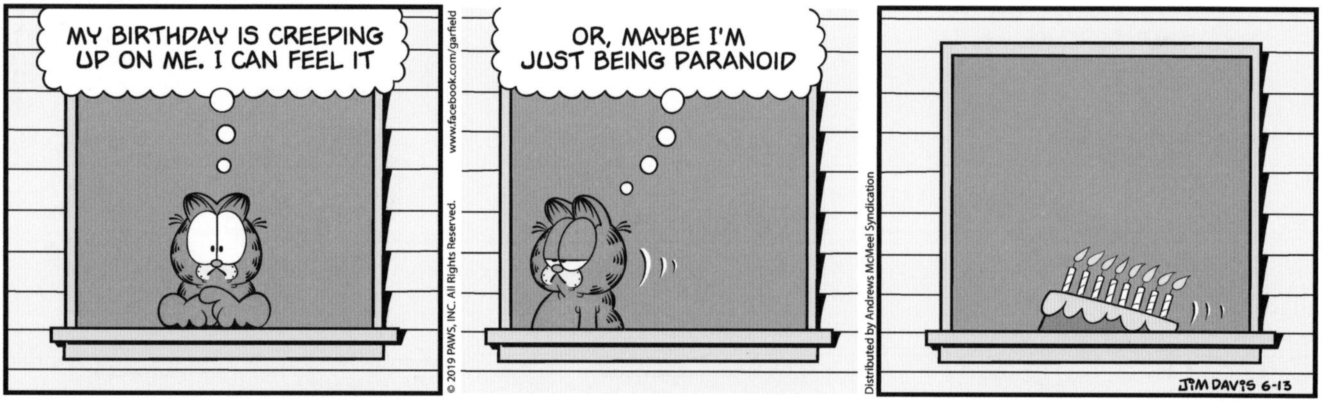
MY BIRTHDAY IS CREEPING UP ON ME. I CAN FEEL IT
OR, MAYBE I'M JUST BEING PARANOID
© 2019 PAWS, INC. All Rights Reserved. www.facebook.com/garfield
Distributed by Andrews McMeel Syndication
JIM DAVIS 6-13

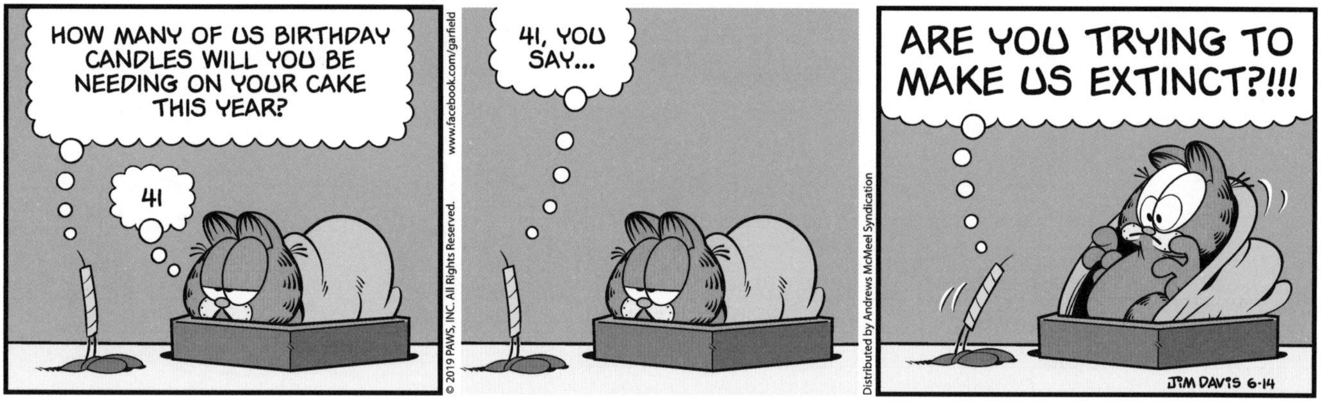
HOW MANY OF US BIRTHDAY CANDLES WILL YOU BE NEEDING ON YOUR CAKE THIS YEAR?
41
41, YOU SAY...
ARE YOU TRYING TO MAKE US EXTINCT?!!!
© 2019 PAWS, INC. All Rights Reserved. www.facebook.com/garfield
Distributed by Andrews McMeel Syndication
JIM DAVIS 6-14

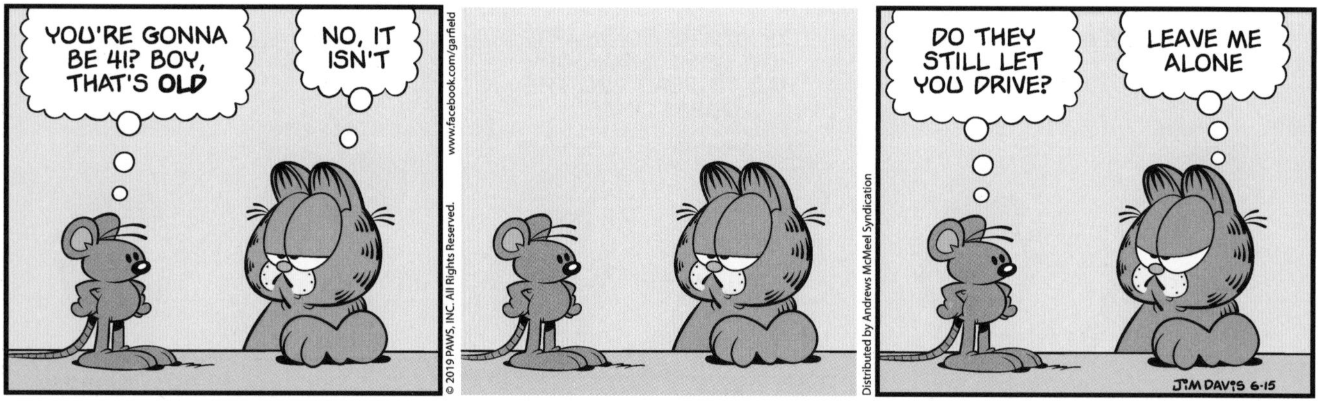
YOU'RE GONNA BE 41? BOY, THAT'S **OLD**
NO, IT ISN'T
DO THEY STILL LET YOU DRIVE?
LEAVE ME ALONE
© 2019 PAWS, INC. All Rights Reserved. www.facebook.com/garfield
Distributed by Andrews McMeel Syndication
JIM DAVIS 6-15

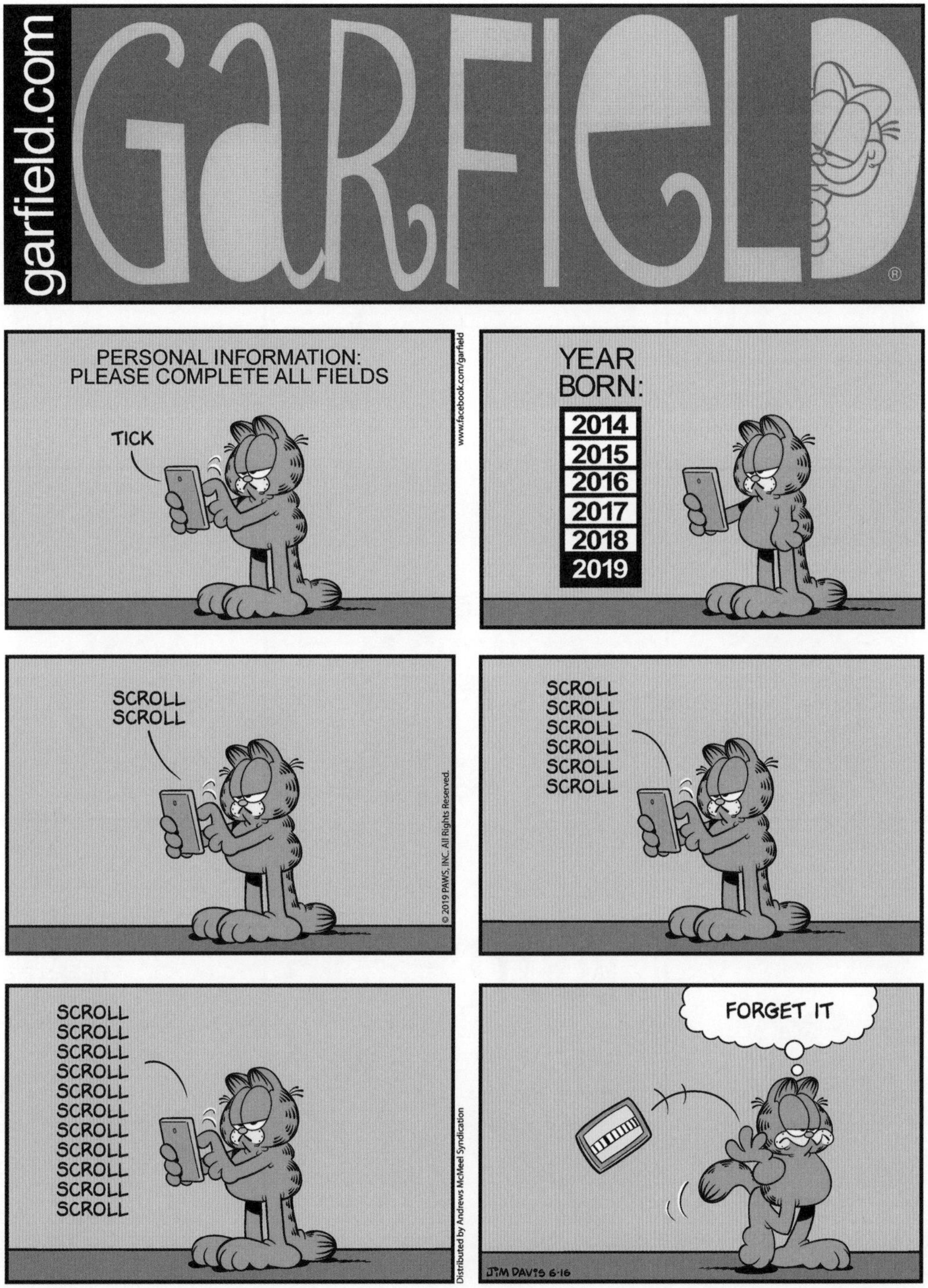
garfield.com
GARFIELD
PERSONAL INFORMATION:
PLEASE COMPLETE ALL FIELDS
TICK
YEAR BORN:
2014
2015
2016
2017
2018
2019
SCROLL
SCROLL
SCROLL
SCROLL
SCROLL
SCROLL
SCROLL
SCROLL
SCROLL
SCROLL
SCROLL
SCROLL
SCROLL
SCROLL
SCROLL
SCROLL
SCROLL
SCROLL
SCROLL
FORGET IT
JIM DAVIS 6-16

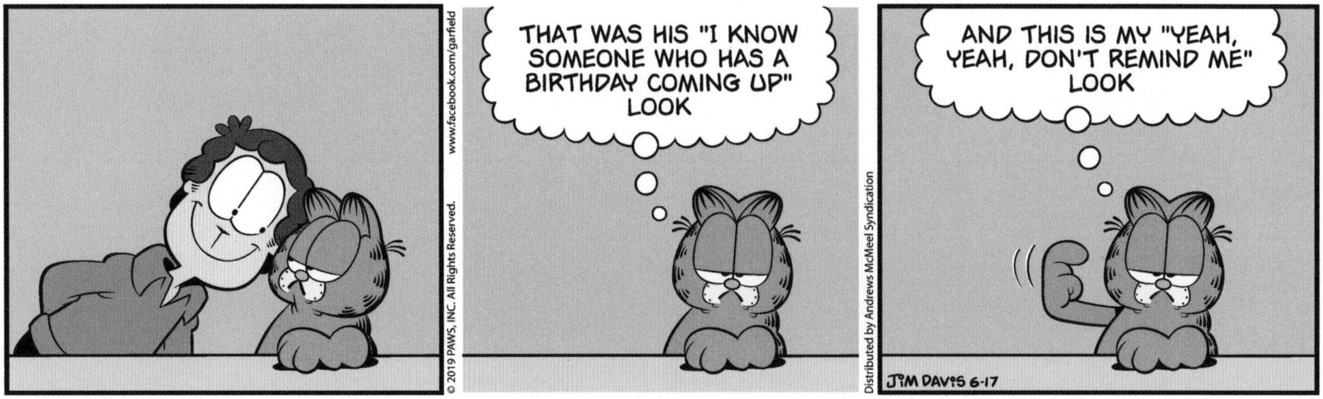
THAT WAS HIS "I KNOW SOMEONE WHO HAS A BIRTHDAY COMING UP" LOOK
AND THIS IS MY "YEAH, YEAH, DON'T REMIND ME" LOOK
JIM DAVIS 6-17
© 2019 PAWS, INC. All Rights Reserved. www.facebook.com/garfield
Distributed by Andrews McMeel Syndication

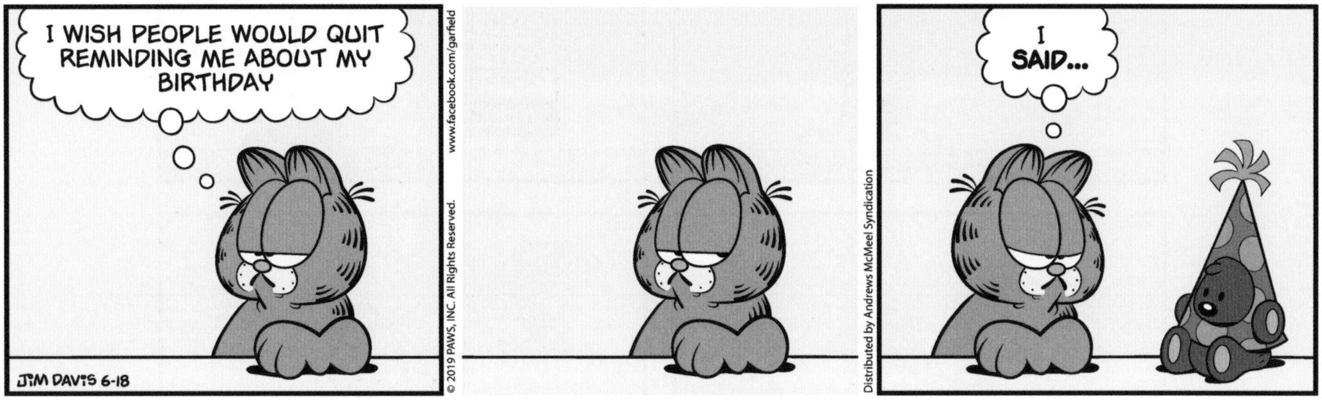
I WISH PEOPLE WOULD QUIT REMINDING ME ABOUT MY BIRTHDAY
I **SAID...**
JIM DAVIS 6-18
© 2019 PAWS, INC. All Rights Reserved. www.facebook.com/garfield
Distributed by Andrews McMeel Syndication

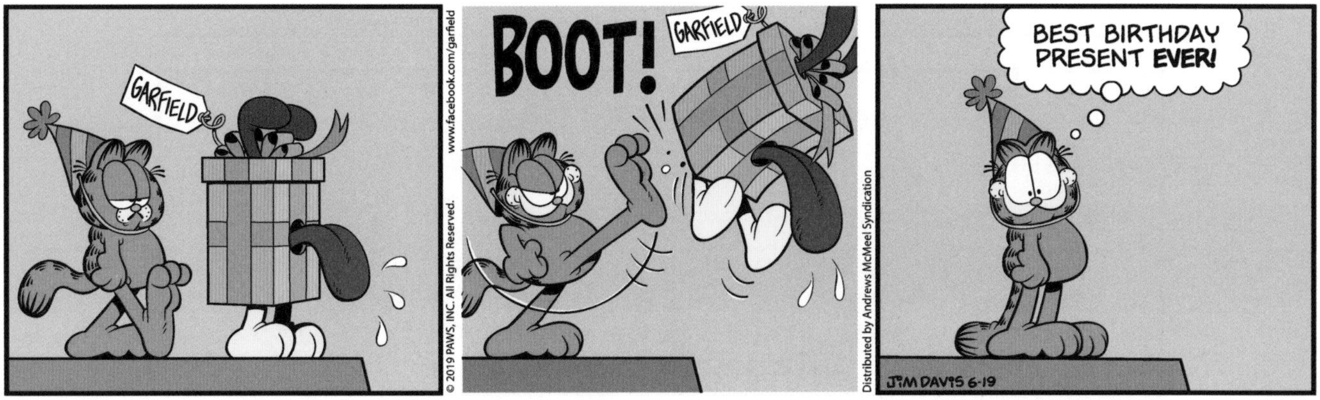
GARFIELD
BOOT!
GARFIELD
BEST BIRTHDAY PRESENT **EVER!**
JIM DAVIS 6-19
© 2019 PAWS, INC. All Rights Reserved. www.facebook.com/garfield
Distributed by Andrews McMeel Syndication

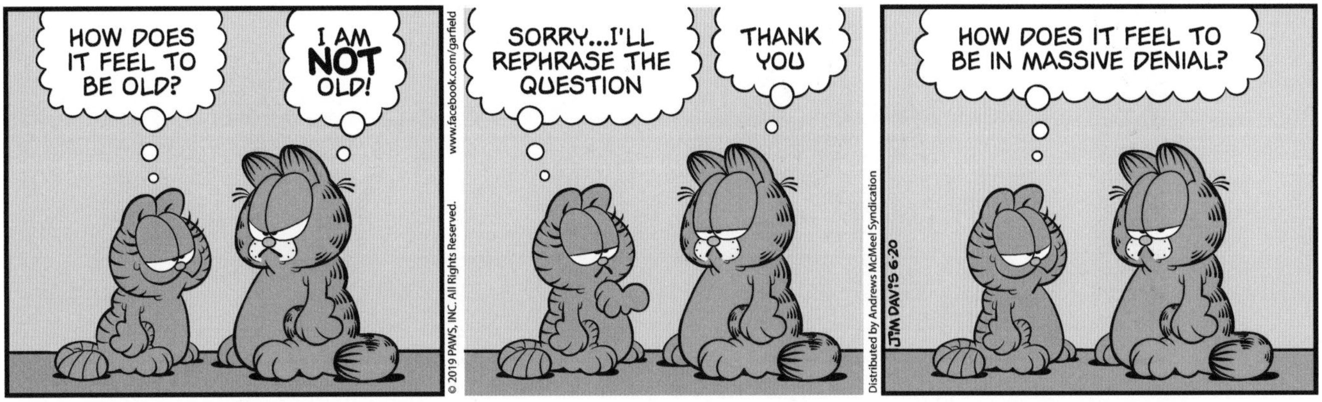
HOW DOES IT FEEL TO BE OLD?
I AM **NOT** OLD!
SORRY...I'LL REPHRASE THE QUESTION
THANK YOU
HOW DOES IT FEEL TO BE IN MASSIVE DENIAL?
© 2019 PAWS, INC. All Rights Reserved. www.facebook.com/garfield
Distributed by Andrews McMeel Syndication
JIM DAVIS 6-20

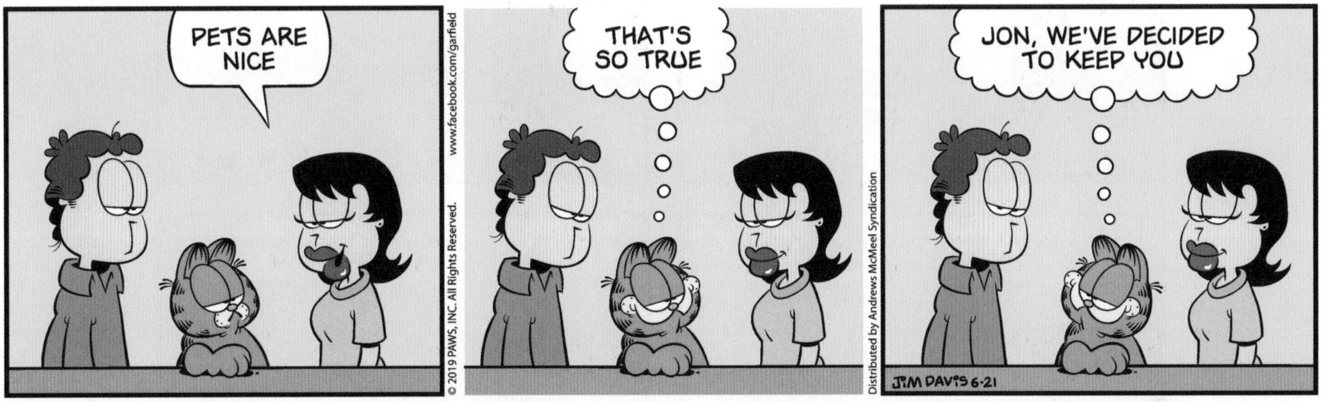
PETS ARE NICE
THAT'S SO TRUE
JON, WE'VE DECIDED TO KEEP YOU
© 2019 PAWS, INC. All Rights Reserved. www.facebook.com/garfield
Distributed by Andrews McMeel Syndication
JIM DAVIS 6-21

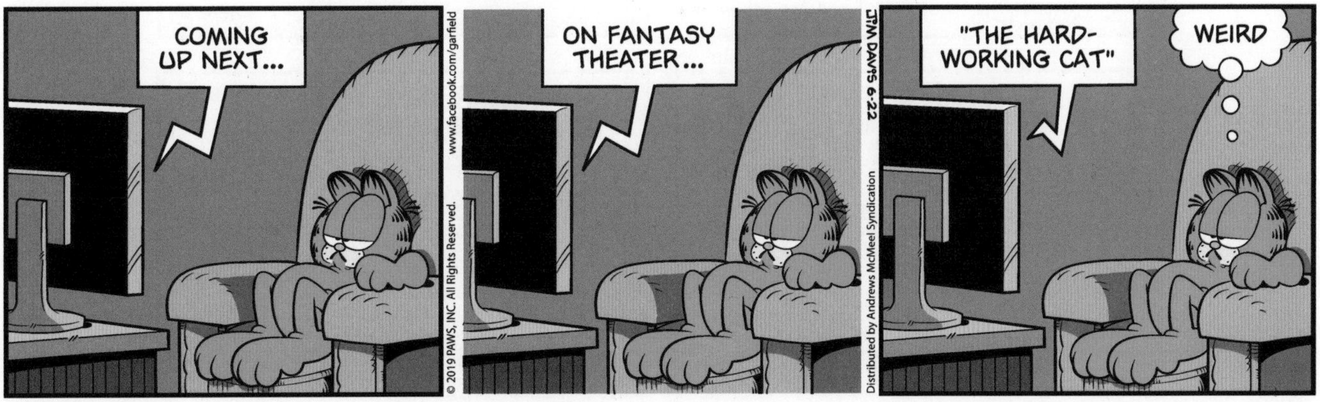
COMING UP NEXT...
ON FANTASY THEATER...
"THE HARD-WORKING CAT"
WEIRD
© 2019 PAWS, INC. All Rights Reserved. www.facebook.com/garfield
JIM DAVIS 6-22
Distributed by Andrews McMeel Syndication

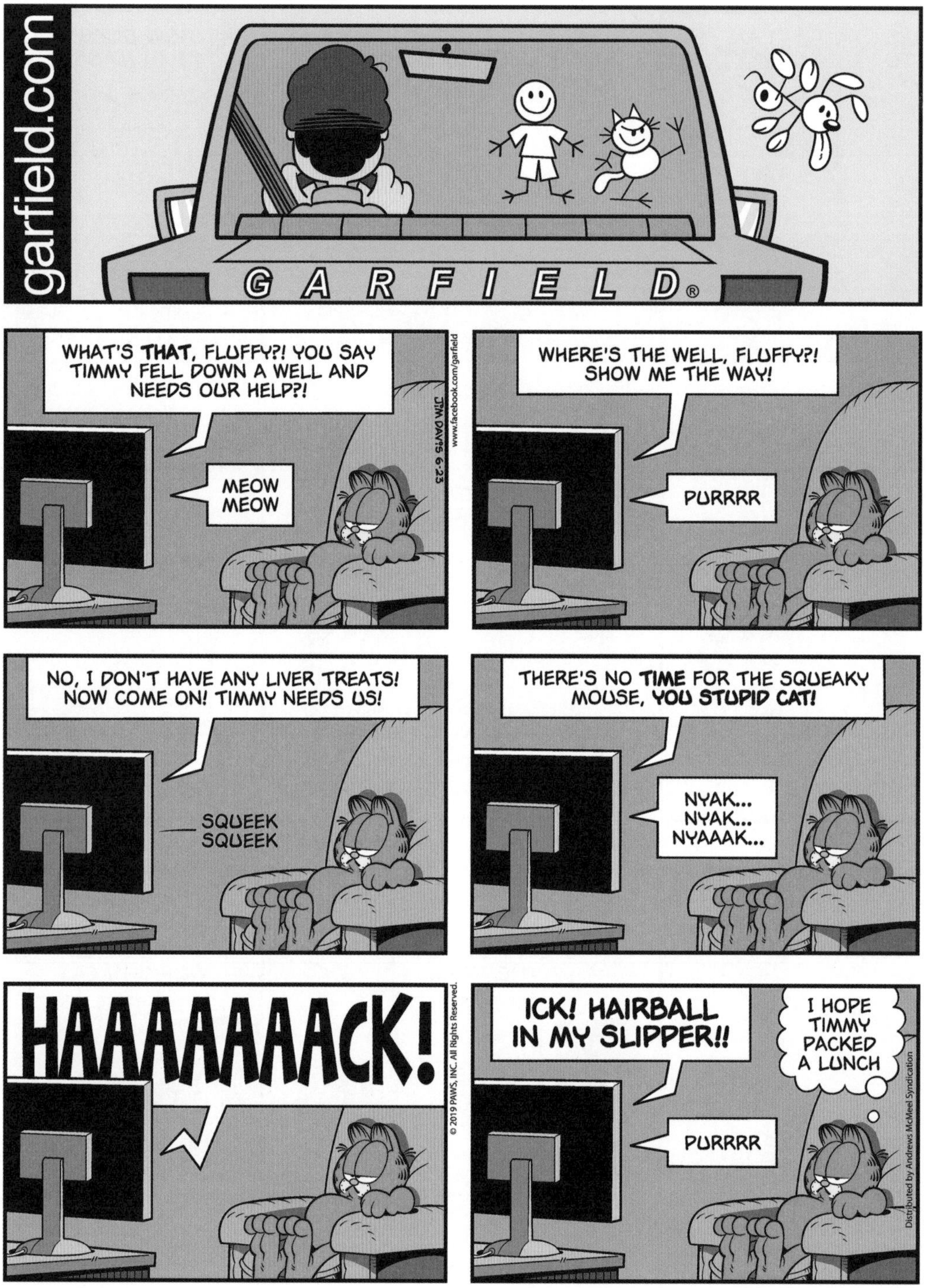
garfield.com
GARFIELD®
WHAT'S THAT, FLUFFY?! YOU SAY TIMMY FELL DOWN A WELL AND NEEDS OUR HELP?!
MEOW MEOW
JIM DAVIS 6-23
www.facebook.com/garfield
WHERE'S THE WELL, FLUFFY?! SHOW ME THE WAY!
PURRRR
NO, I DON'T HAVE ANY LIVER TREATS! NOW COME ON! TIMMY NEEDS US!
SQUEEK SQUEEK
THERE'S NO TIME FOR THE SQUEAKY MOUSE, YOU STUPID CAT!
NYAK... NYAK... NYAAAK...
HAAAAAAACK!
© 2019 PAWS, INC. All Rights Reserved.
ICK! HAIRBALL IN MY SLIPPER!!
I HOPE TIMMY PACKED A LUNCH
PURRRR
Distributed by Andrews McMeel Syndication

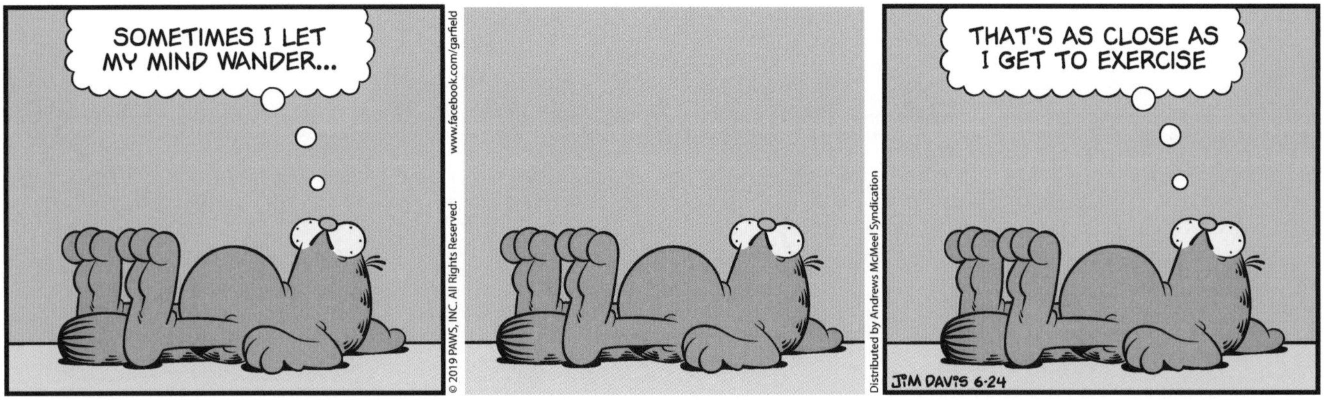
SOMETIMES I LET MY MIND WANDER...
THAT'S AS CLOSE AS I GET TO EXERCISE
© 2019 PAWS, INC. All Rights Reserved. www.facebook.com/garfield
Distributed by Andrews McMeel Syndication
JIM DAVIS 6-24

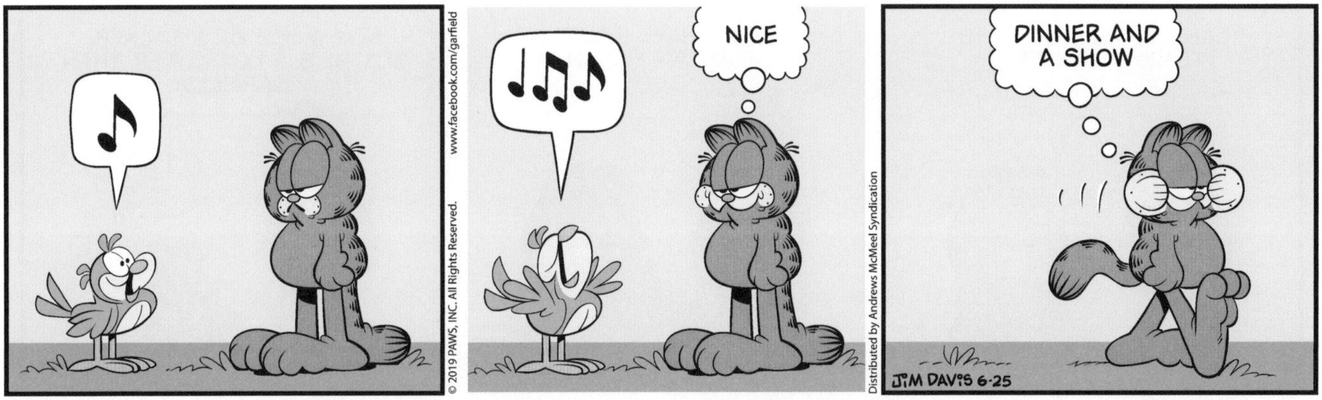
NICE
DINNER AND A SHOW
© 2019 PAWS, INC. All Rights Reserved. www.facebook.com/garfield
Distributed by Andrews McMeel Syndication
JIM DAVIS 6-25

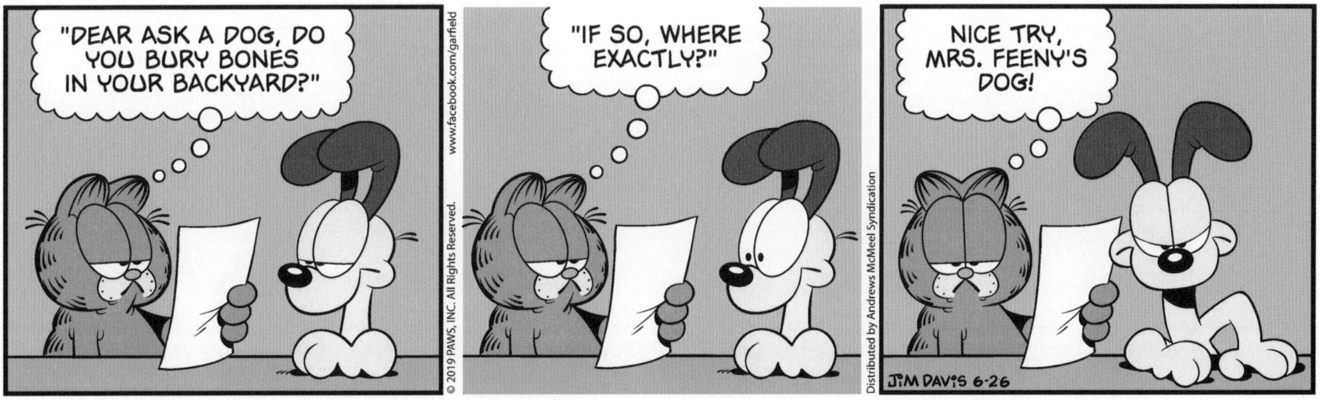
"DEAR ASK A DOG, DO YOU BURY BONES IN YOUR BACKYARD?"
"IF SO, WHERE EXACTLY?"
NICE TRY, MRS. FEENY'S DOG!
© 2019 PAWS, INC. All Rights Reserved. www.facebook.com/garfield
Distributed by Andrews McMeel Syndication
JIM DAVIS 6-26

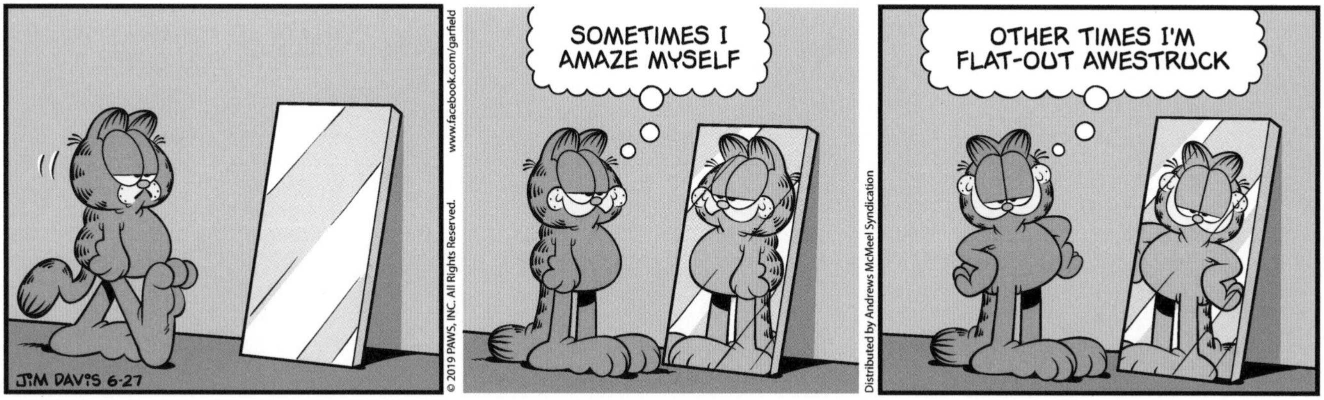
JIM DAVIS 6-27
© 2019 PAWS, INC. All Rights Reserved. www.facebook.com/garfield
SOMETIMES I AMAZE MYSELF
Distributed by Andrews McMeel Syndication
OTHER TIMES I'M FLAT-OUT AWESTRUCK

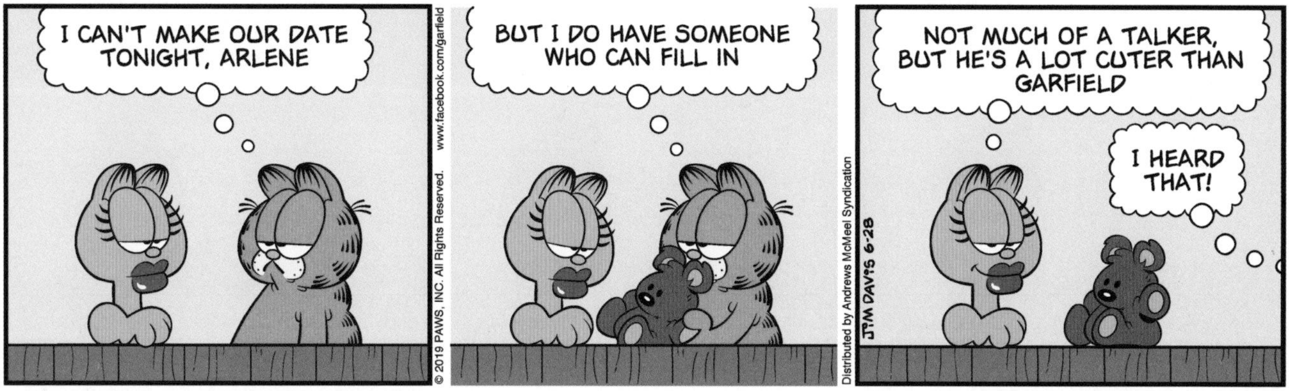
I CAN'T MAKE OUR DATE TONIGHT, ARLENE
© 2019 PAWS, INC. All Rights Reserved. www.facebook.com/garfield
BUT I DO HAVE SOMEONE WHO CAN FILL IN
Distributed by Andrews McMeel Syndication
JIM DAVIS 6-28
NOT MUCH OF A TALKER, BUT HE'S A LOT CUTER THAN GARFIELD
I HEARD THAT!

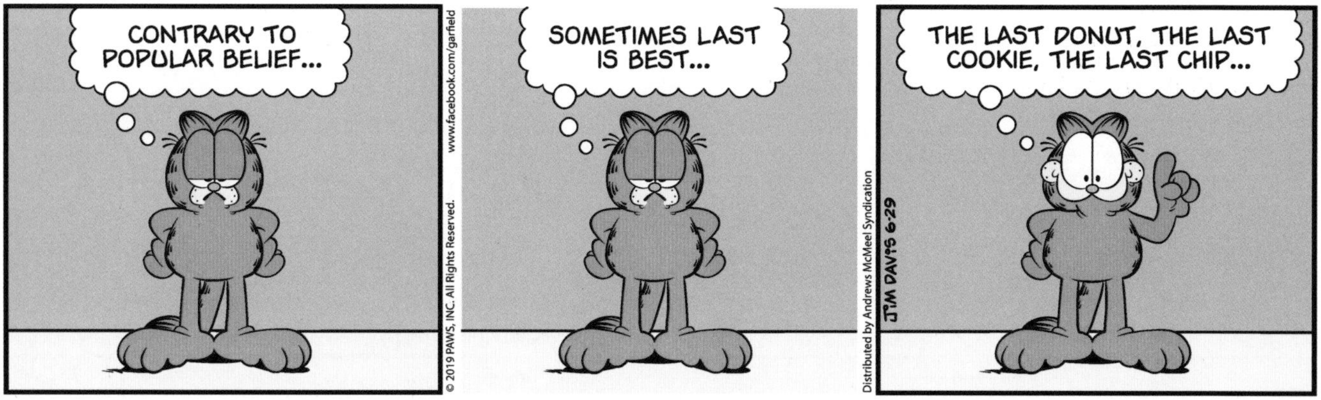
CONTRARY TO POPULAR BELIEF...
© 2019 PAWS, INC. All Rights Reserved. www.facebook.com/garfield
SOMETIMES LAST IS BEST...
Distributed by Andrews McMeel Syndication
JIM DAVIS 6-29
THE LAST DONUT, THE LAST COOKIE, THE LAST CHIP...

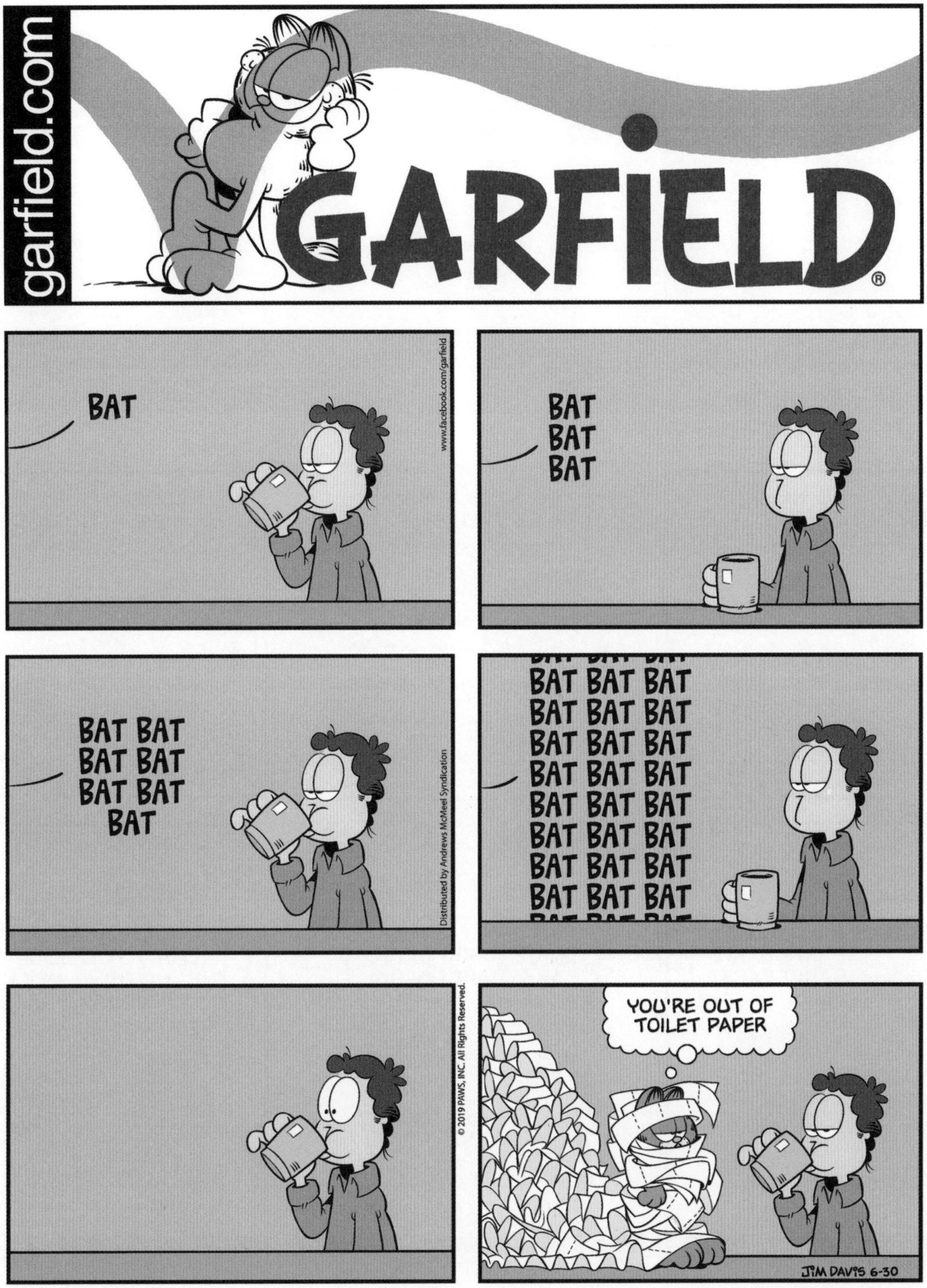
garfield.com
GARFIELD®
BAT
www.facebook.com/garfield
BAT
BAT
BAT
BAT BAT
BAT BAT
BAT BAT
BAT
Distributed by Andrews McMeel Syndication
BAT BAT BAT
BAT BAT BAT
BAT BAT BAT
BAT BAT BAT
BAT BAT BAT
BAT BAT BAT
BAT BAT BAT
BAT BAT BAT
© 2019 PAWS, INC. All Rights Reserved.
YOU'RE OUT OF TOILET PAPER
JIM DAVIS 6-30

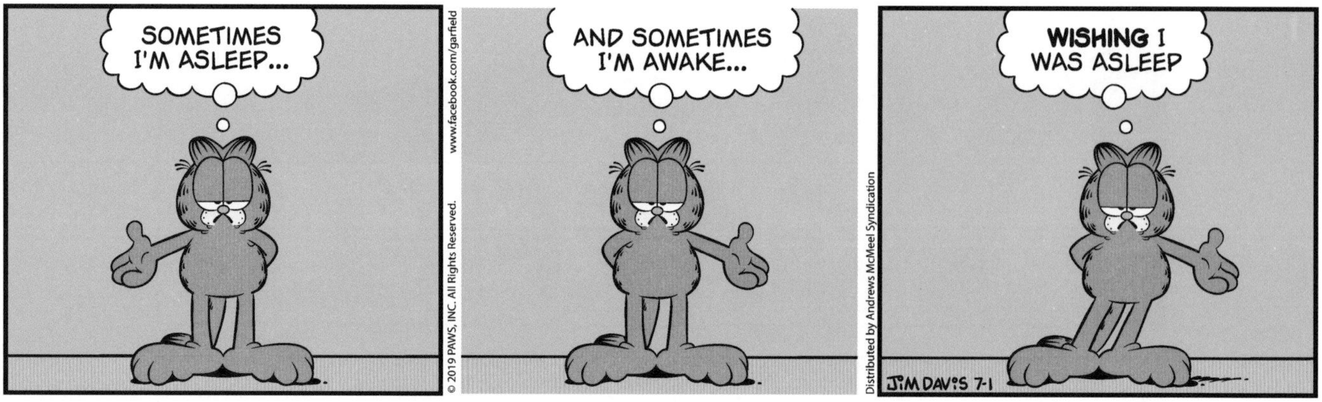
SOMETIMES I'M ASLEEP...
AND SOMETIMES I'M AWAKE...
WISHING I WAS ASLEEP
JIM DAVIS 7-1
© 2019 PAWS, INC. All Rights Reserved. www.facebook.com/garfield
Distributed by Andrews McMeel Syndication

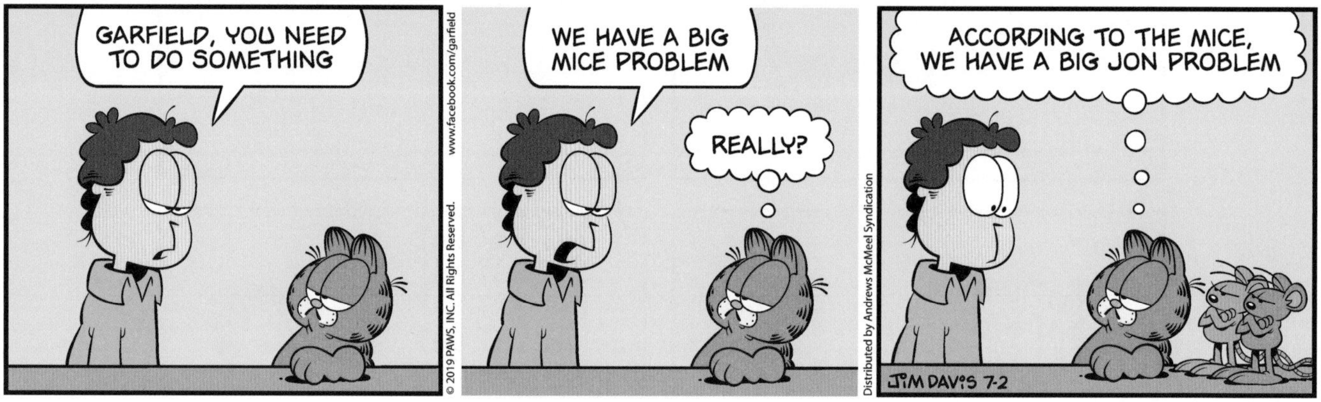
GARFIELD, YOU NEED TO DO SOMETHING
WE HAVE A BIG MICE PROBLEM
REALLY?
ACCORDING TO THE MICE, WE HAVE A BIG JON PROBLEM
JIM DAVIS 7-2
© 2019 PAWS, INC. All Rights Reserved. www.facebook.com/garfield
Distributed by Andrews McMeel Syndication

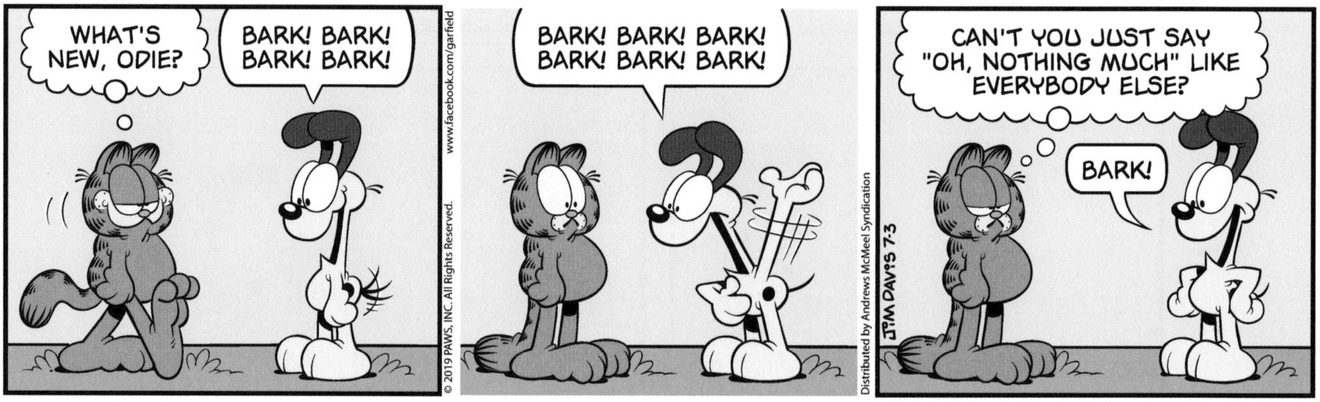
WHAT'S NEW, ODIE?
BARK! BARK! BARK! BARK!
BARK! BARK! BARK! BARK! BARK! BARK!
CAN'T YOU JUST SAY "OH, NOTHING MUCH" LIKE EVERYBODY ELSE?
BARK!
JIM DAVIS 7-3
© 2019 PAWS, INC. All Rights Reserved. www.facebook.com/garfield
Distributed by Andrews McMeel Syndication

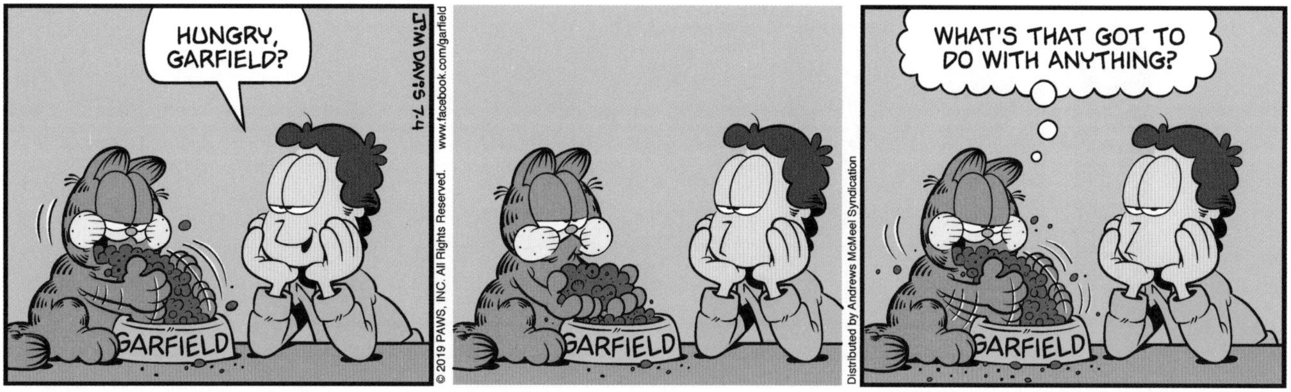
HUNGRY, GARFIELD?
JIM DAVIS 7-4
© 2019 PAWS, INC. All Rights Reserved. www.facebook.com/garfield
GARFIELD
GARFIELD
Distributed by Andrews McMeel Syndication
WHAT'S THAT GOT TO DO WITH ANYTHING?
GARFIELD

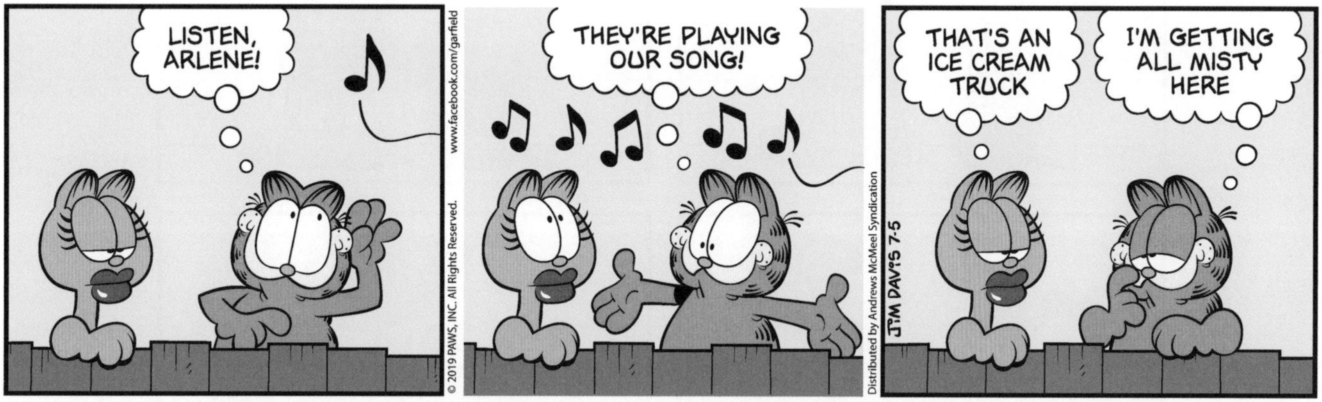
LISTEN, ARLENE!
© 2019 PAWS, INC. All Rights Reserved. www.facebook.com/garfield
THEY'RE PLAYING OUR SONG!
Distributed by Andrews McMeel Syndication
JIM DAVIS 7-5
THAT'S AN ICE CREAM TRUCK
I'M GETTING ALL MISTY HERE

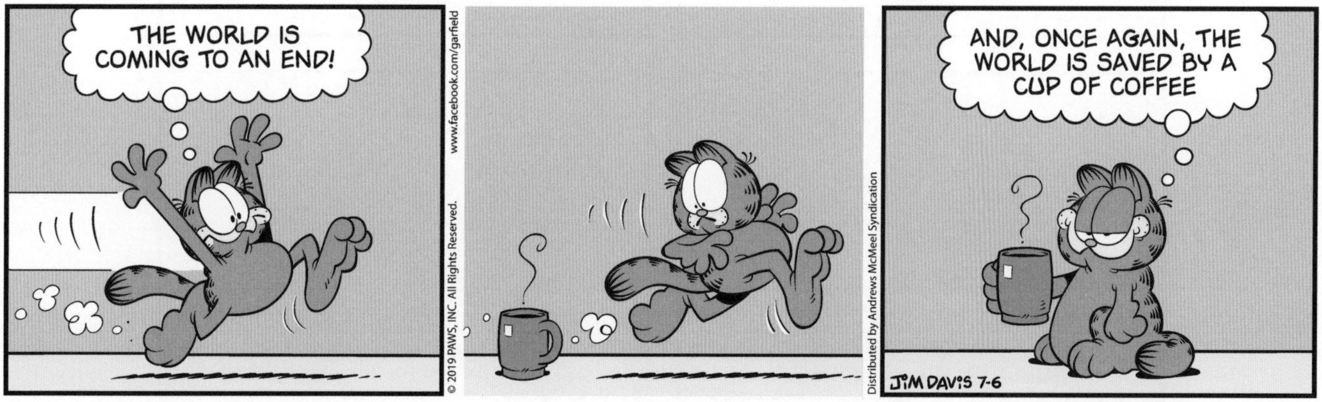
THE WORLD IS COMING TO AN END!
© 2019 PAWS, INC. All Rights Reserved. www.facebook.com/garfield
Distributed by Andrews McMeel Syndication
AND, ONCE AGAIN, THE WORLD IS SAVED BY A CUP OF COFFEE
JIM DAVIS 7-6

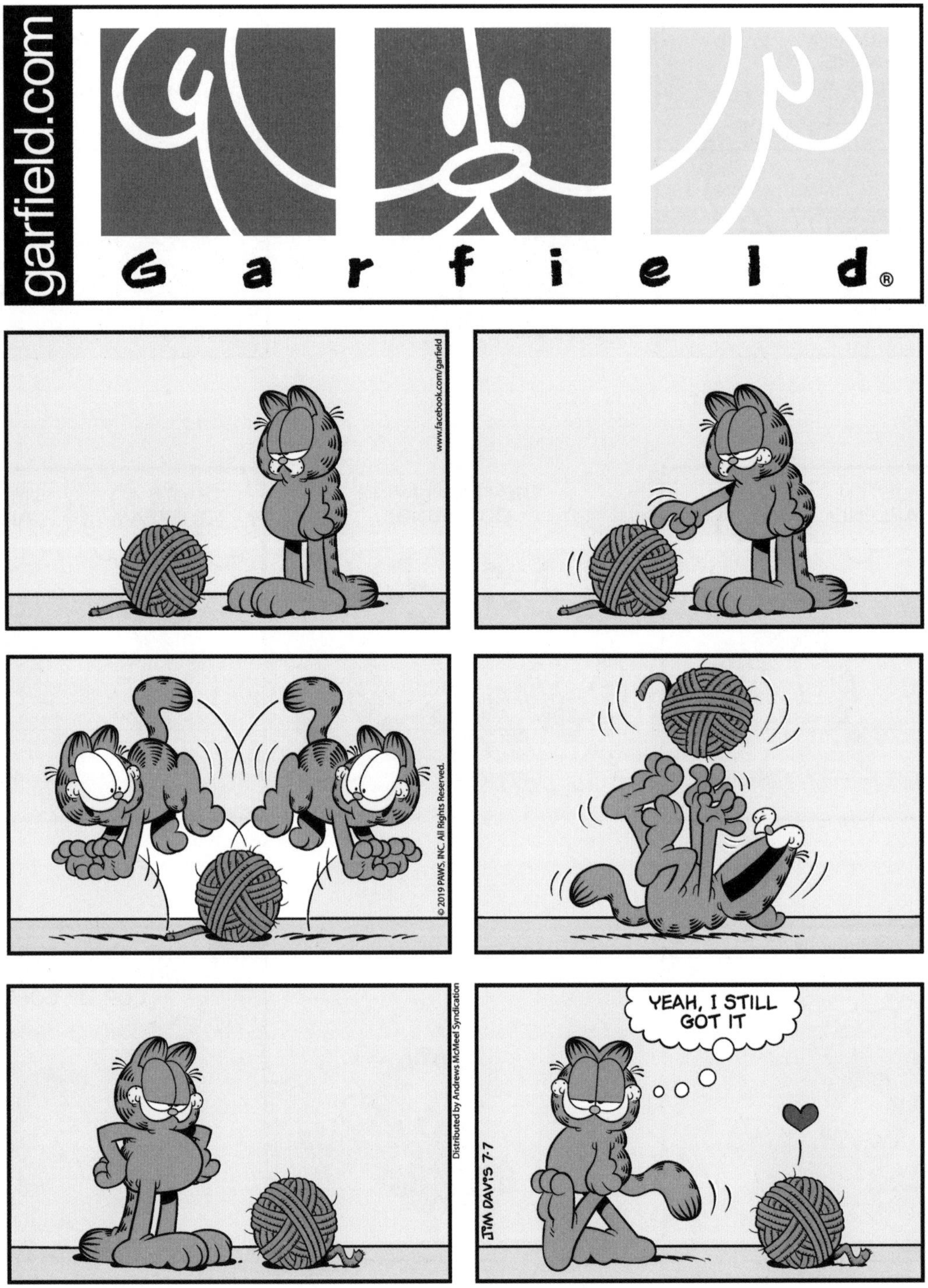
garfield.com
Garfield®
www.facebook.com/garfield
© 2019 PAWS, INC. All Rights Reserved.
Distributed by Andrews McMeel Syndication
JIM DAVIS 7-7
YEAH, I STILL GOT IT

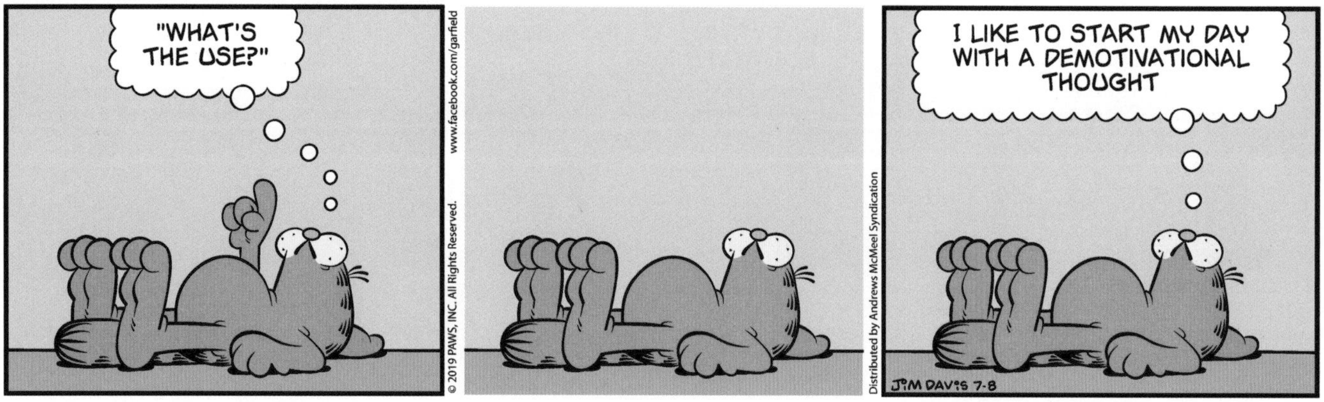
"WHAT'S THE USE?"
I LIKE TO START MY DAY WITH A DEMOTIVATIONAL THOUGHT
JIM DAVIS 7-8
© 2019 PAWS, INC. All Rights Reserved. www.facebook.com/garfield
Distributed by Andrews McMeel Syndication

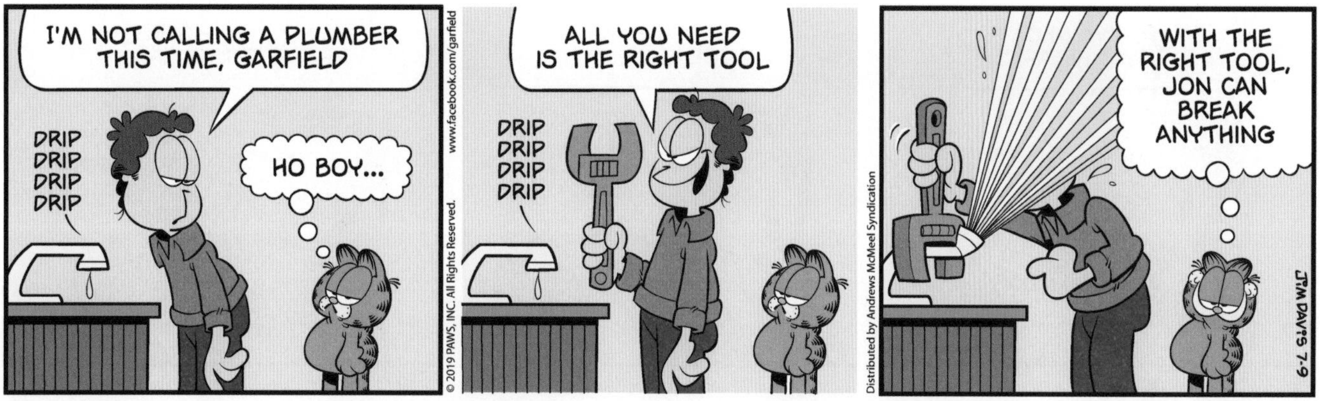
I'M NOT CALLING A PLUMBER THIS TIME, GARFIELD
DRIP DRIP DRIP DRIP
HO BOY...
ALL YOU NEED IS THE RIGHT TOOL
DRIP DRIP DRIP DRIP
WITH THE RIGHT TOOL, JON CAN BREAK ANYTHING
JIM DAVIS 7-9
© 2019 PAWS, INC. All Rights Reserved. www.facebook.com/garfield
Distributed by Andrews McMeel Syndication

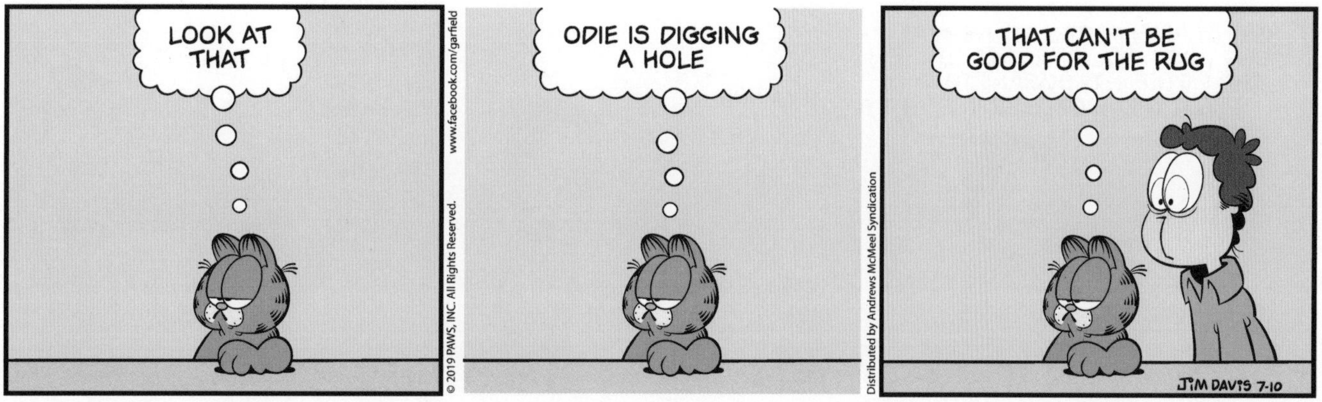
LOOK AT THAT
ODIE IS DIGGING A HOLE
THAT CAN'T BE GOOD FOR THE RUG
JIM DAVIS 7-10
© 2019 PAWS, INC. All Rights Reserved. www.facebook.com/garfield
Distributed by Andrews McMeel Syndication

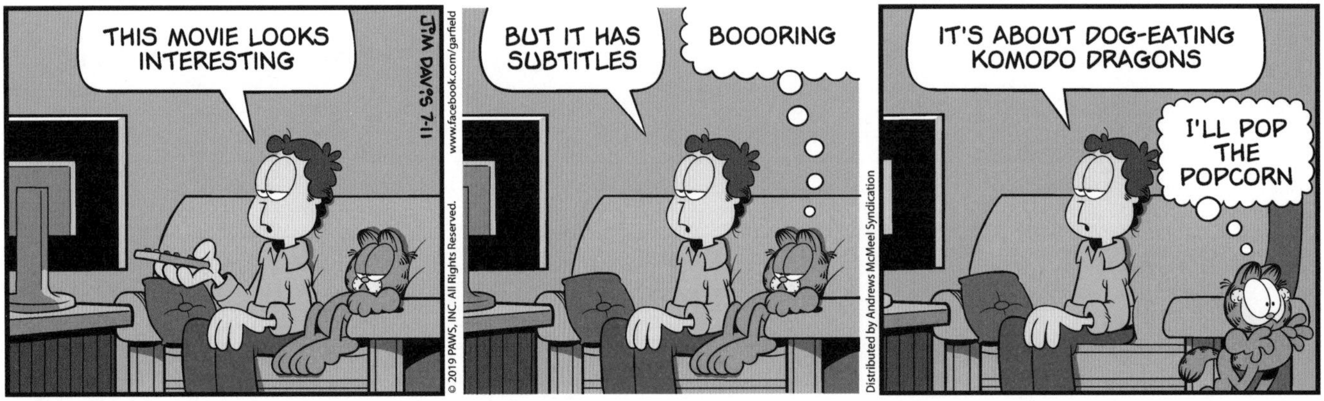
THIS MOVIE LOOKS INTERESTING
JIM DAVIS 7-11
© 2019 PAWS, INC. All Rights Reserved. www.facebook.com/garfield
BUT IT HAS SUBTITLES
BOOORING
IT'S ABOUT DOG-EATING KOMODO DRAGONS
I'LL POP THE POPCORN
Distributed by Andrews McMeel Syndication

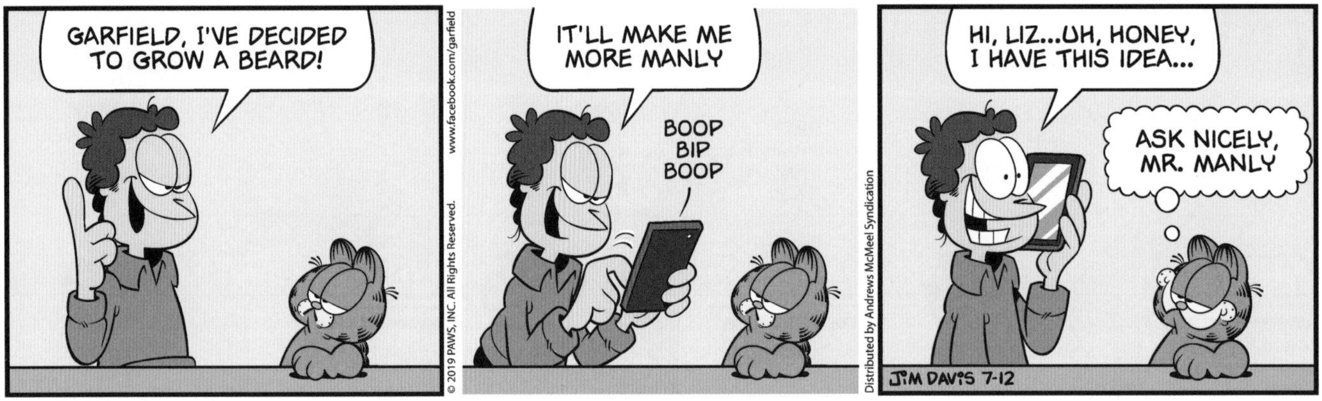
GARFIELD, I'VE DECIDED TO GROW A BEARD!
© 2019 PAWS, INC. All Rights Reserved. www.facebook.com/garfield
IT'LL MAKE ME MORE MANLY
BOOP BIP BOOP
HI, LIZ...UH, HONEY, I HAVE THIS IDEA...
ASK NICELY, MR. MANLY
Distributed by Andrews McMeel Syndication
JIM DAVIS 7-12

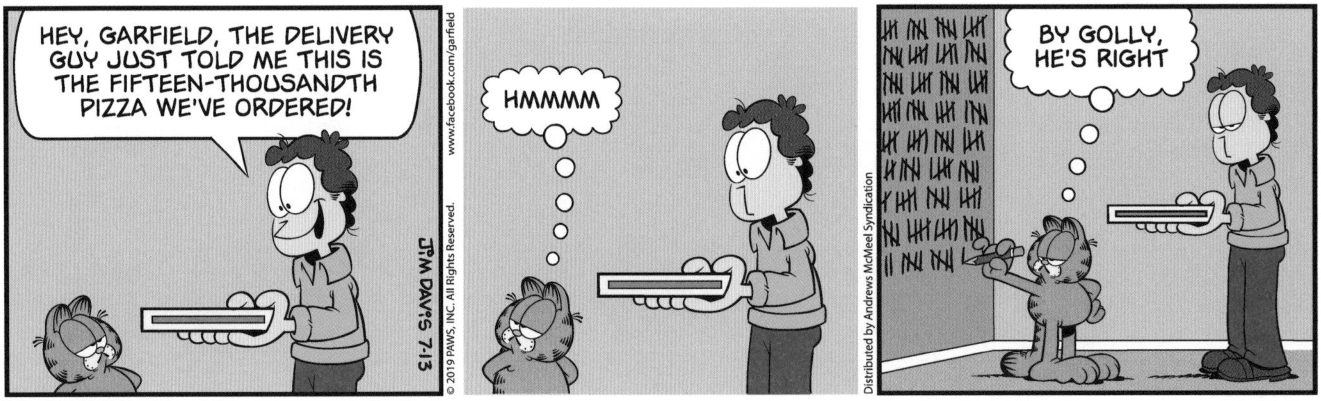
HEY, GARFIELD, THE DELIVERY GUY JUST TOLD ME THIS IS THE FIFTEEN-THOUSANDTH PIZZA WE'VE ORDERED!
JIM DAVIS 7-13
© 2019 PAWS, INC. All Rights Reserved. www.facebook.com/garfield
HMMMM
BY GOLLY, HE'S RIGHT
Distributed by Andrews McMeel Syndication

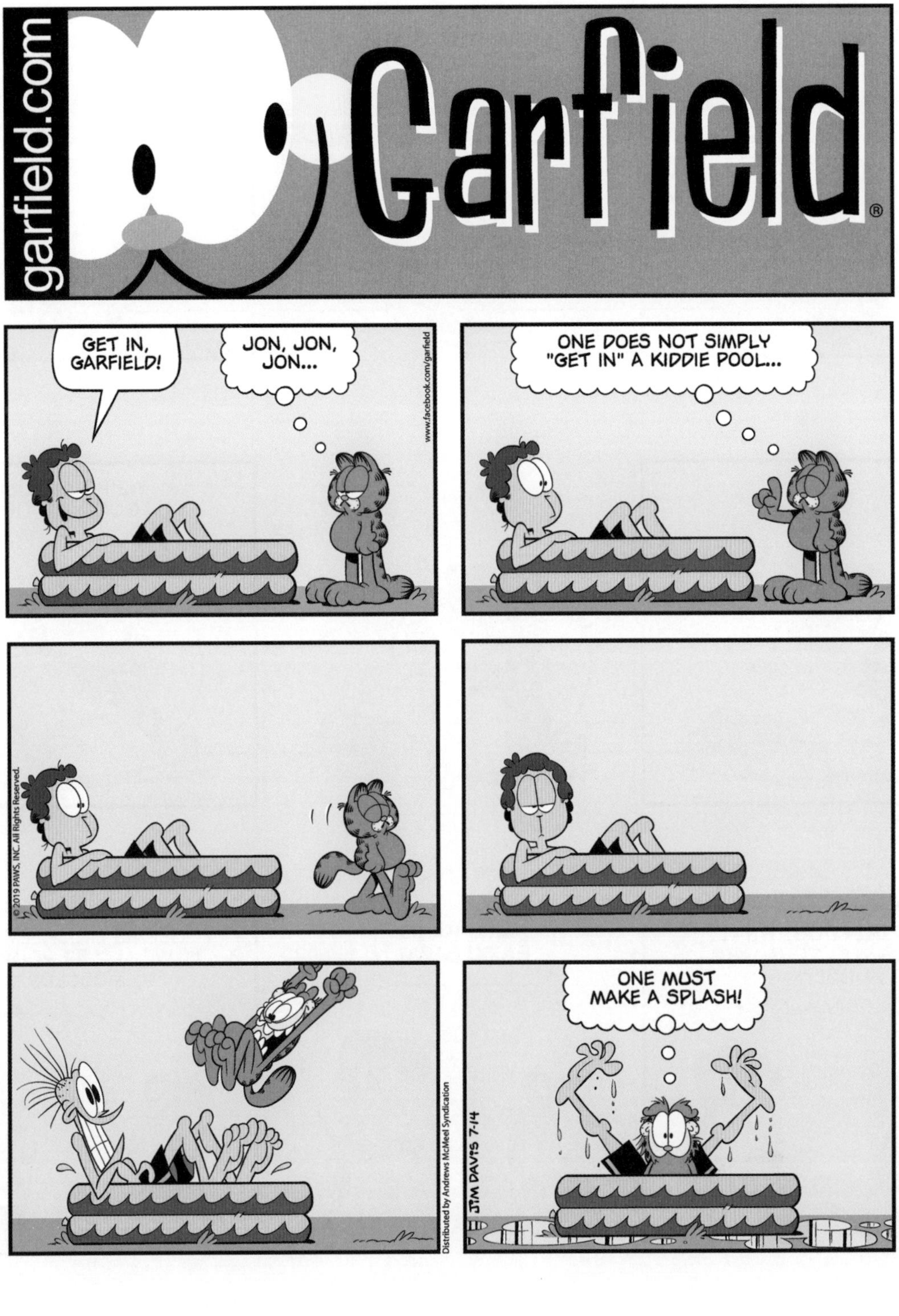
garfield.com
Garfield®
GET IN, GARFIELD!
JON, JON, JON...
www.facebook.com/garfield
ONE DOES NOT SIMPLY "GET IN" A KIDDIE POOL...
© 2019 PAWS, INC. All Rights Reserved.
Distributed by Andrews McMeel Syndication
JIM DAVIS 7-14
ONE MUST MAKE A SPLASH!

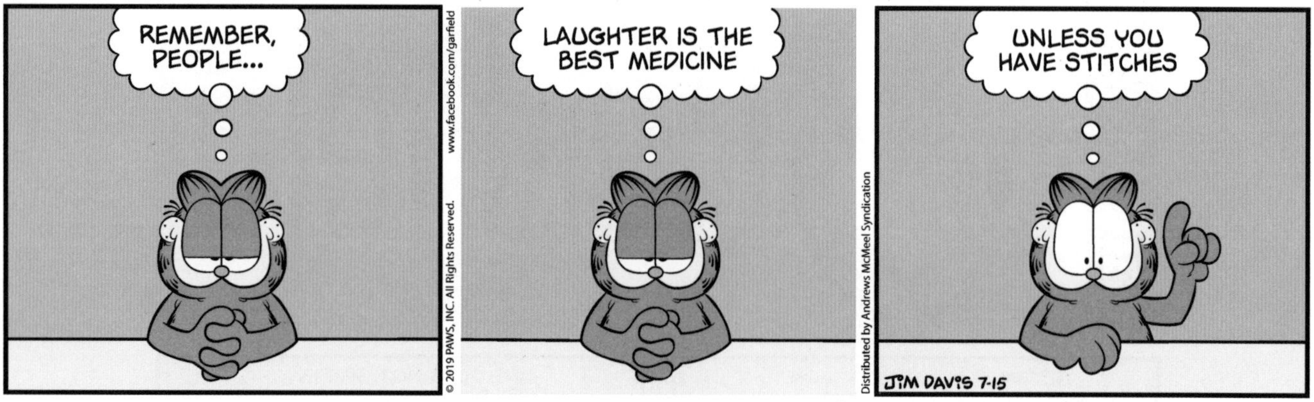
REMEMBER, PEOPLE...
© 2019 PAWS, INC. All Rights Reserved. www.facebook.com/garfield
LAUGHTER IS THE BEST MEDICINE
Distributed by Andrews McMeel Syndication
UNLESS YOU HAVE STITCHES
JIM DAVIS 7-15

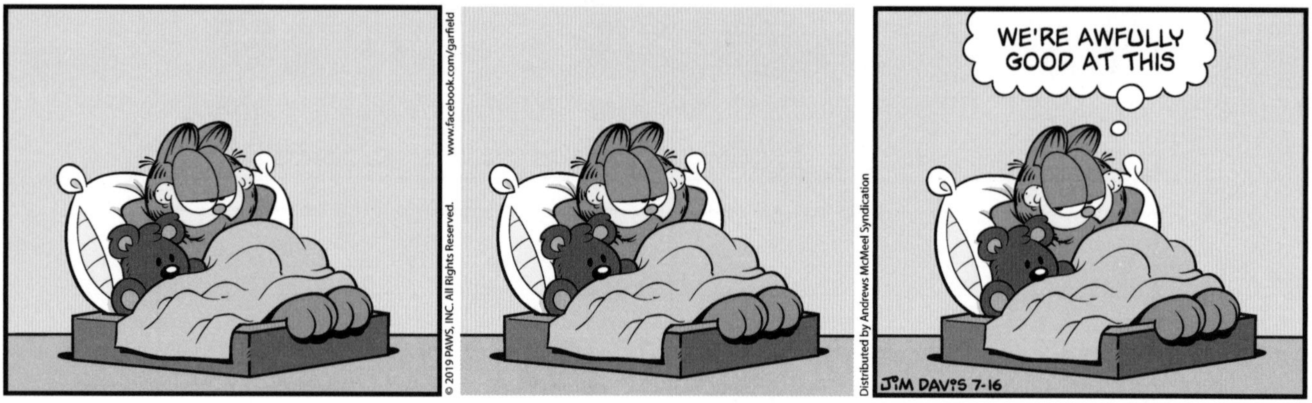
© 2019 PAWS, INC. All Rights Reserved. www.facebook.com/garfield
Distributed by Andrews McMeel Syndication
WE'RE AWFULLY GOOD AT THIS
JIM DAVIS 7-16

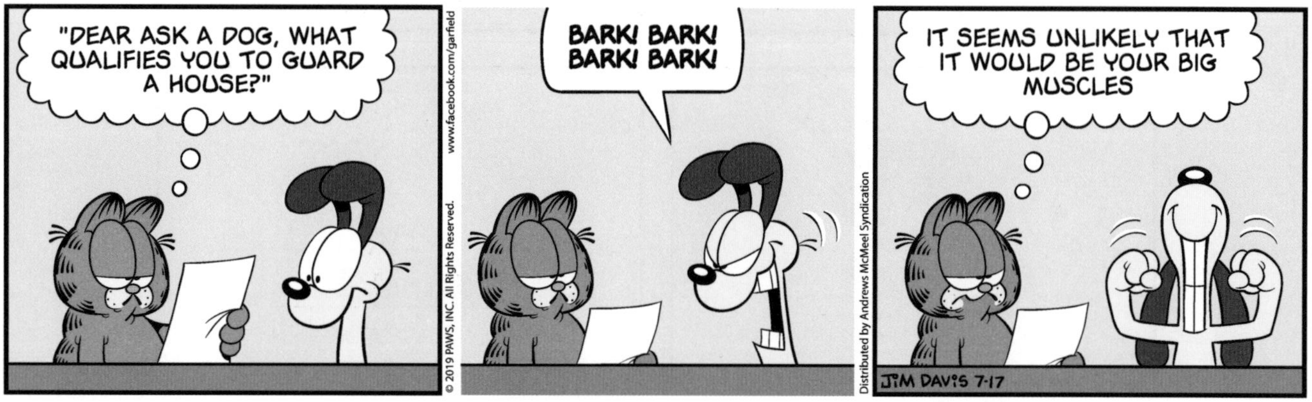
"DEAR ASK A DOG, WHAT QUALIFIES YOU TO GUARD A HOUSE?"
© 2019 PAWS, INC. All Rights Reserved. www.facebook.com/garfield
BARK! BARK! BARK! BARK!
Distributed by Andrews McMeel Syndication
IT SEEMS UNLIKELY THAT IT WOULD BE YOUR BIG MUSCLES
JIM DAVIS 7-17

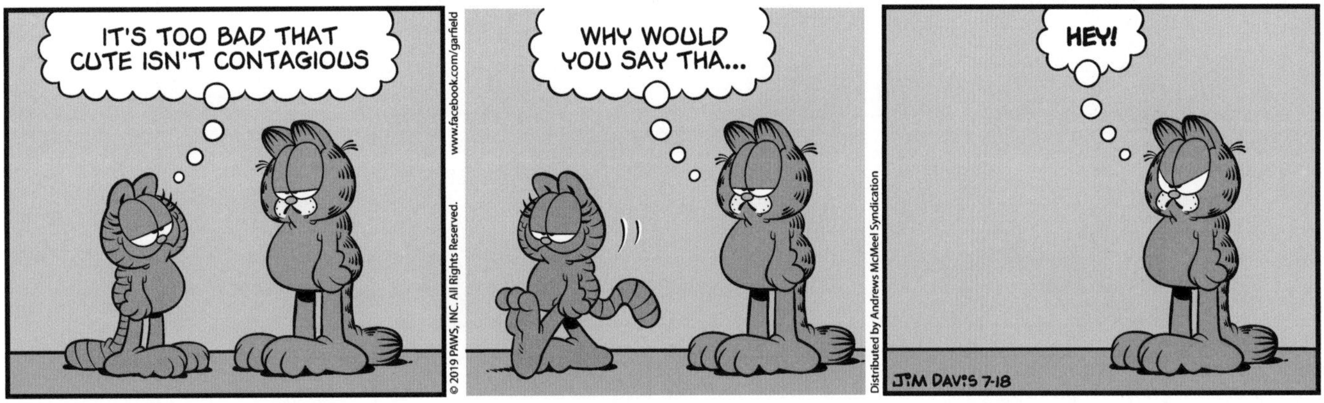
IT'S TOO BAD THAT CUTE ISN'T CONTAGIOUS
WHY WOULD YOU SAY THA...
HEY!
JIM DAVIS 7-18
© 2019 PAWS, INC. All Rights Reserved. www.facebook.com/garfield
Distributed by Andrews McMeel Syndication

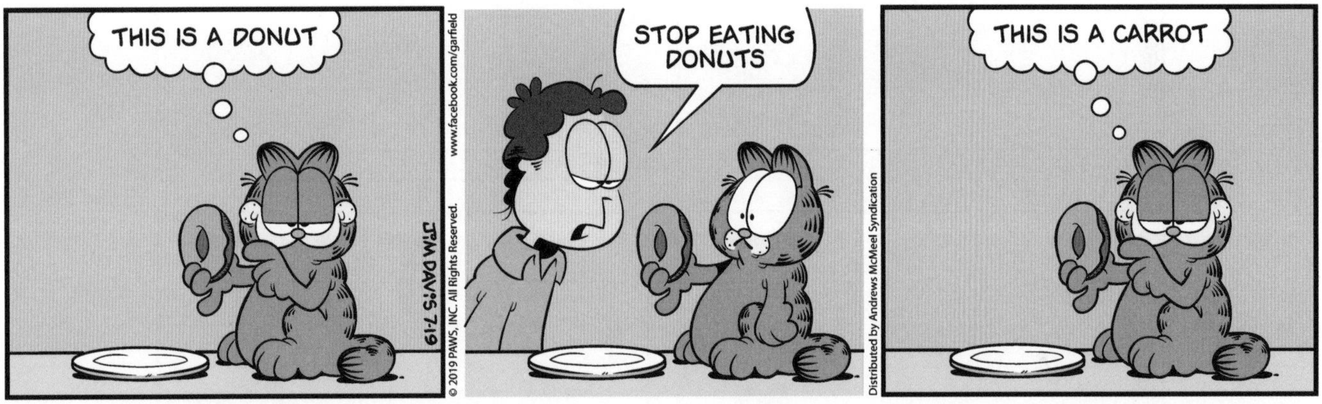
THIS IS A DONUT
STOP EATING DONUTS
THIS IS A CARROT
JIM DAVIS 7-19
© 2019 PAWS, INC. All Rights Reserved. www.facebook.com/garfield
Distributed by Andrews McMeel Syndication

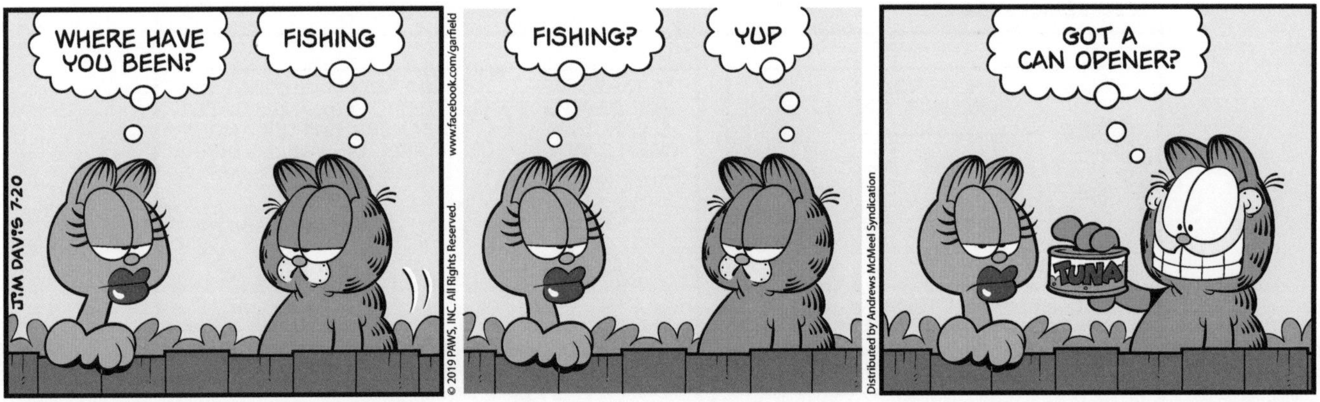
WHERE HAVE YOU BEEN?
FISHING
FISHING?
YUP
GOT A CAN OPENER?
TUNA
JIM DAVIS 7-20
© 2019 PAWS, INC. All Rights Reserved. www.facebook.com/garfield
Distributed by Andrews McMeel Syndication

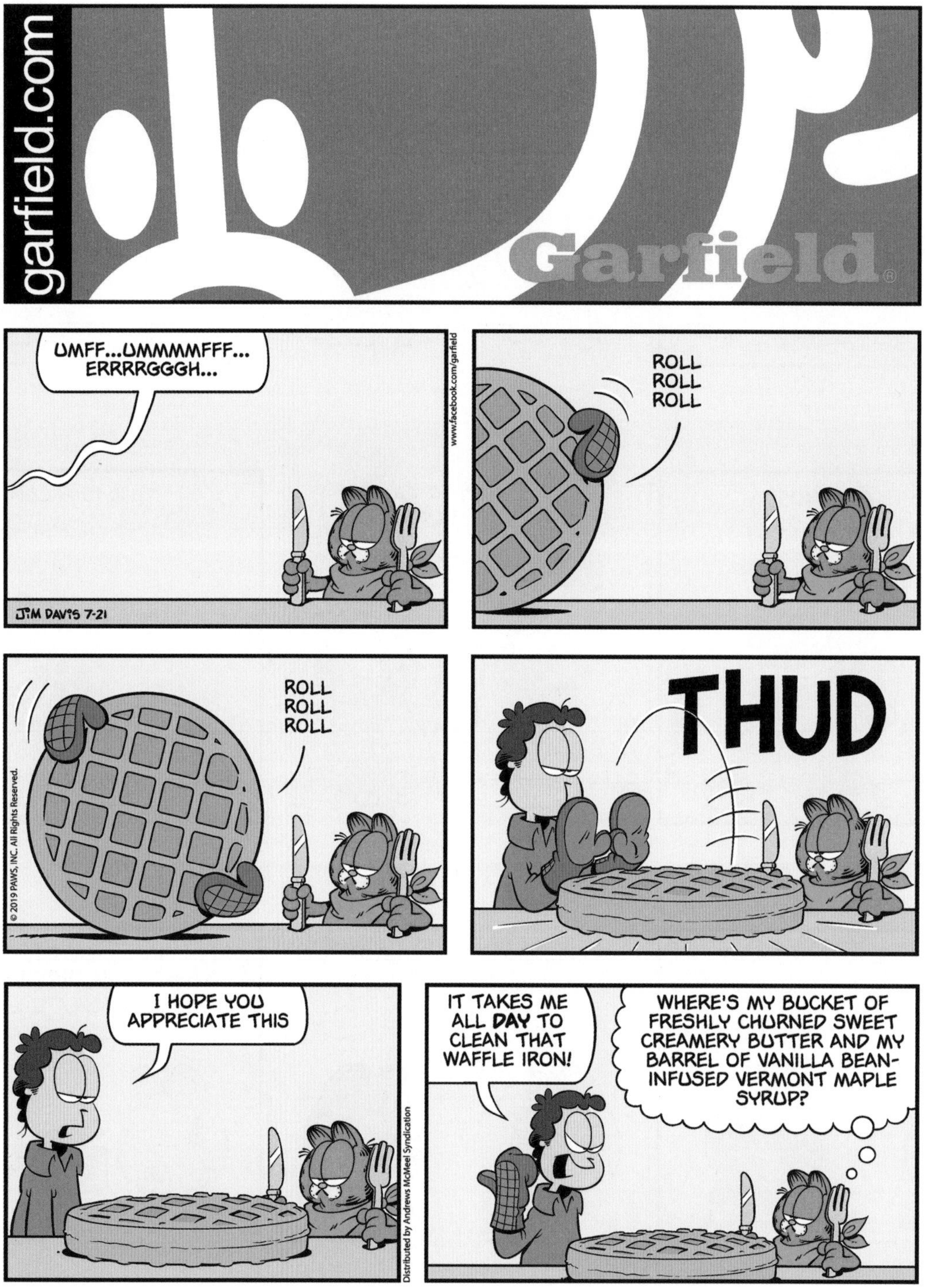
garfield.com
Garfield®
UMFF...UMMMMFFF... ERRRRGGGH...
JIM DAVIS 7-21
www.facebook.com/garfield
ROLL
ROLL
ROLL
© 2019 PAWS, INC. All Rights Reserved.
ROLL
ROLL
ROLL
THUD
I HOPE YOU APPRECIATE THIS
Distributed by Andrews McMeel Syndication
IT TAKES ME ALL **DAY** TO CLEAN THAT WAFFLE IRON!
WHERE'S MY BUCKET OF FRESHLY CHURNED SWEET CREAMERY BUTTER AND MY BARREL OF VANILLA BEAN-INFUSED VERMONT MAPLE SYRUP?

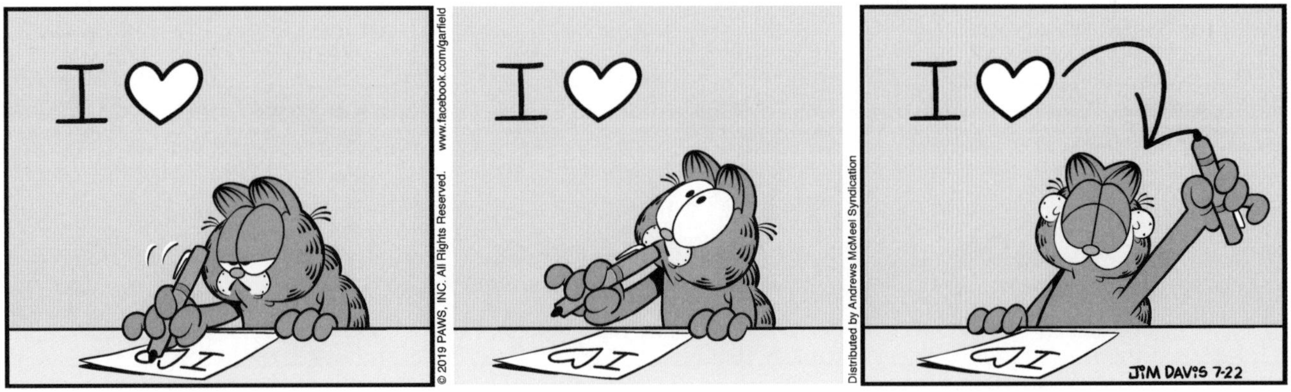
I ♡
© 2019 PAWS, INC. All Rights Reserved. www.facebook.com/garfield
Distributed by Andrews McMeel Syndication
JIM DAVIS 7-22

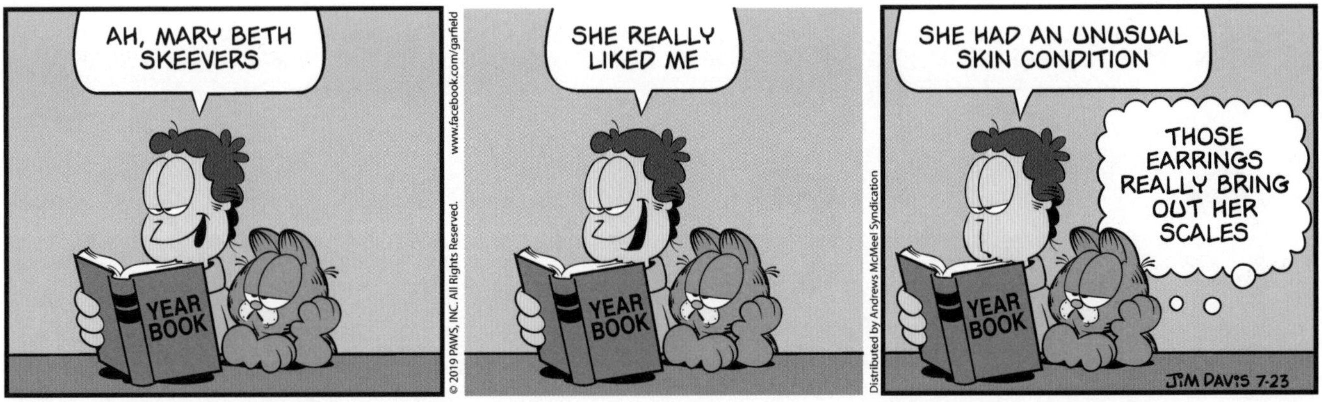
AH, MARY BETH SKEEVERS
YEAR BOOK
SHE REALLY LIKED ME
SHE HAD AN UNUSUAL SKIN CONDITION
THOSE EARRINGS REALLY BRING OUT HER SCALES
© 2019 PAWS, INC. All Rights Reserved. www.facebook.com/garfield
Distributed by Andrews McMeel Syndication
JIM DAVIS 7-23

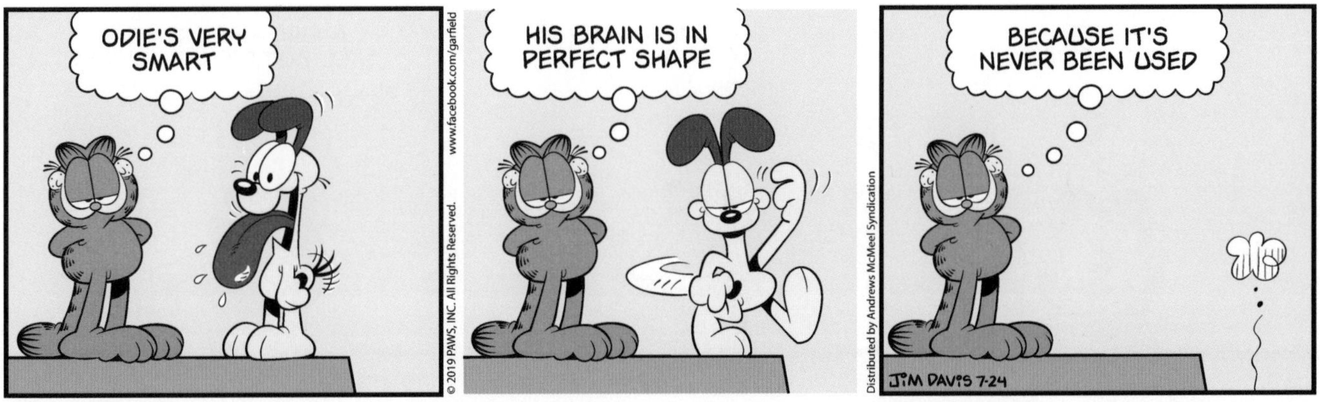
ODIE'S VERY SMART
HIS BRAIN IS IN PERFECT SHAPE
BECAUSE IT'S NEVER BEEN USED
© 2019 PAWS, INC. All Rights Reserved. www.facebook.com/garfield
Distributed by Andrews McMeel Syndication
JIM DAVIS 7-24

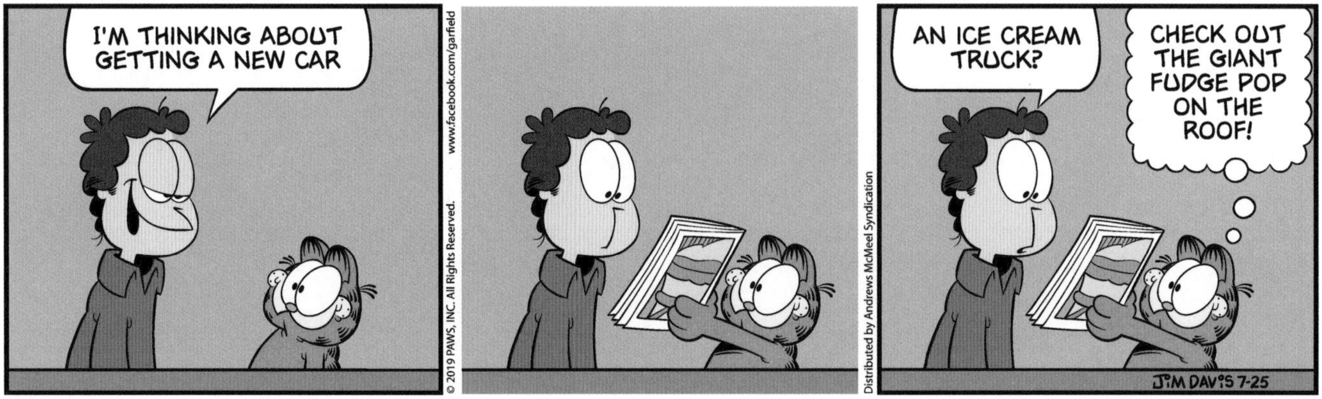
I'M THINKING ABOUT GETTING A NEW CAR
AN ICE CREAM TRUCK?
CHECK OUT THE GIANT FUDGE POP ON THE ROOF!
© 2019 PAWS, INC. All Rights Reserved. www.facebook.com/garfield
Distributed by Andrews McMeel Syndication
JIM DAVIS 7-25

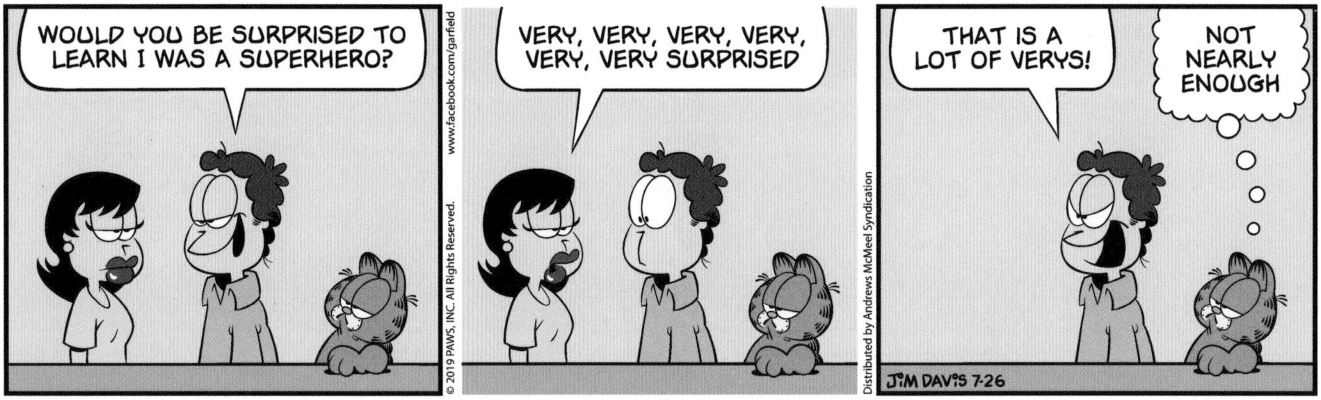
WOULD YOU BE SURPRISED TO LEARN I WAS A SUPERHERO?
VERY, VERY, VERY, VERY, VERY, VERY SURPRISED
THAT IS A LOT OF VERYS!
NOT NEARLY ENOUGH
© 2019 PAWS, INC. All Rights Reserved. www.facebook.com/garfield
Distributed by Andrews McMeel Syndication
JIM DAVIS 7-26

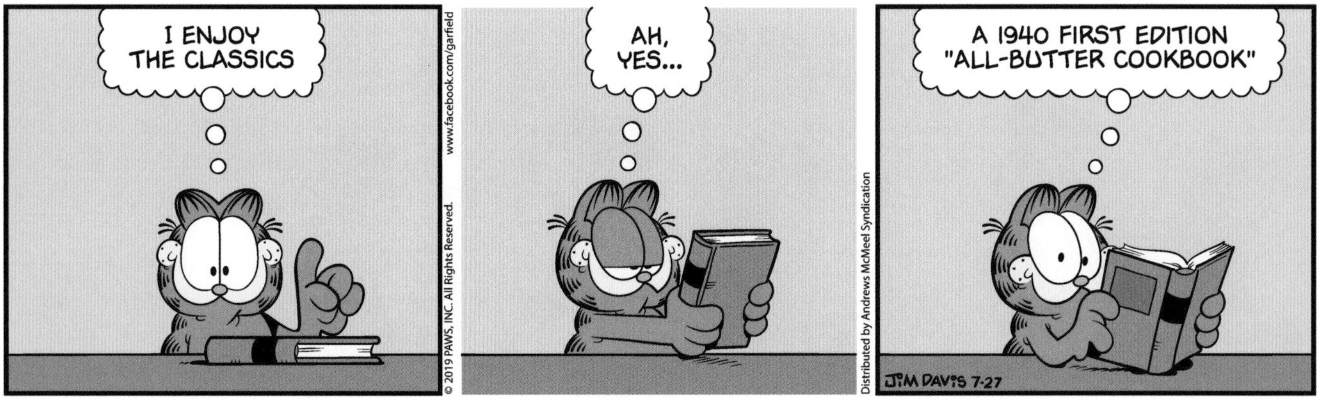
I ENJOY THE CLASSICS
AH, YES...
A 1940 FIRST EDITION "ALL-BUTTER COOKBOOK"
© 2019 PAWS, INC. All Rights Reserved. www.facebook.com/garfield
Distributed by Andrews McMeel Syndication
JIM DAVIS 7-27

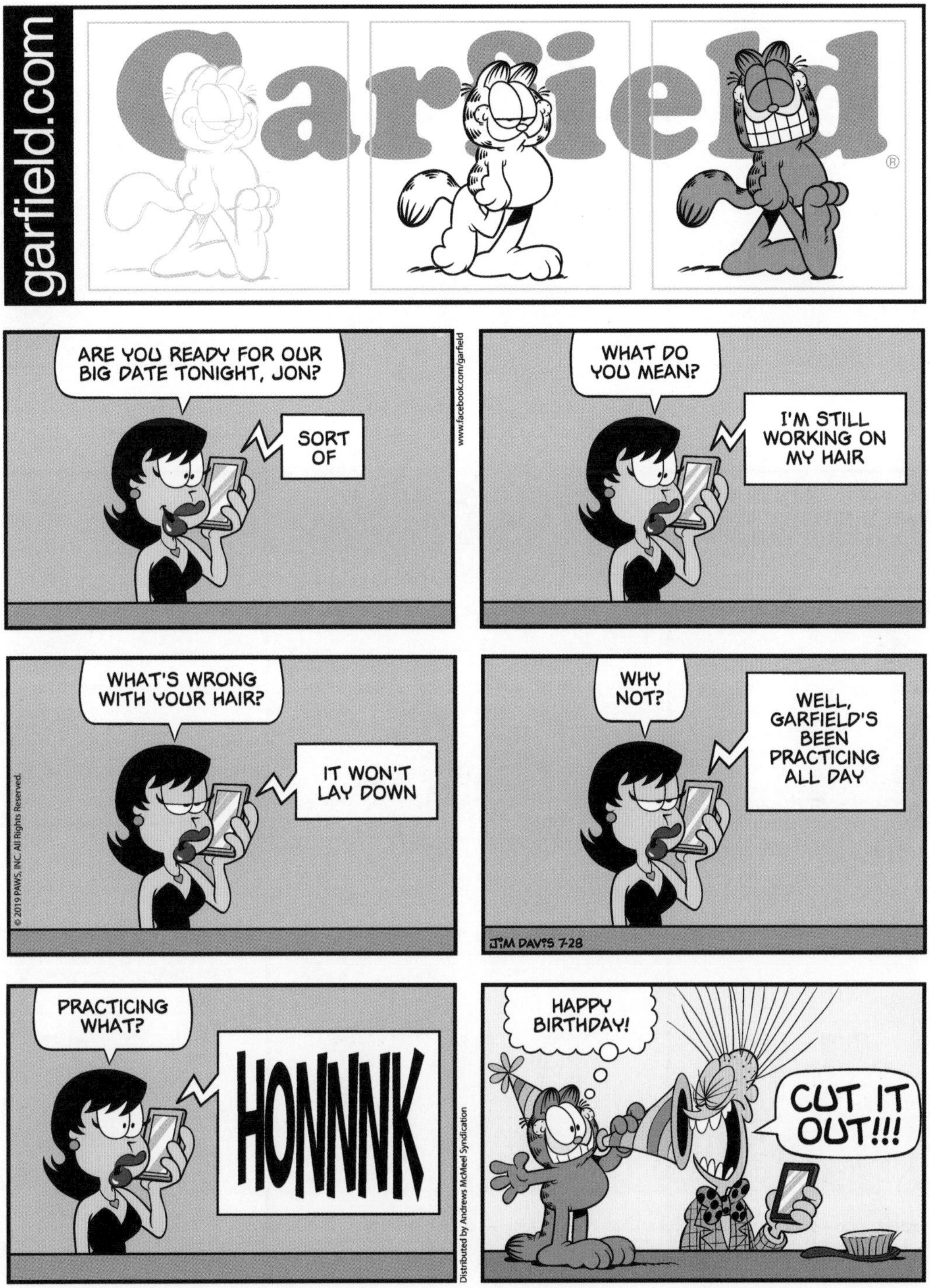
garfield.com
Garfield®
ARE YOU READY FOR OUR BIG DATE TONIGHT, JON?
SORT OF
www.facebook.com/garfield
WHAT DO YOU MEAN?
I'M STILL WORKING ON MY HAIR
WHAT'S WRONG WITH YOUR HAIR?
IT WON'T LAY DOWN
© 2019 PAWS, INC. All Rights Reserved.
WHY NOT?
WELL, GARFIELD'S BEEN PRACTICING ALL DAY
JIM DAVIS 7-28
PRACTICING WHAT?
HONNNK
Distributed by Andrews McMeel Syndication
HAPPY BIRTHDAY!
CUT IT OUT!!!

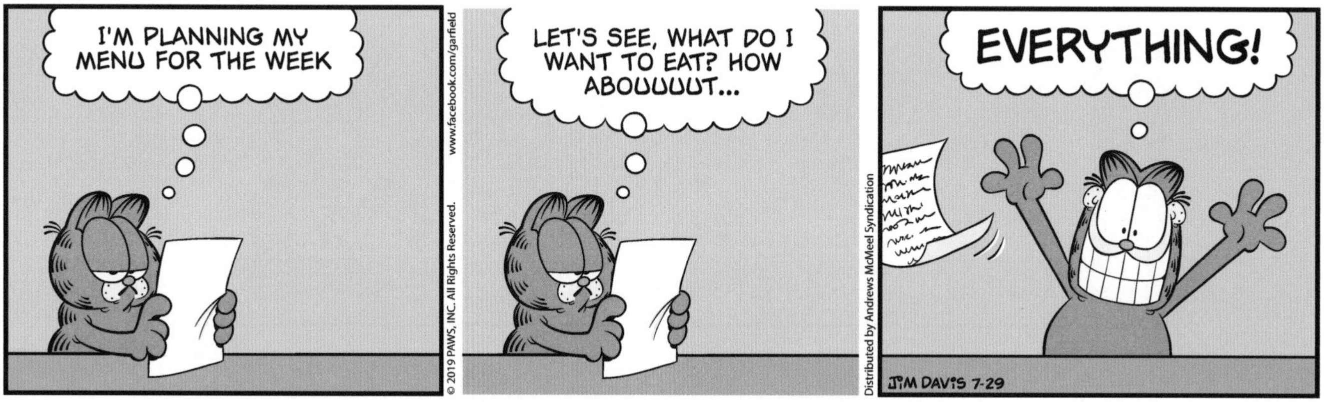
I'M PLANNING MY MENU FOR THE WEEK
LET'S SEE, WHAT DO I WANT TO EAT? HOW ABOUUUUT...
EVERYTHING!
JIM DAVIS 7-29

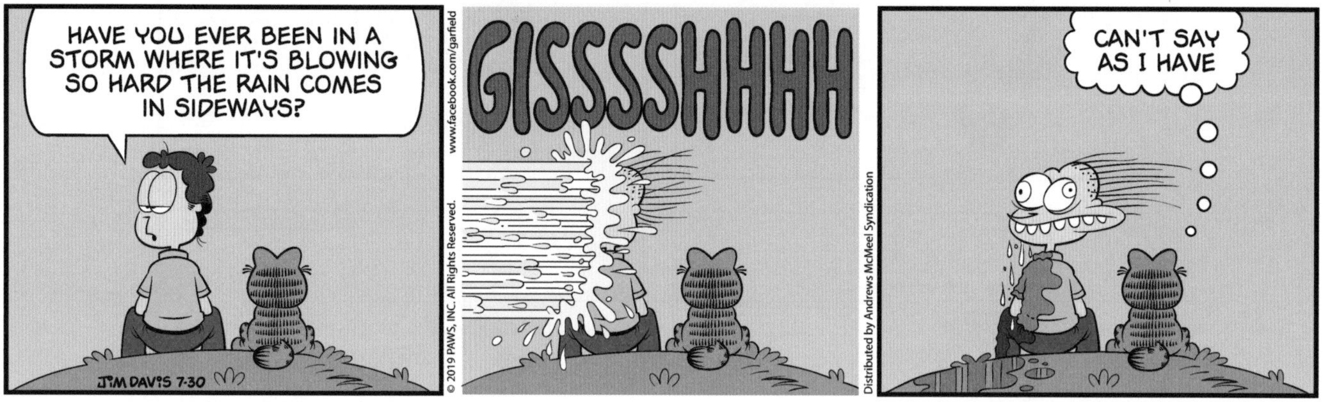
HAVE YOU EVER BEEN IN A STORM WHERE IT'S BLOWING SO HARD THE RAIN COMES IN SIDEWAYS?
JIM DAVIS 7-30
GISSSSHHHH
CAN'T SAY AS I HAVE

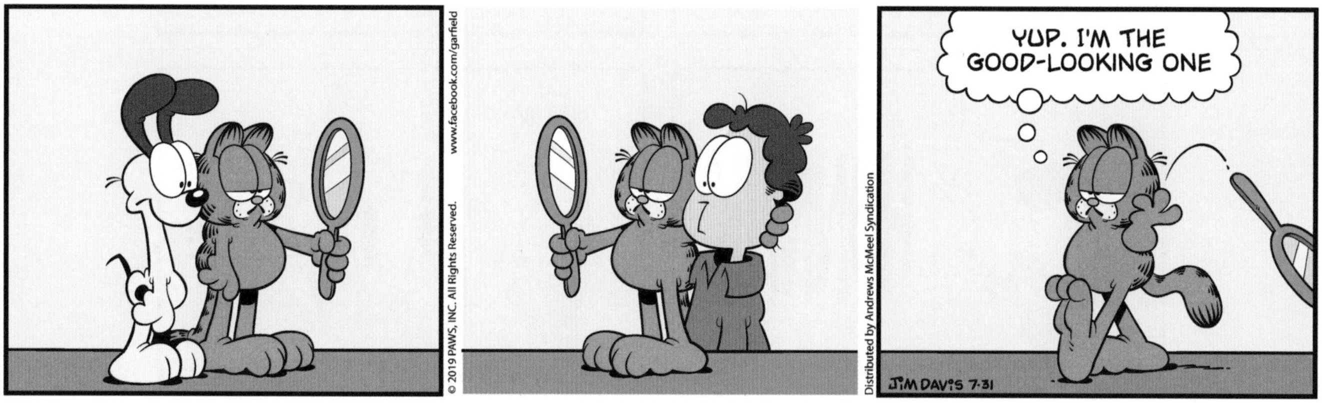
YUP. I'M THE GOOD-LOOKING ONE
JIM DAVIS 7-31

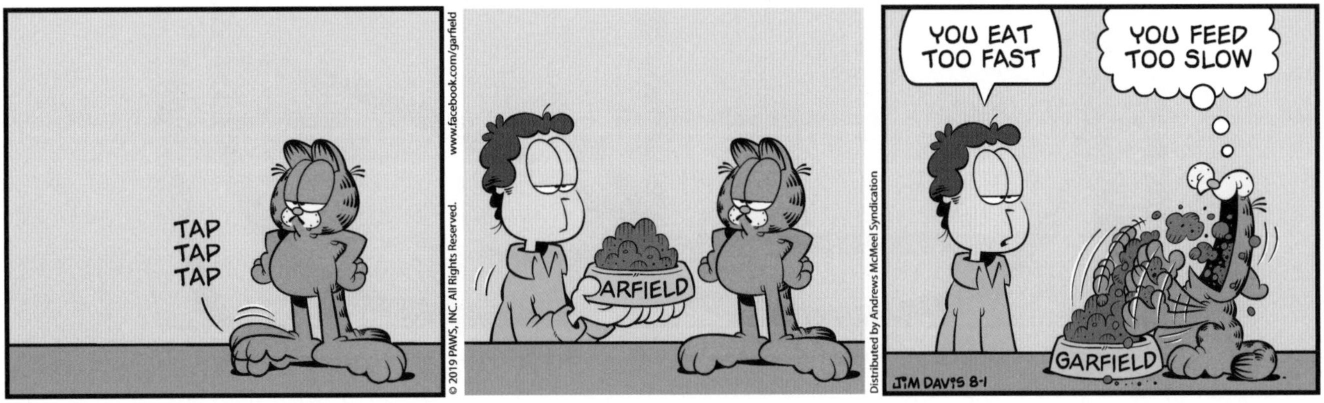
TAP
TAP
TAP
YOU EAT TOO FAST
YOU FEED TOO SLOW
GARFIELD
JIM DAVIS 8-1
© 2019 PAWS, INC. All Rights Reserved. www.facebook.com/garfield
Distributed by Andrews McMeel Syndication

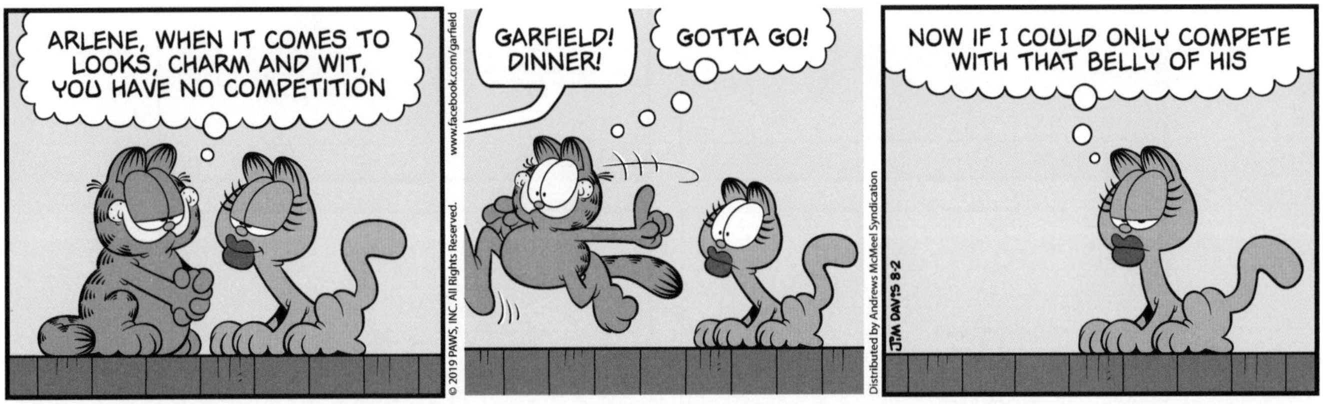
ARLENE, WHEN IT COMES TO LOOKS, CHARM AND WIT, YOU HAVE NO COMPETITION
GARFIELD! DINNER!
GOTTA GO!
NOW IF I COULD ONLY COMPETE WITH THAT BELLY OF HIS
JIM DAVIS 8-2
© 2019 PAWS, INC. All Rights Reserved. www.facebook.com/garfield
Distributed by Andrews McMeel Syndication

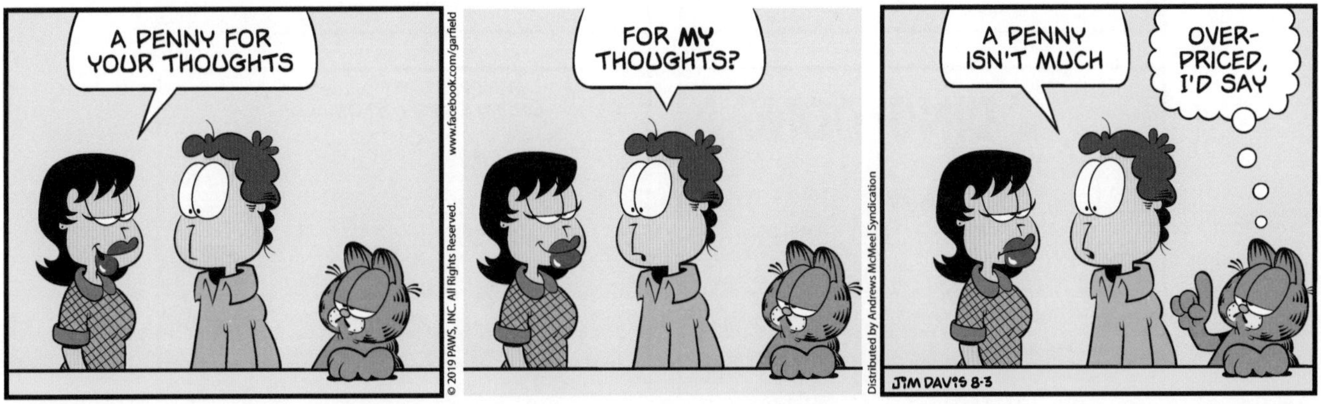
A PENNY FOR YOUR THOUGHTS
FOR MY THOUGHTS?
A PENNY ISN'T MUCH
OVER-PRICED, I'D SAY
JIM DAVIS 8-3
© 2019 PAWS, INC. All Rights Reserved. www.facebook.com/garfield
Distributed by Andrews McMeel Syndication

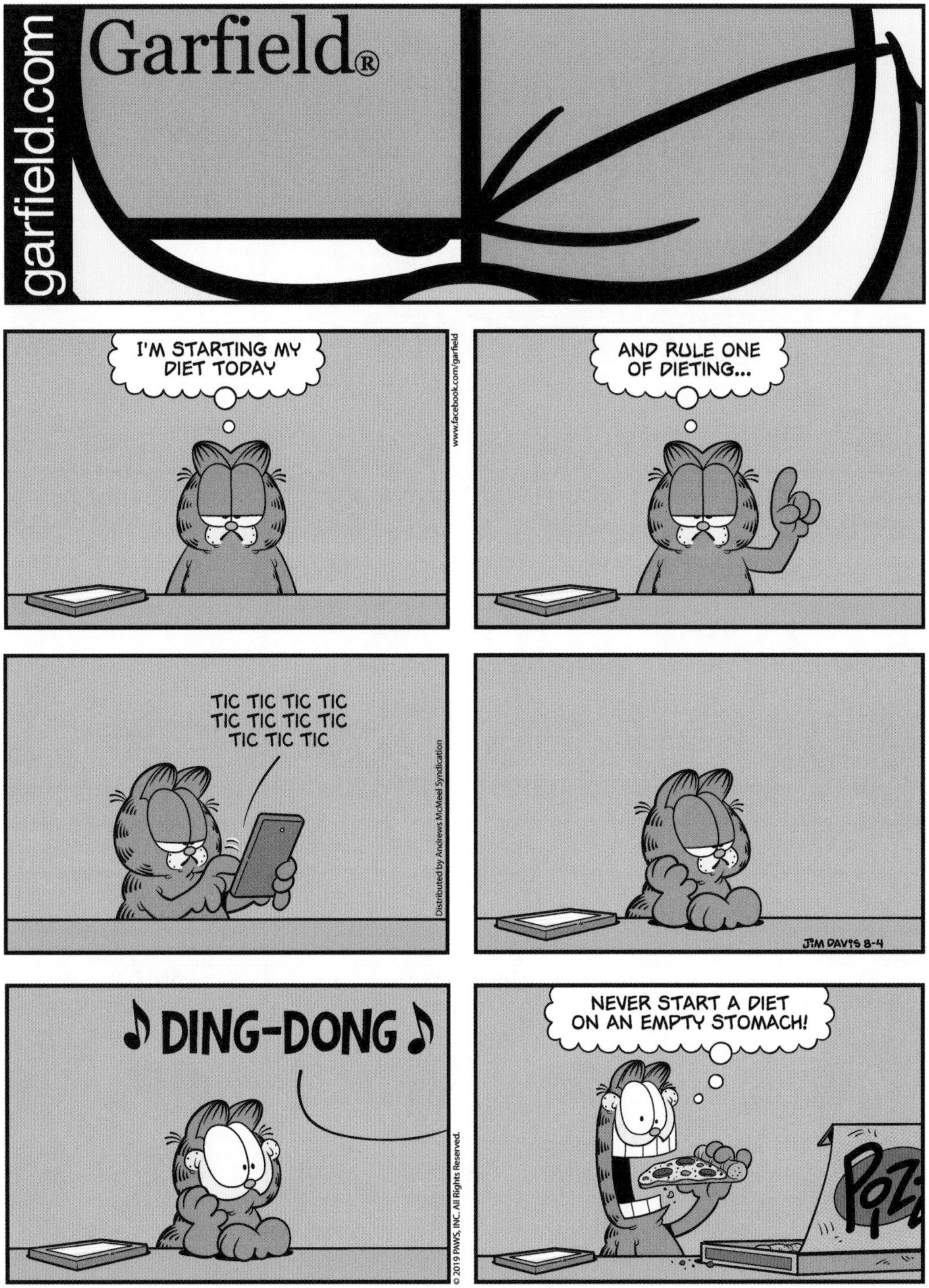
garfield.com
Garfield®
I'M STARTING MY DIET TODAY
www.facebook.com/garfield
AND RULE ONE OF DIETING...
TIC TIC TIC TIC TIC TIC TIC TIC TIC TIC TIC
Distributed by Andrews McMeel Syndication
JIM DAVIS 8-4
♪ DING-DONG ♪
© 2019 PAWS, INC. All Rights Reserved.
NEVER START A DIET ON AN EMPTY STOMACH!

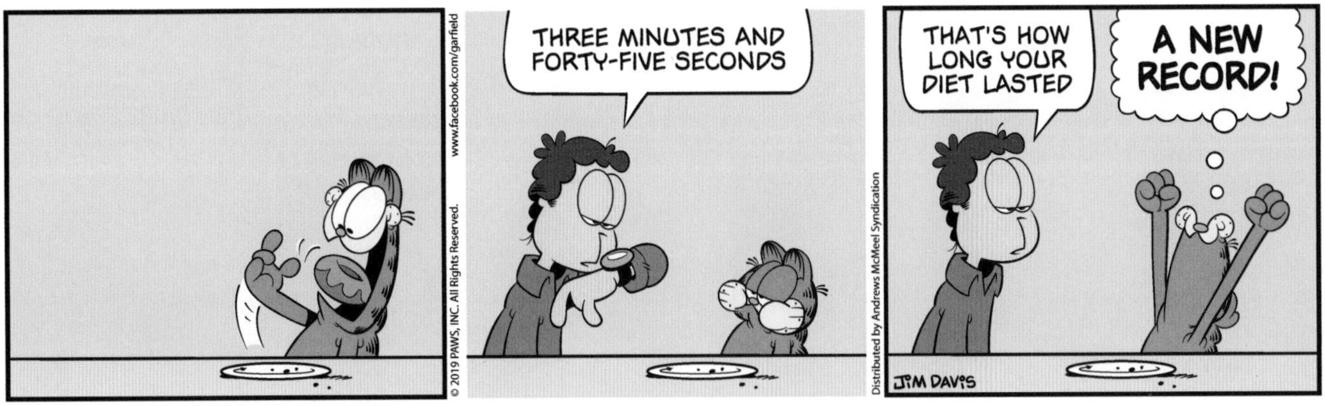
© 2019 PAWS, INC. All Rights Reserved. www.facebook.com/garfield
THREE MINUTES AND FORTY-FIVE SECONDS
Distributed by Andrews McMeel Syndication
THAT'S HOW LONG YOUR DIET LASTED
A NEW RECORD!
JIM DAVIS

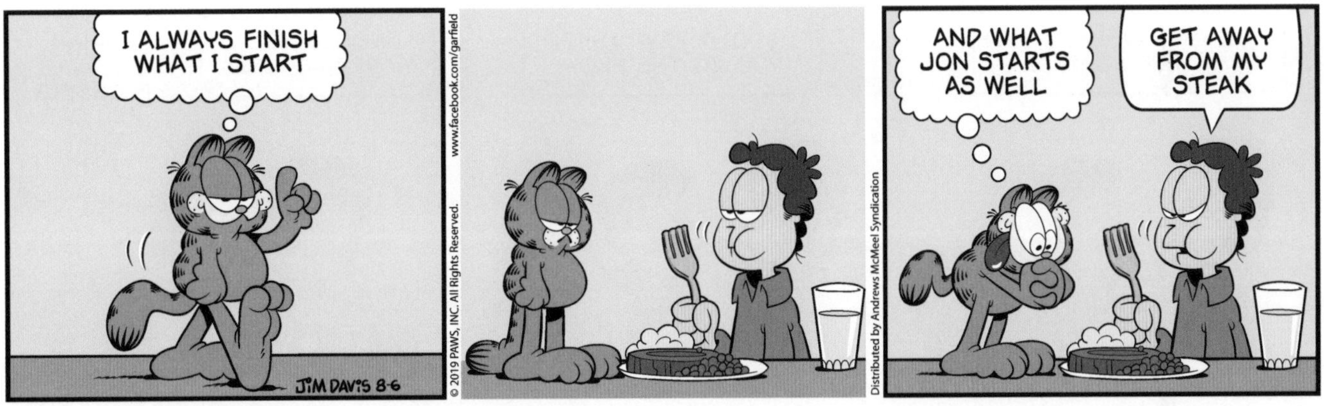
I ALWAYS FINISH WHAT I START
JIM DAVIS 8-6
© 2019 PAWS, INC. All Rights Reserved. www.facebook.com/garfield
Distributed by Andrews McMeel Syndication
AND WHAT JON STARTS AS WELL
GET AWAY FROM MY STEAK

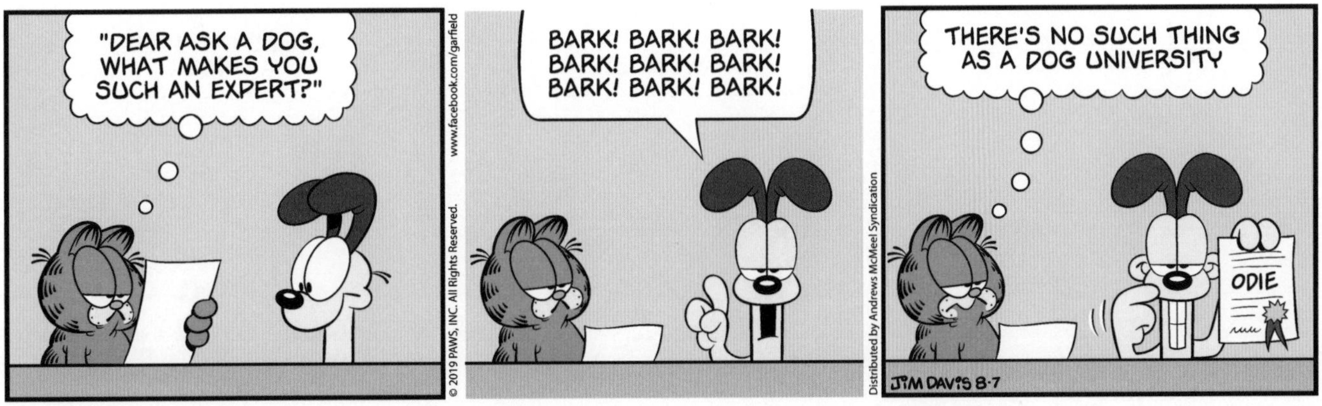
"DEAR ASK A DOG, WHAT MAKES YOU SUCH AN EXPERT?"
© 2019 PAWS, INC. All Rights Reserved. www.facebook.com/garfield
BARK! BARK! BARK! BARK! BARK! BARK! BARK! BARK! BARK!
Distributed by Andrews McMeel Syndication
THERE'S NO SUCH THING AS A DOG UNIVERSITY
ODIE
JIM DAVIS 8-7

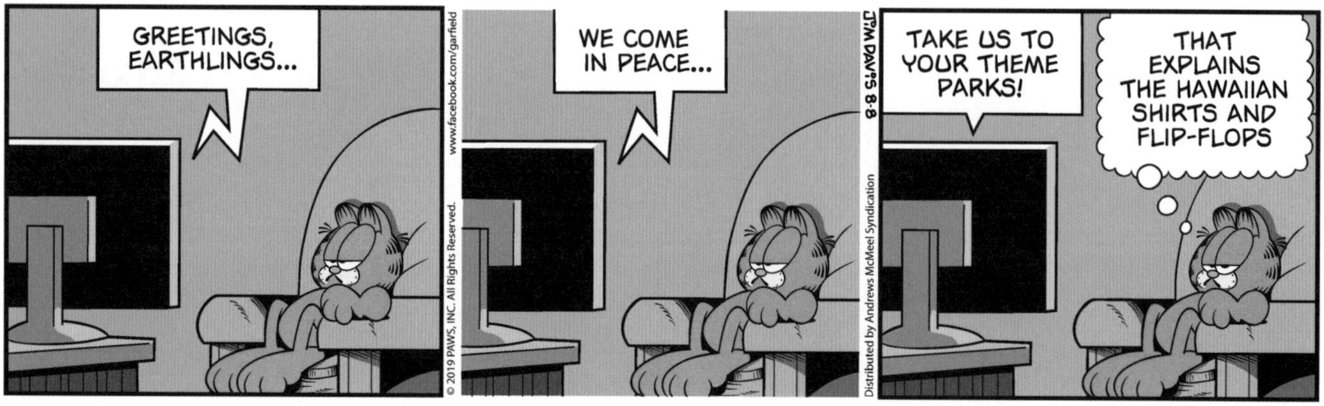
GREETINGS, EARTHLINGS...
© 2019 PAWS, INC. All Rights Reserved. www.facebook.com/garfield
WE COME IN PEACE...
JIM DAVIS 8-8
Distributed by Andrews McMeel Syndication
TAKE US TO YOUR THEME PARKS!
THAT EXPLAINS THE HAWAIIAN SHIRTS AND FLIP-FLOPS

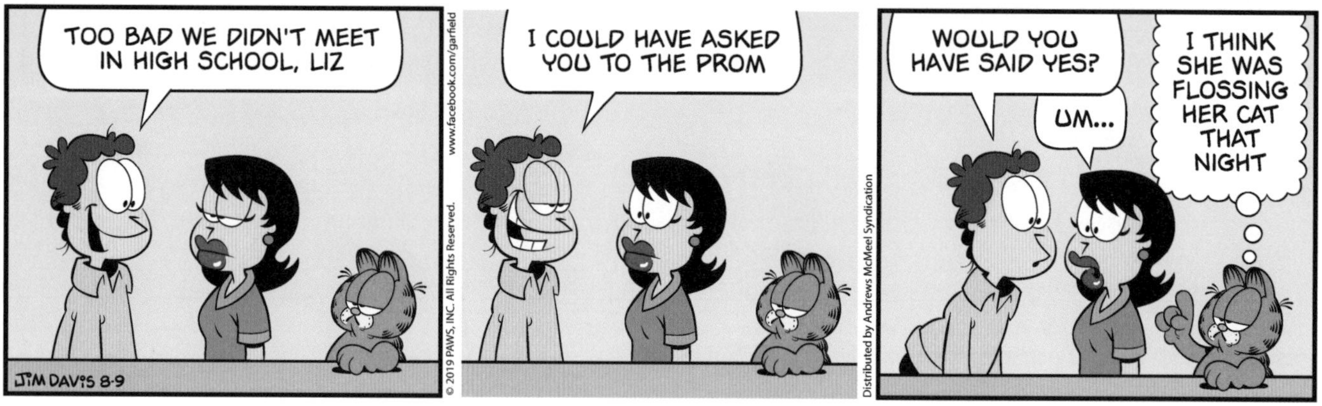
TOO BAD WE DIDN'T MEET IN HIGH SCHOOL, LIZ
JIM DAVIS 8-9
© 2019 PAWS, INC. All Rights Reserved. www.facebook.com/garfield
I COULD HAVE ASKED YOU TO THE PROM
Distributed by Andrews McMeel Syndication
WOULD YOU HAVE SAID YES?
UM...
I THINK SHE WAS FLOSSING HER CAT THAT NIGHT

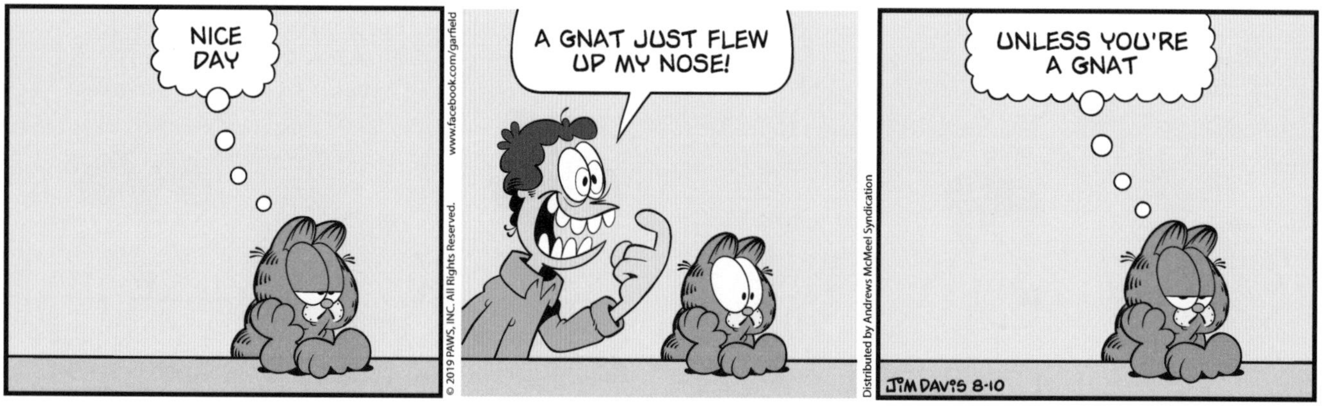
NICE DAY
© 2019 PAWS, INC. All Rights Reserved. www.facebook.com/garfield
A GNAT JUST FLEW UP MY NOSE!
Distributed by Andrews McMeel Syndication
UNLESS YOU'RE A GNAT
JIM DAVIS 8-10

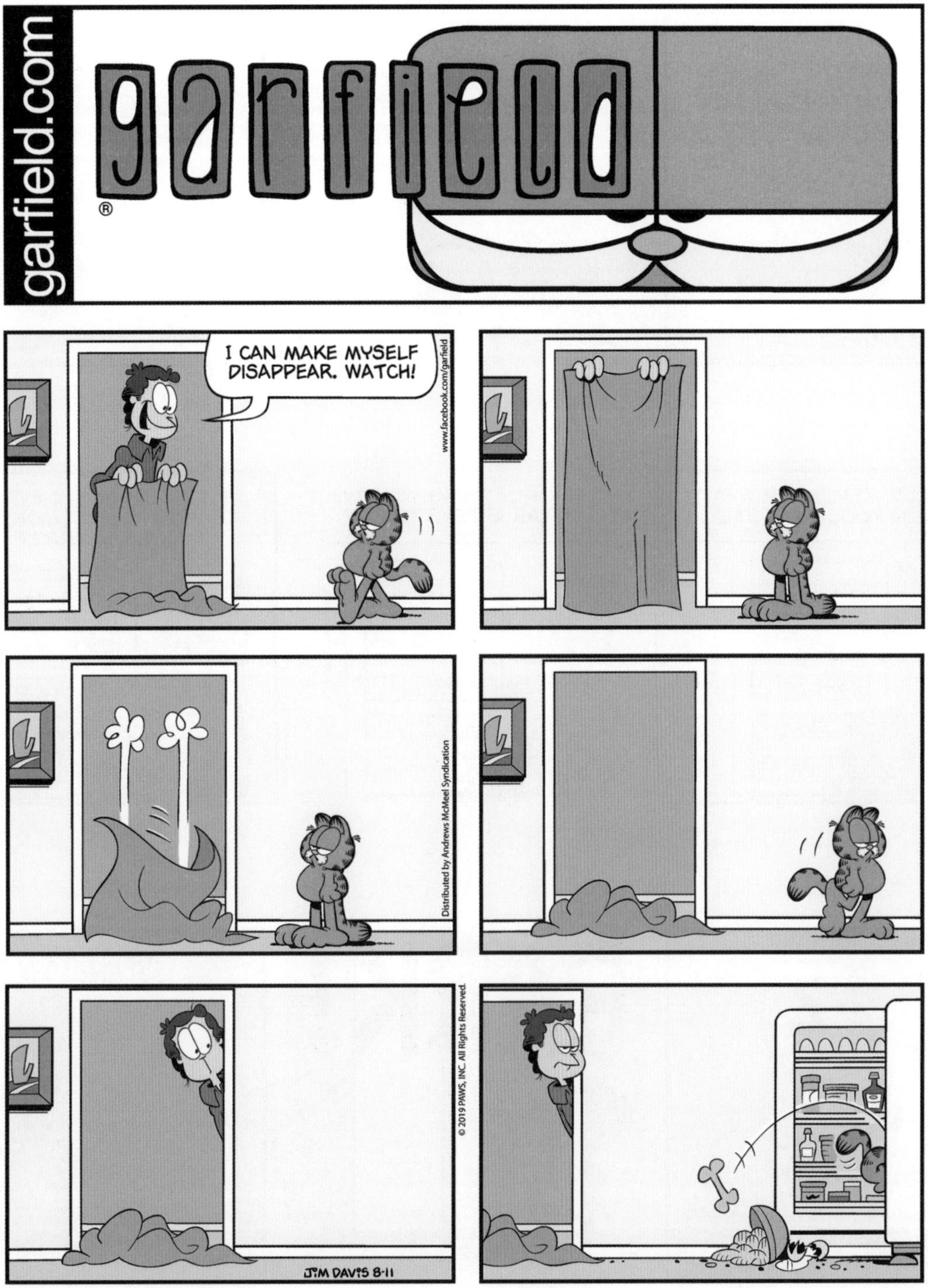
garfield.com
garfield
I CAN MAKE MYSELF DISAPPEAR. WATCH!
www.facebook.com/garfield
Distributed by Andrews McMeel Syndication
© 2019 PAWS, INC. All Rights Reserved.
JIM DAVIS 8-11

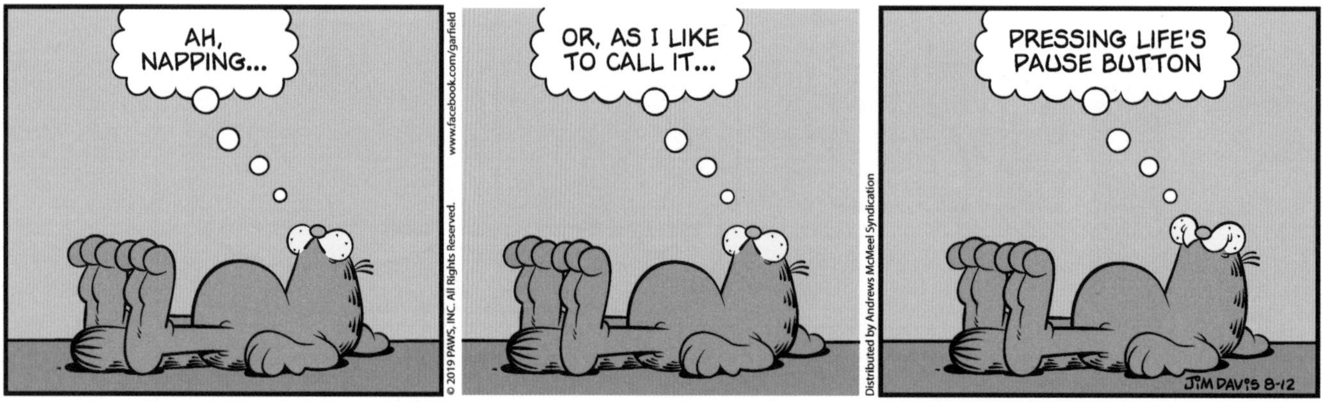
AH, NAPPING...
OR, AS I LIKE TO CALL IT...
PRESSING LIFE'S PAUSE BUTTON
JIM DAVIS 8-12

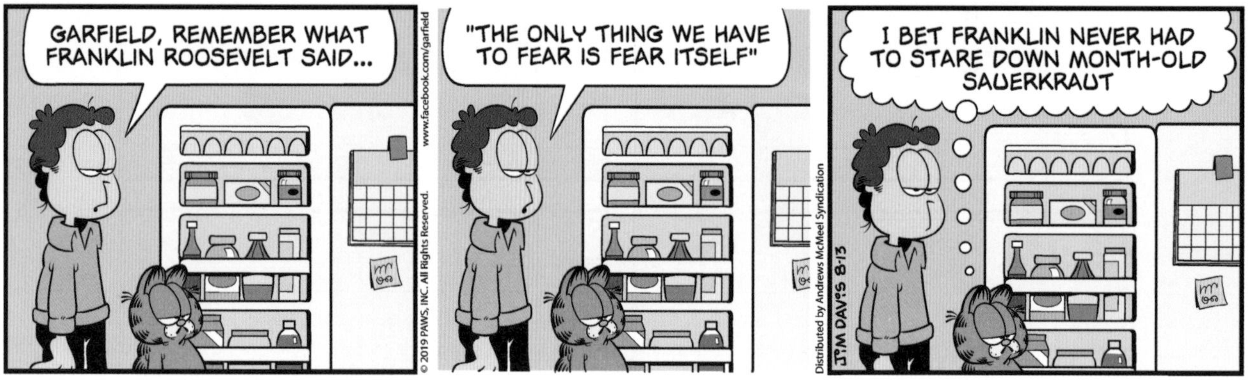
GARFIELD, REMEMBER WHAT FRANKLIN ROOSEVELT SAID...
"THE ONLY THING WE HAVE TO FEAR IS FEAR ITSELF"
I BET FRANKLIN NEVER HAD TO STARE DOWN MONTH-OLD SAUERKRAUT
JIM DAVIS 8-13

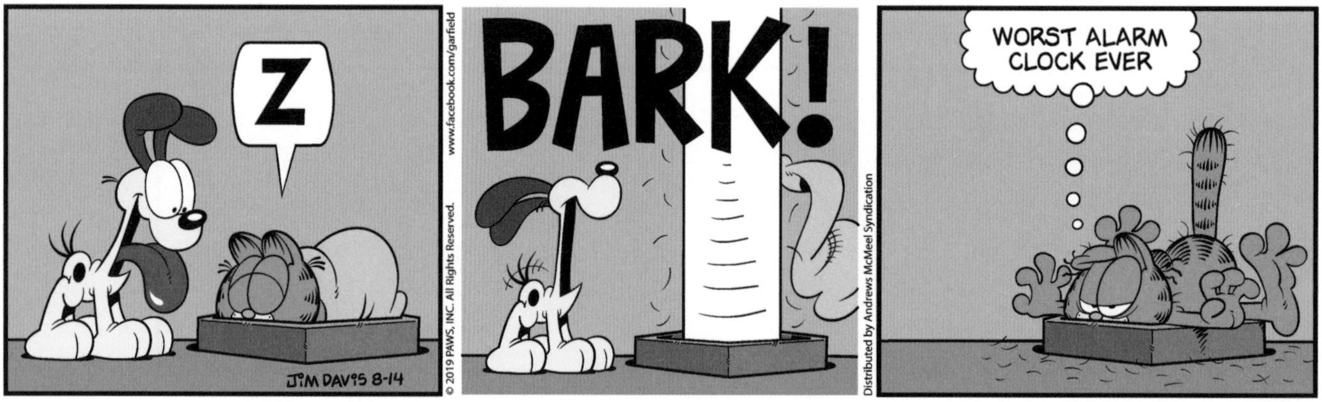
Z
BARK!
WORST ALARM CLOCK EVER
JIM DAVIS 8-14

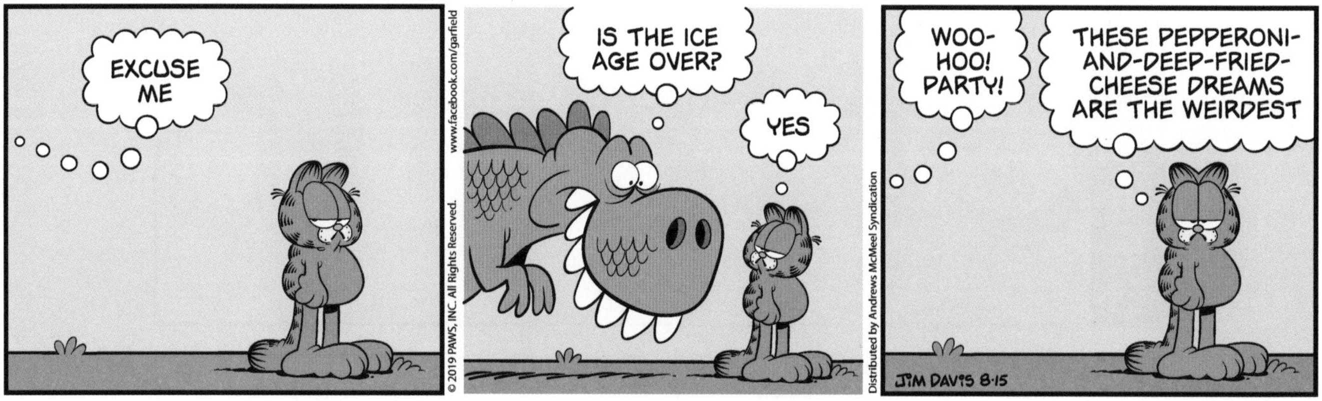
EXCUSE ME
IS THE ICE AGE OVER?
YES
WOO-HOO! PARTY!
THESE PEPPERONI-AND-DEEP-FRIED-CHEESE DREAMS ARE THE WEIRDEST
JIM DAVIS 8-15
© 2019 PAWS, INC. All Rights Reserved. www.facebook.com/garfield
Distributed by Andrews McMeel Syndication

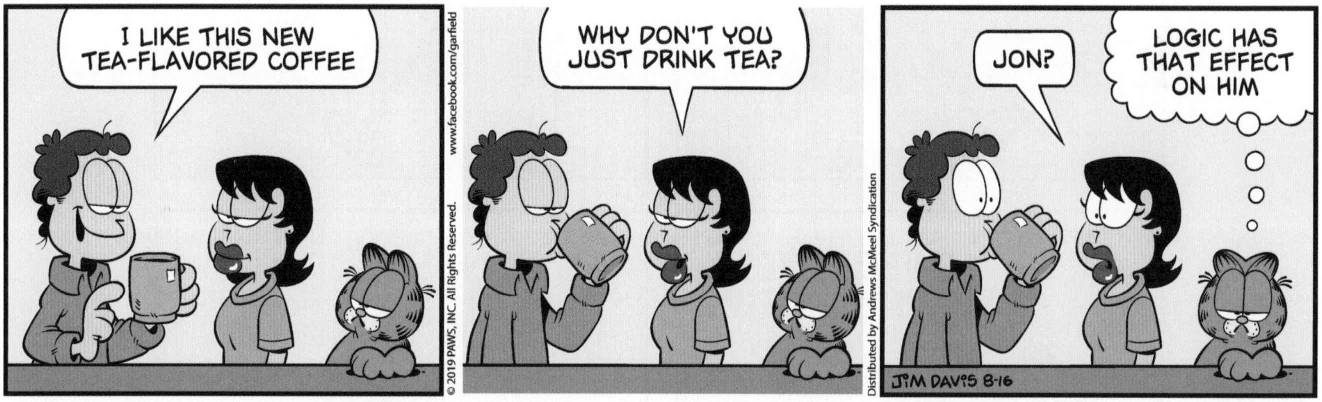
I LIKE THIS NEW TEA-FLAVORED COFFEE
WHY DON'T YOU JUST DRINK TEA?
JON?
LOGIC HAS THAT EFFECT ON HIM
JIM DAVIS 8-16
© 2019 PAWS, INC. All Rights Reserved. www.facebook.com/garfield
Distributed by Andrews McMeel Syndication

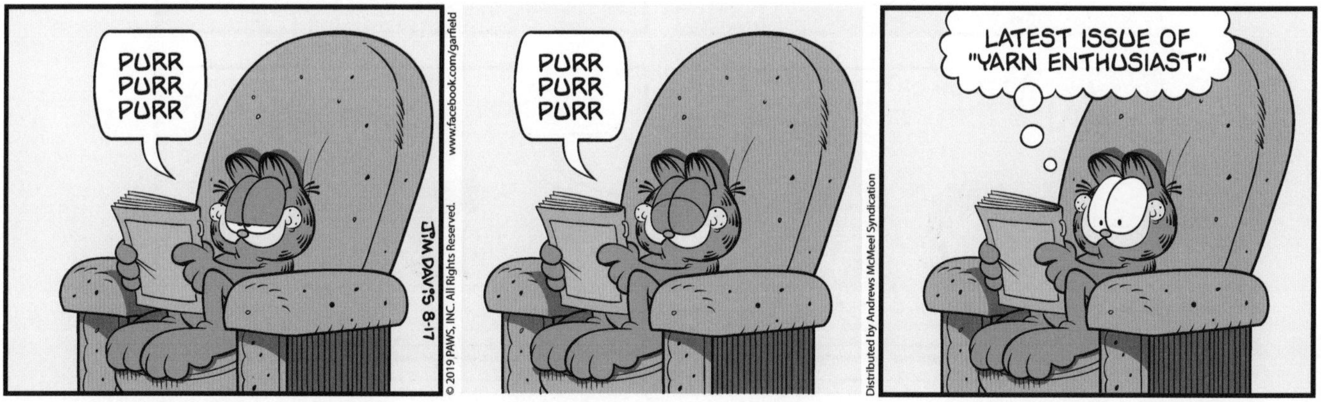
PURR PURR PURR
PURR PURR PURR
LATEST ISSUE OF "YARN ENTHUSIAST"
JIM DAVIS 8-17
© 2019 PAWS, INC. All Rights Reserved. www.facebook.com/garfield
Distributed by Andrews McMeel Syndication

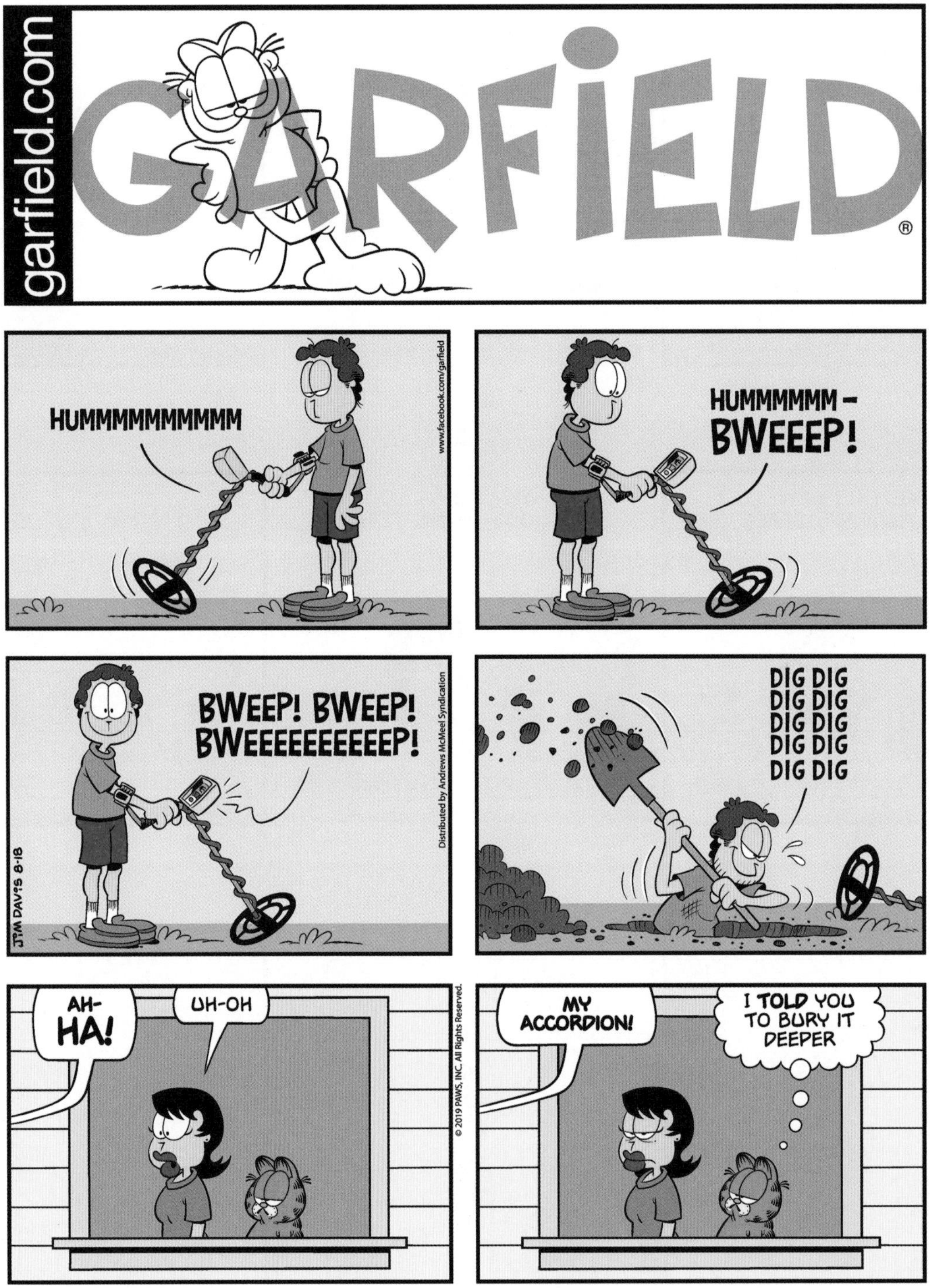
garfield.com
GARFIELD®
HUMMMMMMMMMM
www.facebook.com/garfield
HUMMMMMM –
BWEEEP!
BWEEP! BWEEP!
BWEEEEEEEEEP!
JIM DAVIS 8-18
Distributed by Andrews McMeel Syndication
DIG DIG
DIG DIG
DIG DIG
DIG DIG
DIG DIG
AH-
HA!
UH-OH
© 2019 PAWS, INC. All Rights Reserved.
MY
ACCORDION!
I TOLD YOU
TO BURY IT
DEEPER

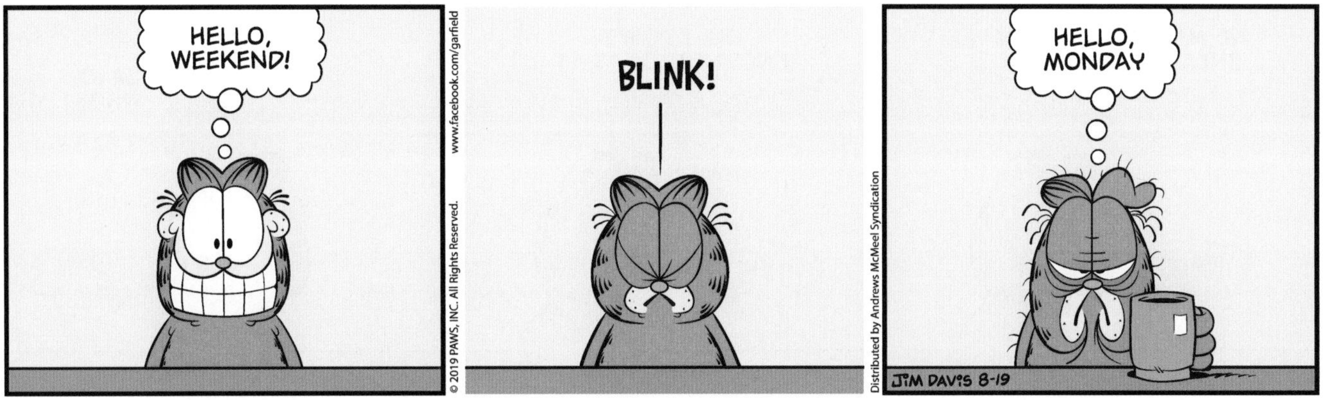
HELLO, WEEKEND!
© 2019 PAWS, INC. All Rights Reserved. www.facebook.com/garfield
BLINK!
Distributed by Andrews McMeel Syndication
HELLO, MONDAY
JIM DAVIS 8-19

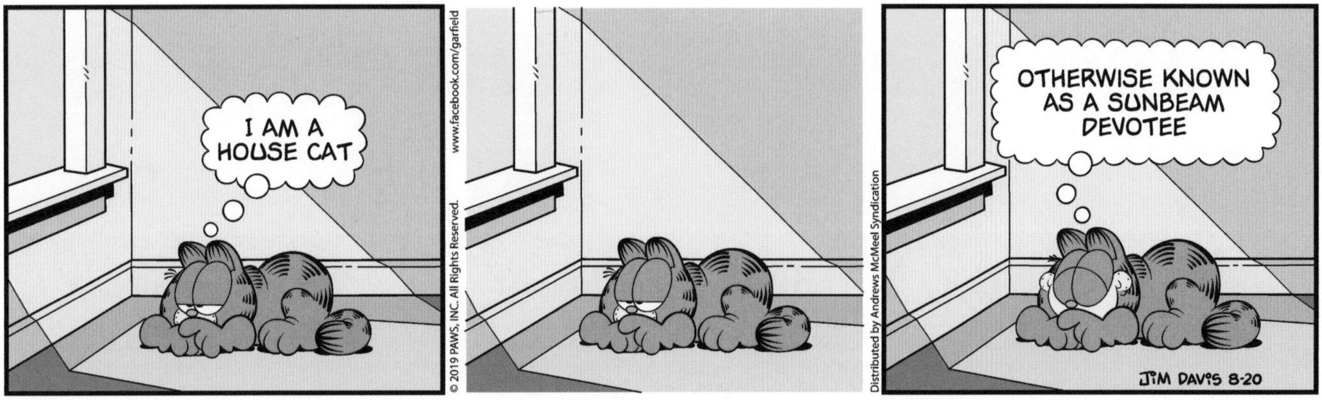
I AM A HOUSE CAT
© 2019 PAWS, INC. All Rights Reserved. www.facebook.com/garfield
Distributed by Andrews McMeel Syndication
OTHERWISE KNOWN AS A SUNBEAM DEVOTEE
JIM DAVIS 8-20

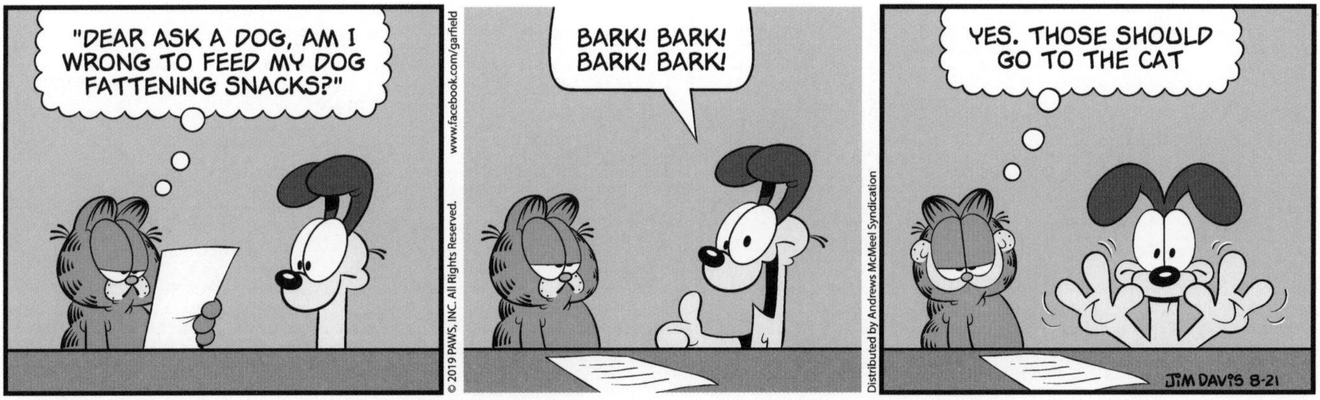
"DEAR ASK A DOG, AM I WRONG TO FEED MY DOG FATTENING SNACKS?"
© 2019 PAWS, INC. All Rights Reserved. www.facebook.com/garfield
BARK! BARK! BARK! BARK!
Distributed by Andrews McMeel Syndication
YES. THOSE SHOULD GO TO THE CAT
JIM DAVIS 8-21

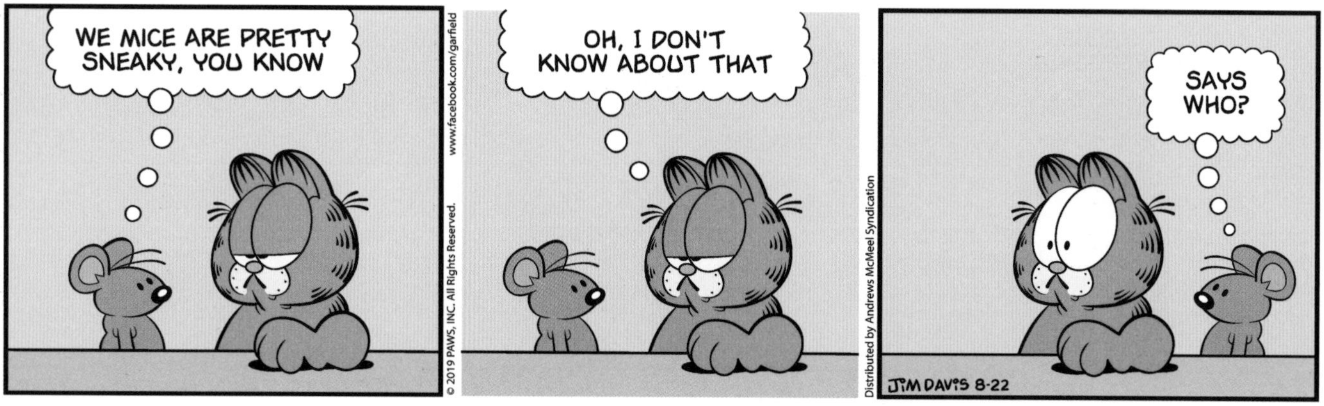
WE MICE ARE PRETTY SNEAKY, YOU KNOW
OH, I DON'T KNOW ABOUT THAT
SAYS WHO?
© 2019 PAWS, INC. All Rights Reserved. www.facebook.com/garfield
Distributed by Andrews McMeel Syndication
JIM DAVIS 8-22

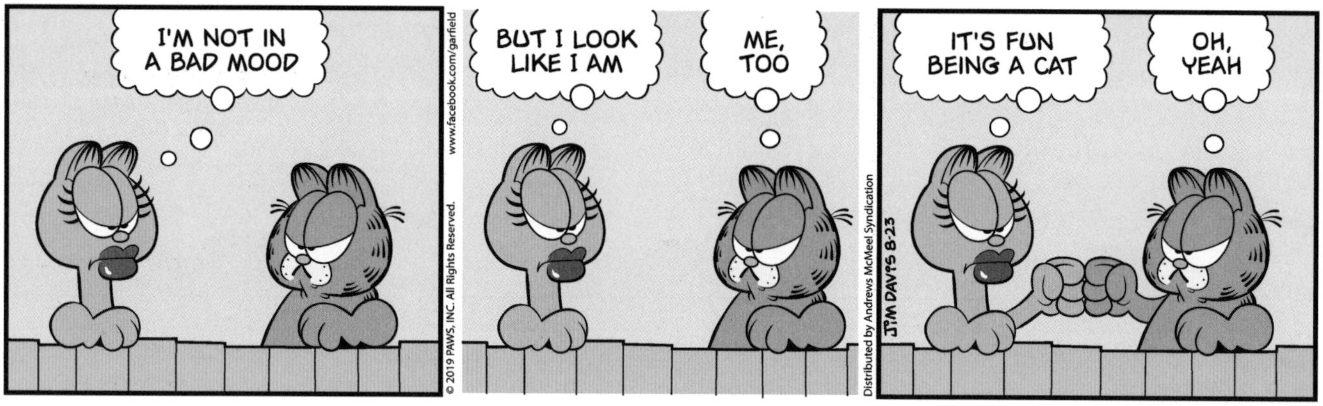
I'M NOT IN A BAD MOOD
BUT I LOOK LIKE I AM
ME, TOO
IT'S FUN BEING A CAT
OH, YEAH
© 2019 PAWS, INC. All Rights Reserved. www.facebook.com/garfield
Distributed by Andrews McMeel Syndication
JIM DAVIS 8-23

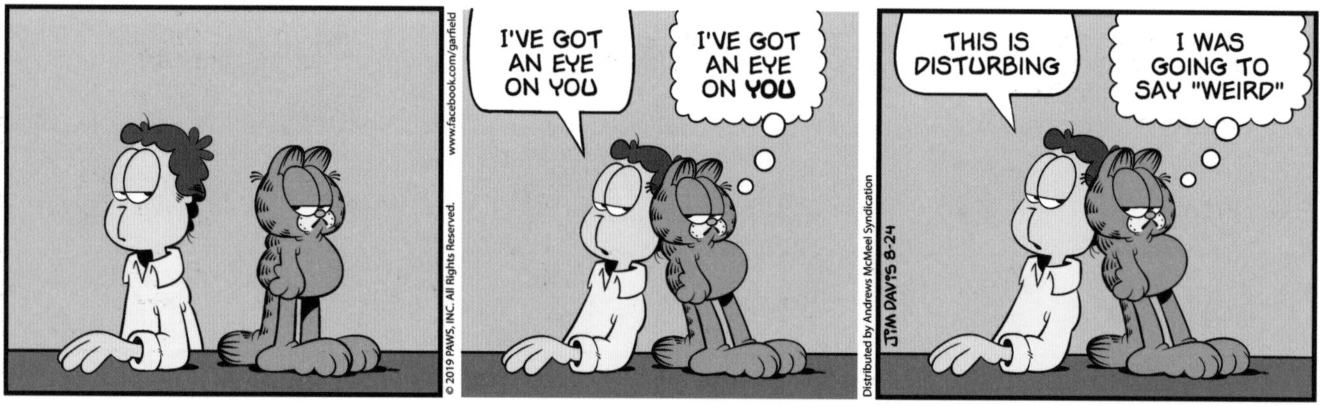
I'VE GOT AN EYE ON YOU
I'VE GOT AN EYE ON **YOU**
THIS IS DISTURBING
I WAS GOING TO SAY "WEIRD"
© 2019 PAWS, INC. All Rights Reserved. www.facebook.com/garfield
Distributed by Andrews McMeel Syndication
JIM DAVIS 8-24

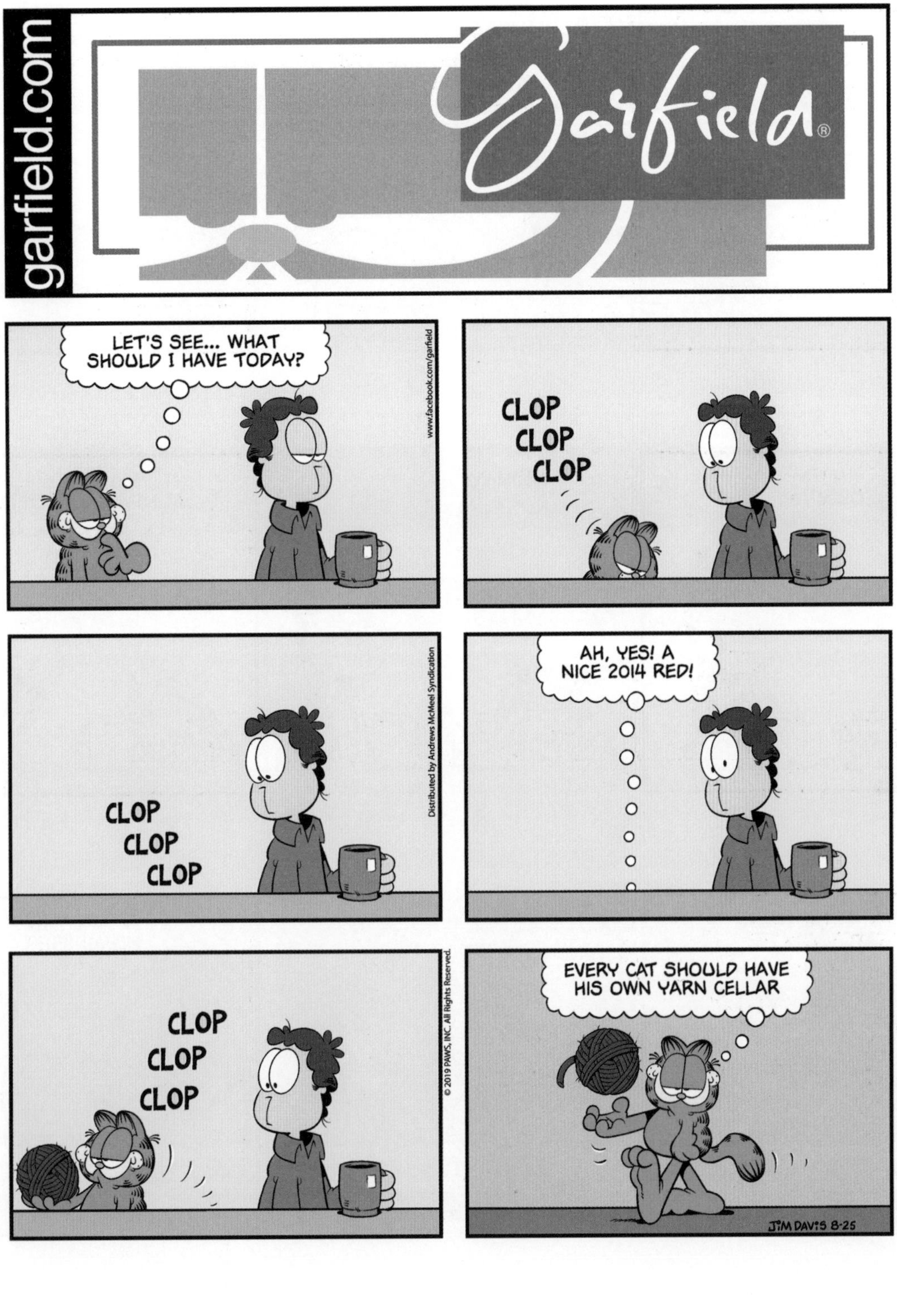
garfield.com
Garfield®
LET'S SEE... WHAT SHOULD I HAVE TODAY?
www.facebook.com/garfield
CLOP CLOP CLOP
Distributed by Andrews McMeel Syndication
CLOP CLOP CLOP
AH, YES! A NICE 2014 RED!
© 2019 PAWS, INC. All Rights Reserved.
CLOP CLOP CLOP
EVERY CAT SHOULD HAVE HIS OWN YARN CELLAR
JIM DAVIS 8-25

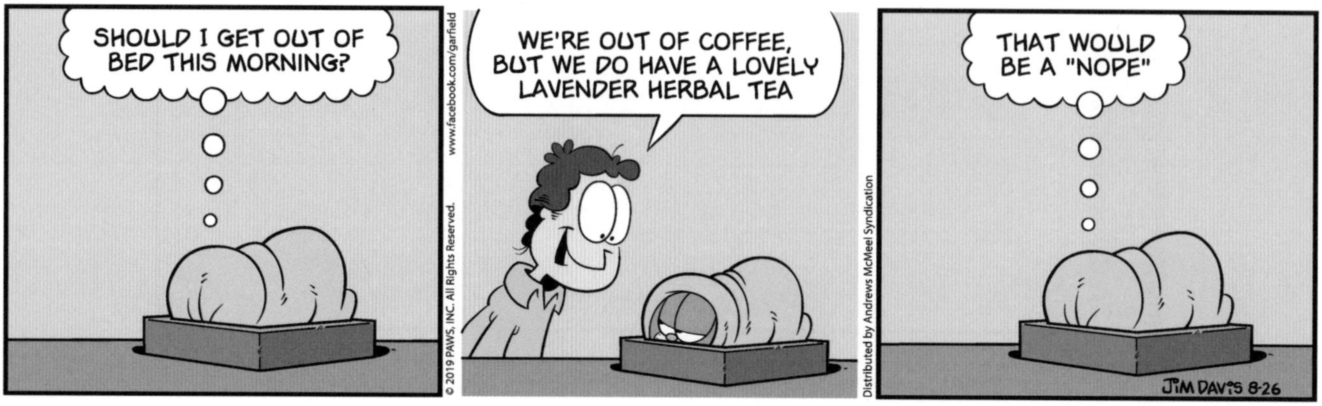
SHOULD I GET OUT OF BED THIS MORNING?
WE'RE OUT OF COFFEE, BUT WE DO HAVE A LOVELY LAVENDER HERBAL TEA
THAT WOULD BE A "NOPE"
JIM DAVIS 8-26
© 2019 PAWS, INC. All Rights Reserved. www.facebook.com/garfield
Distributed by Andrews McMeel Syndication

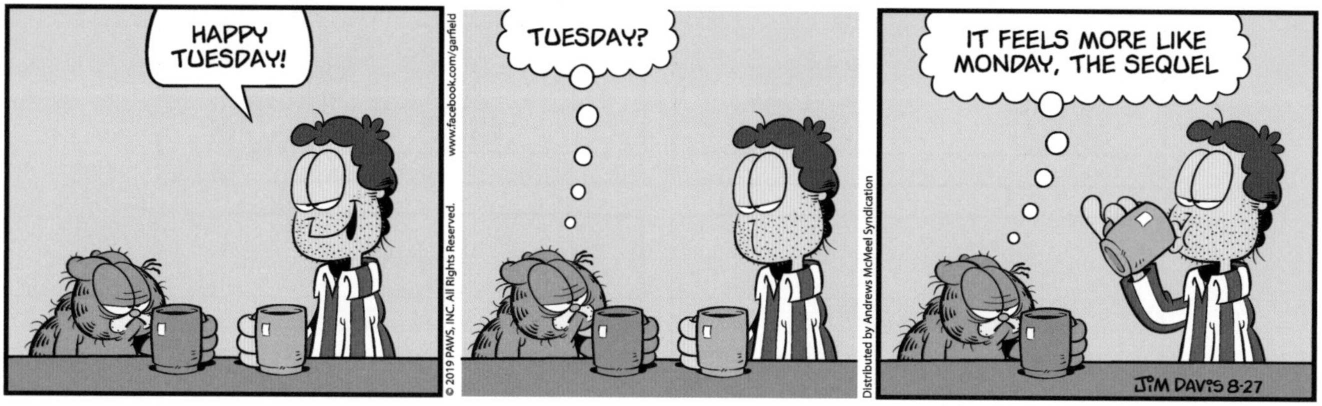
HAPPY TUESDAY!
TUESDAY?
IT FEELS MORE LIKE MONDAY, THE SEQUEL
JIM DAVIS 8-27
© 2019 PAWS, INC. All Rights Reserved. www.facebook.com/garfield
Distributed by Andrews McMeel Syndication

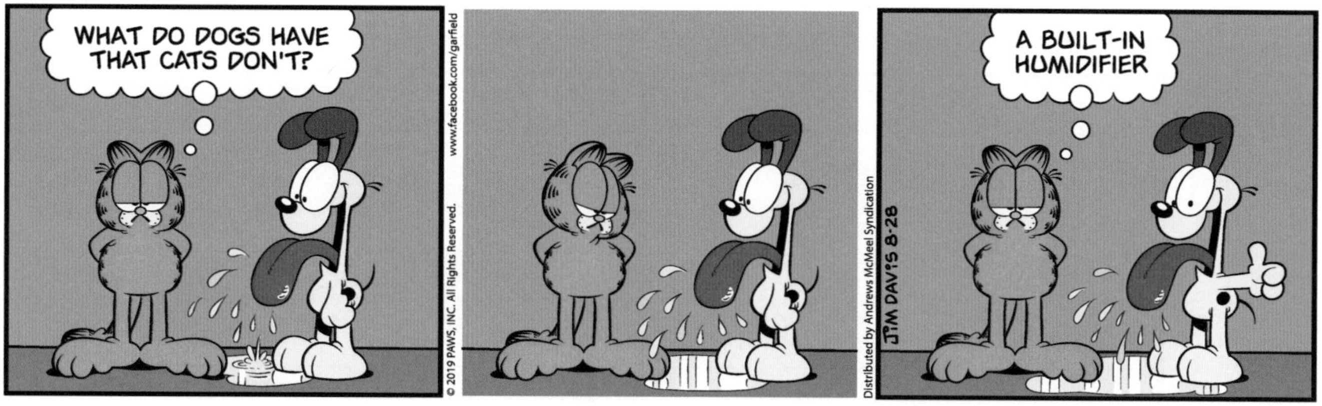
WHAT DO DOGS HAVE THAT CATS DON'T?
A BUILT-IN HUMIDIFIER
JIM DAVIS 8-28
© 2019 PAWS, INC. All Rights Reserved. www.facebook.com/garfield
Distributed by Andrews McMeel Syndication

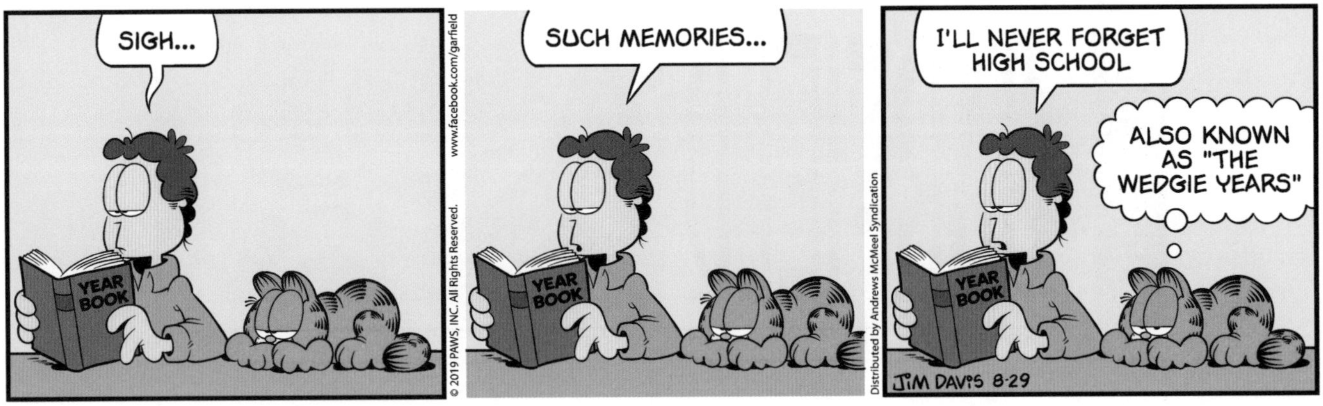
SIGH...
© 2019 PAWS, INC. All Rights Reserved. www.facebook.com/garfield
SUCH MEMORIES...
Distributed by Andrews McMeel Syndication
I'LL NEVER FORGET HIGH SCHOOL
ALSO KNOWN AS "THE WEDGIE YEARS"
YEAR BOOK
JIM DAVIS 8-29

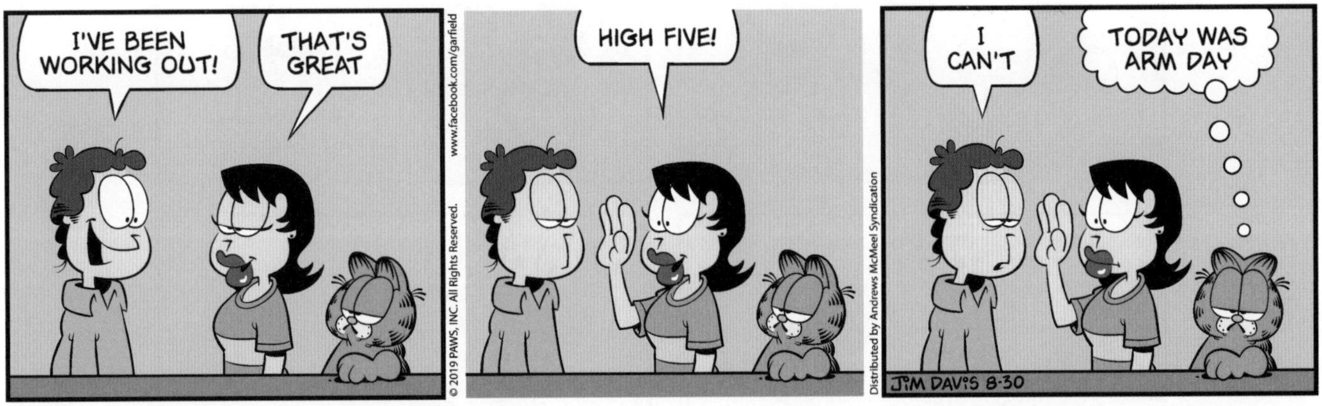
I'VE BEEN WORKING OUT!
THAT'S GREAT
© 2019 PAWS, INC. All Rights Reserved. www.facebook.com/garfield
HIGH FIVE!
Distributed by Andrews McMeel Syndication
I CAN'T
TODAY WAS ARM DAY
JIM DAVIS 8-30

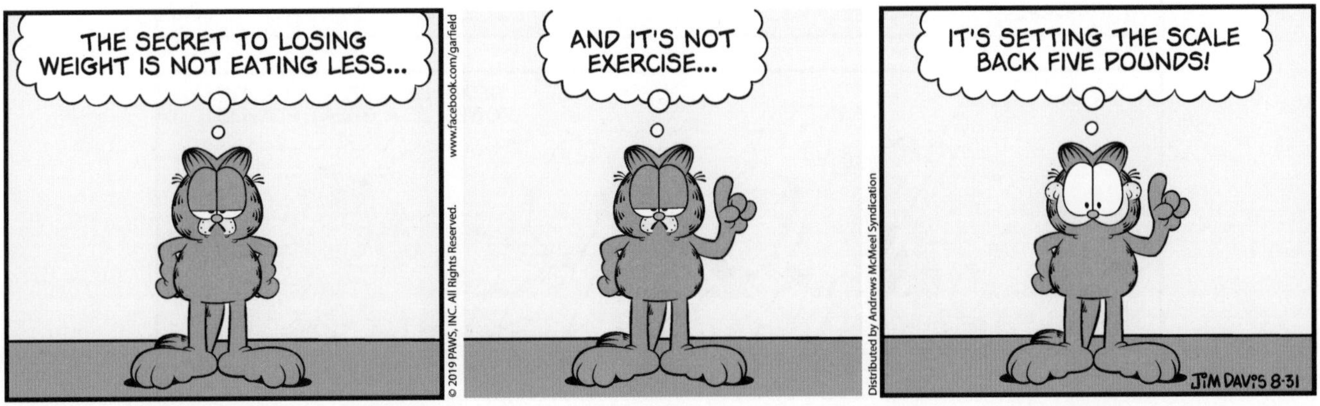
THE SECRET TO LOSING WEIGHT IS NOT EATING LESS...
© 2019 PAWS, INC. All Rights Reserved. www.facebook.com/garfield
AND IT'S NOT EXERCISE...
Distributed by Andrews McMeel Syndication
IT'S SETTING THE SCALE BACK FIVE POUNDS!
JIM DAVIS 8-31

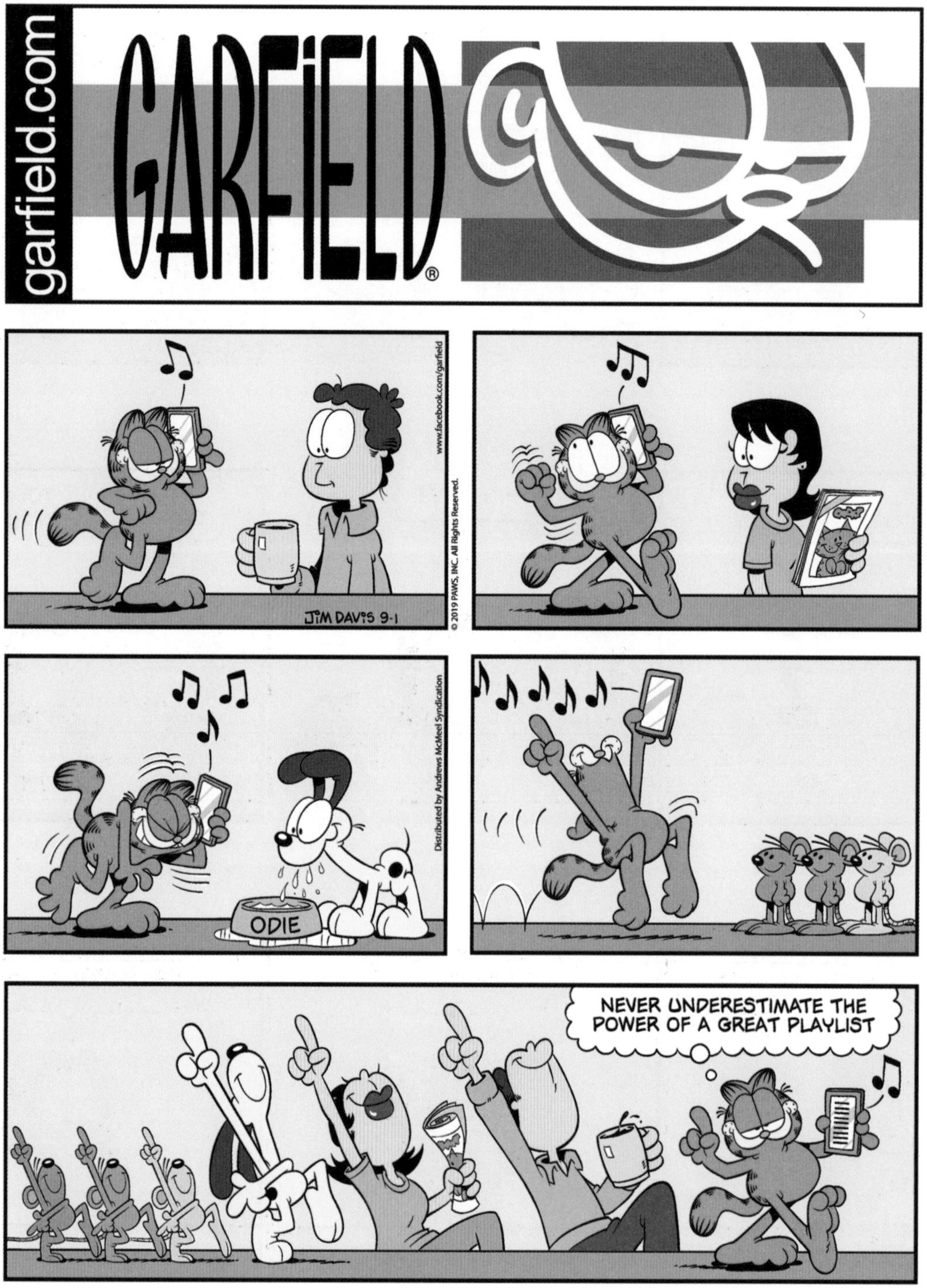
garfield.com
GARFIELD
JIM DAVIS 9-1
www.facebook.com/garfield
© 2019 PAWS, INC. All Rights Reserved.
Distributed by Andrews McMeel Syndication
ODIE
NEVER UNDERESTIMATE THE POWER OF A GREAT PLAYLIST

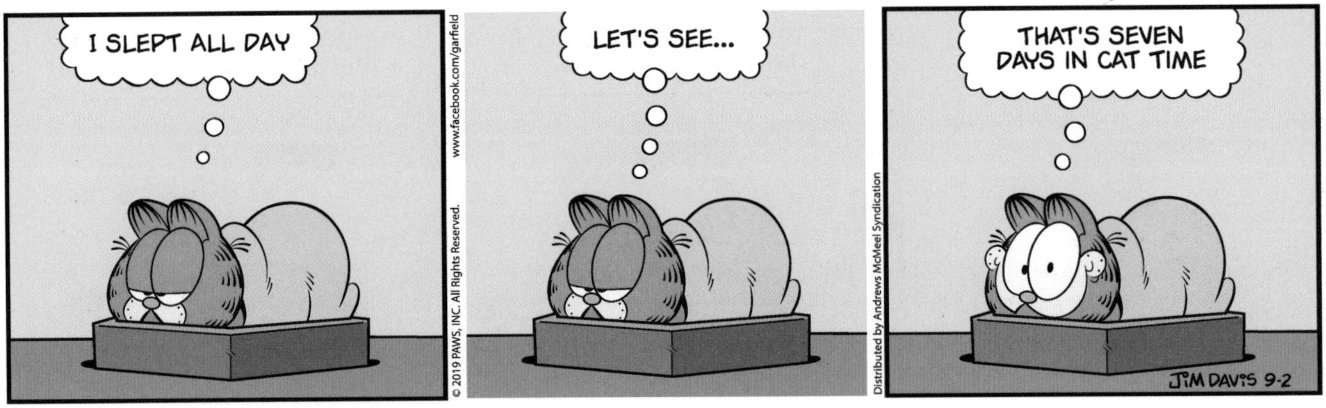
I SLEPT ALL DAY
© 2019 PAWS, INC. All Rights Reserved.
www.facebook.com/garfield
LET'S SEE...
Distributed by Andrews McMeel Syndication
THAT'S SEVEN DAYS IN CAT TIME
JIM DAVIS 9-2

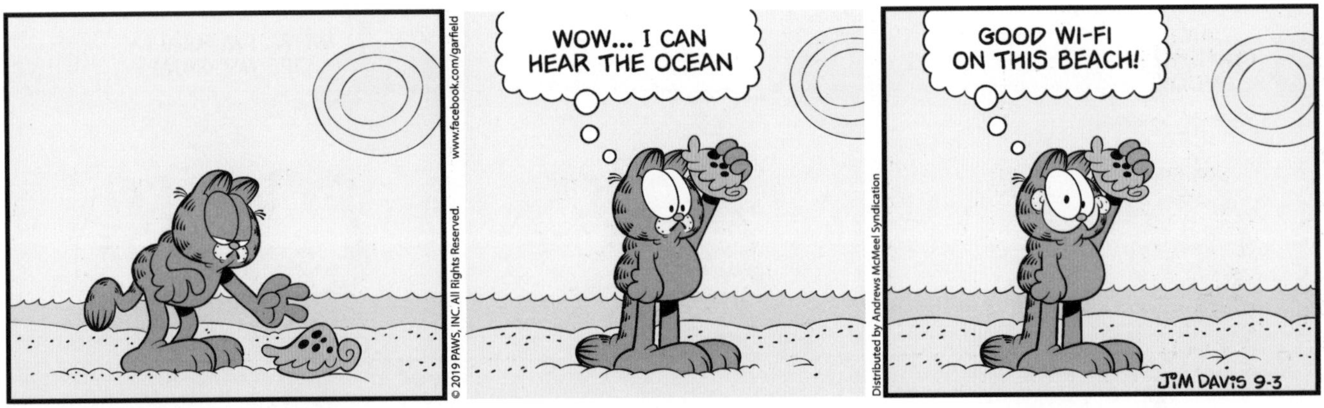
© 2019 PAWS, INC. All Rights Reserved.
www.facebook.com/garfield
WOW... I CAN HEAR THE OCEAN
Distributed by Andrews McMeel Syndication
GOOD WI-FI ON THIS BEACH!
JIM DAVIS 9-3

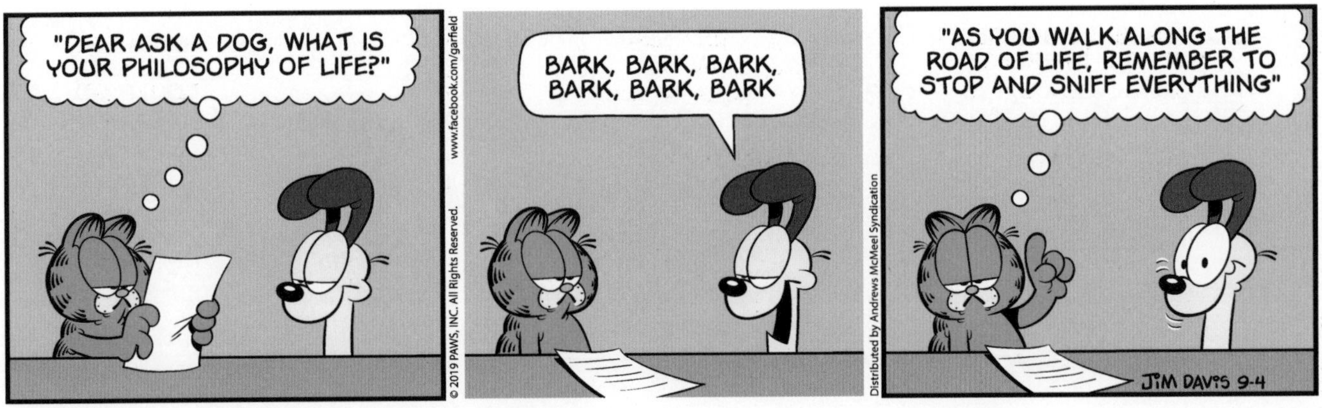
"DEAR ASK A DOG, WHAT IS YOUR PHILOSOPHY OF LIFE?"
© 2019 PAWS, INC. All Rights Reserved.
www.facebook.com/garfield
BARK, BARK, BARK, BARK, BARK, BARK
Distributed by Andrews McMeel Syndication
"AS YOU WALK ALONG THE ROAD OF LIFE, REMEMBER TO STOP AND SNIFF EVERYTHING"
JIM DAVIS 9-4

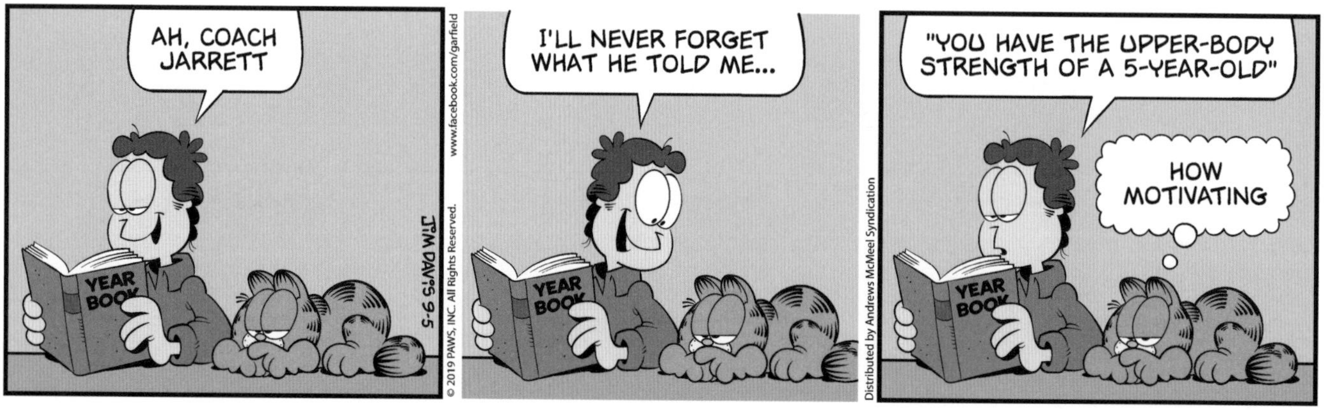
AH, COACH JARRETT
JIM DAVIS 9-5
© 2019 PAWS, INC. All Rights Reserved.
www.facebook.com/garfield
I'LL NEVER FORGET WHAT HE TOLD ME...
Distributed by Andrews McMeel Syndication
"YOU HAVE THE UPPER-BODY STRENGTH OF A 5-YEAR-OLD"
HOW MOTIVATING

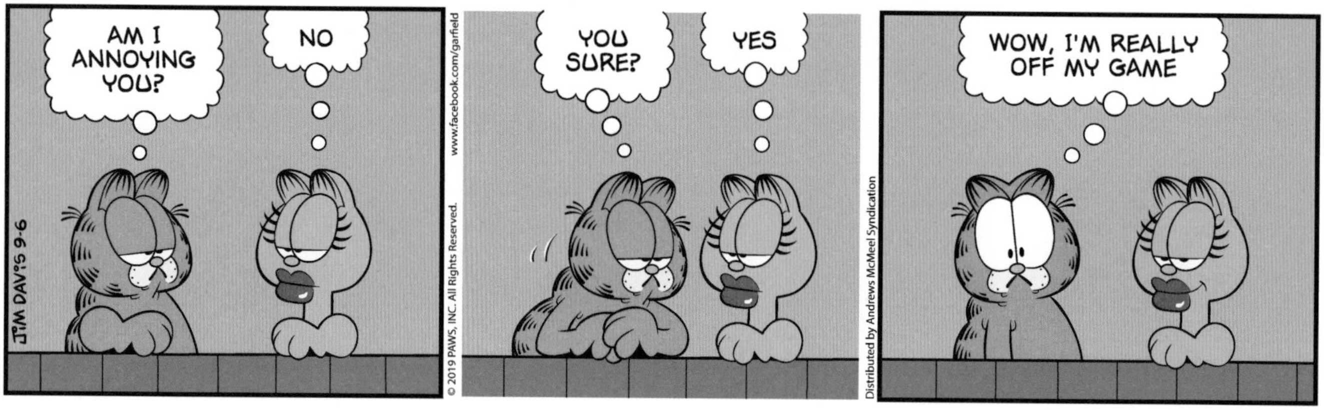
AM I ANNOYING YOU?
NO
JIM DAVIS 9-6
© 2019 PAWS, INC. All Rights Reserved.
www.facebook.com/garfield
YOU SURE?
YES
Distributed by Andrews McMeel Syndication
WOW, I'M REALLY OFF MY GAME

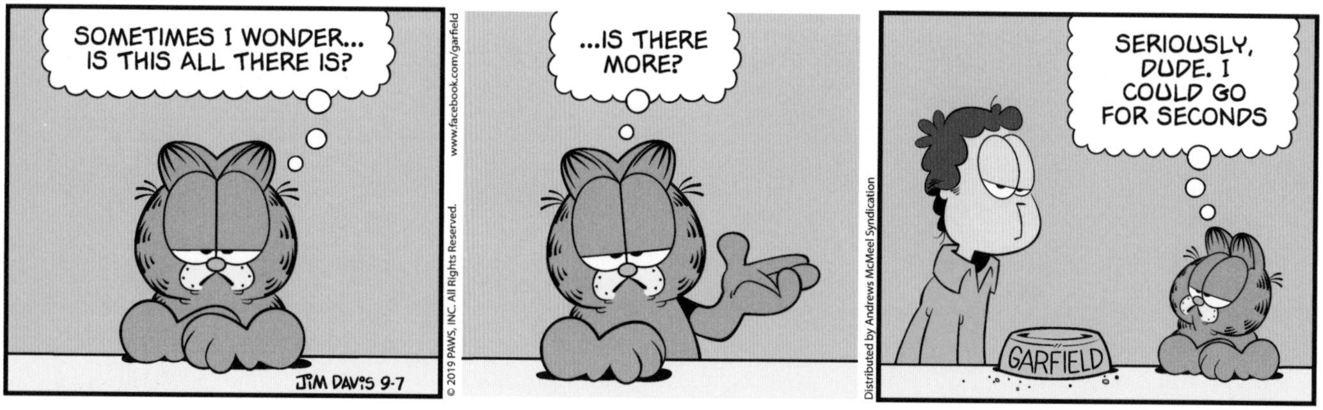
SOMETIMES I WONDER... IS THIS ALL THERE IS?
JIM DAVIS 9-7
© 2019 PAWS, INC. All Rights Reserved.
www.facebook.com/garfield
...IS THERE MORE?
Distributed by Andrews McMeel Syndication
SERIOUSLY, DUDE. I COULD GO FOR SECONDS
GARFIELD

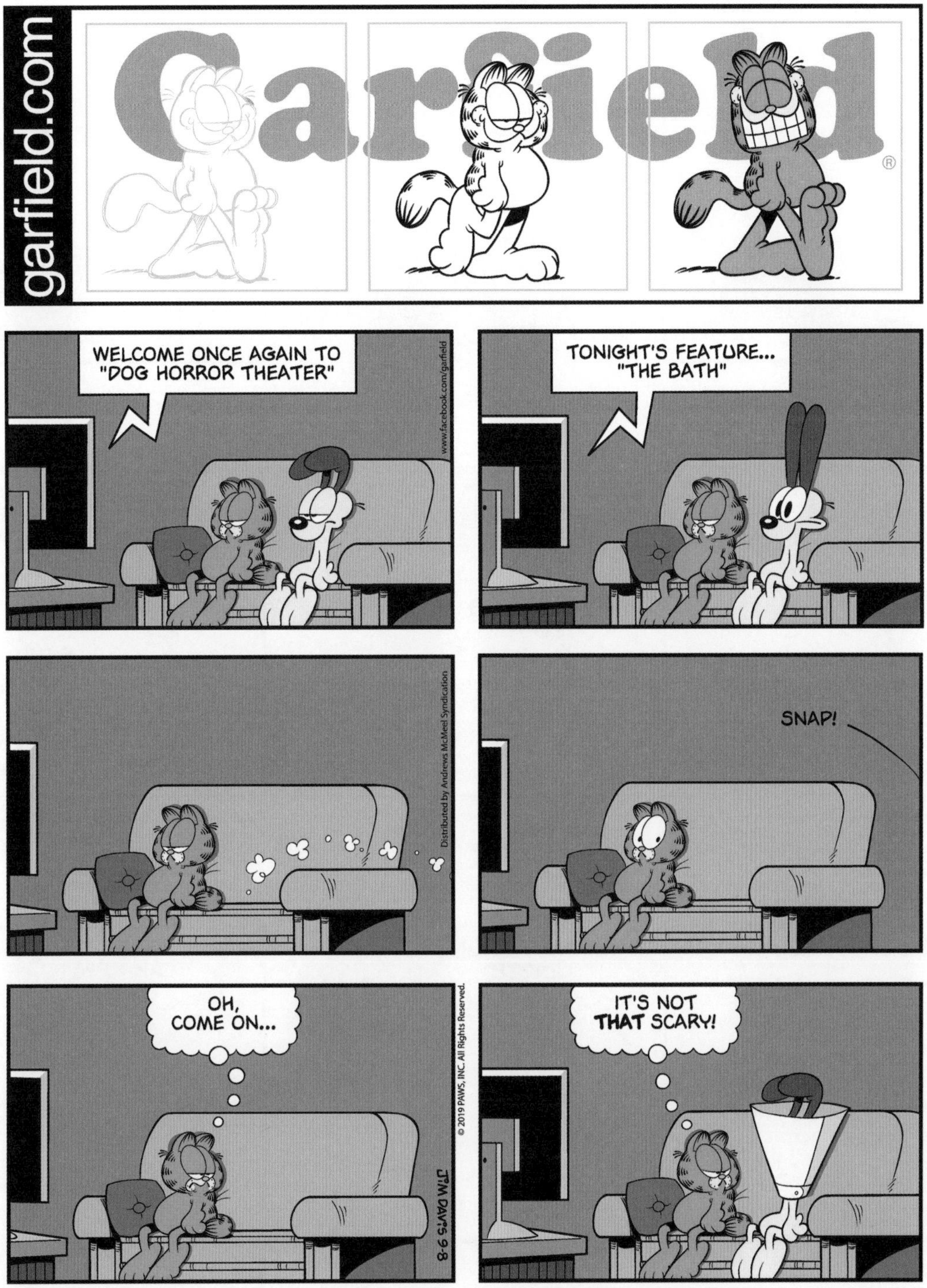
garfield.com
Garfield
WELCOME ONCE AGAIN TO "DOG HORROR THEATER"
www.facebook.com/garfield
TONIGHT'S FEATURE... "THE BATH"
Distributed by Andrews McMeel Syndication
SNAP!
OH, COME ON...
© 2019 PAWS, INC. All Rights Reserved.
JIM DAVIS 9-8
IT'S NOT THAT SCARY!

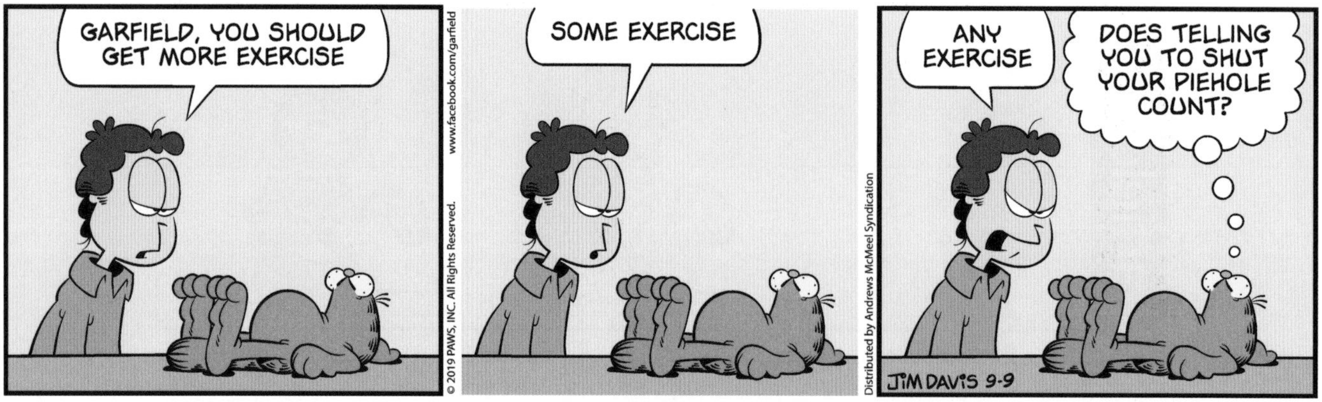
GARFIELD, YOU SHOULD GET MORE EXERCISE
SOME EXERCISE
ANY EXERCISE
DOES TELLING YOU TO SHUT YOUR PIEHOLE COUNT?
JIM DAVIS 9-9
© 2019 PAWS, INC. All Rights Reserved.
www.facebook.com/garfield
Distributed by Andrews McMeel Syndication

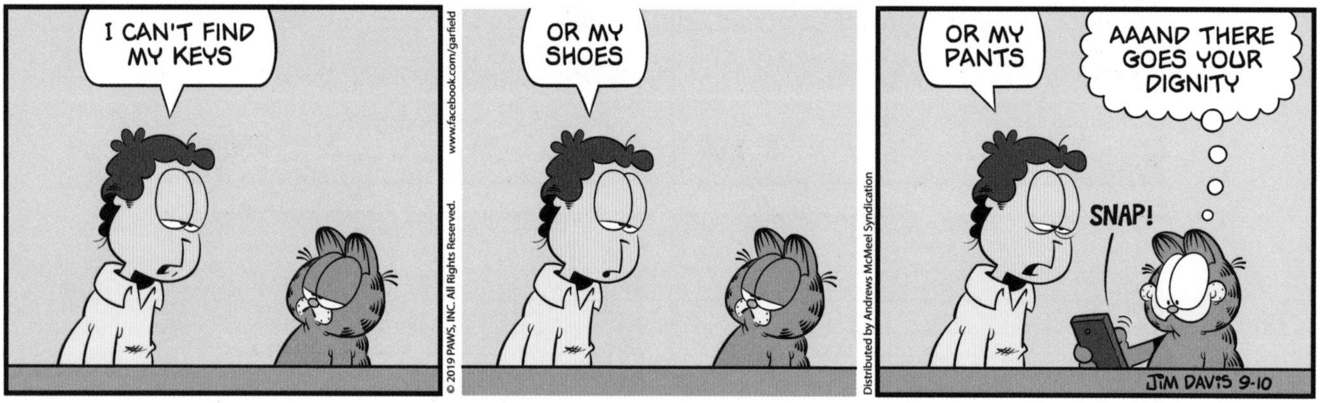
I CAN'T FIND MY KEYS
OR MY SHOES
OR MY PANTS
AAAND THERE GOES YOUR DIGNITY
SNAP!
JIM DAVIS 9-10
© 2019 PAWS, INC. All Rights Reserved.
www.facebook.com/garfield
Distributed by Andrews McMeel Syndication

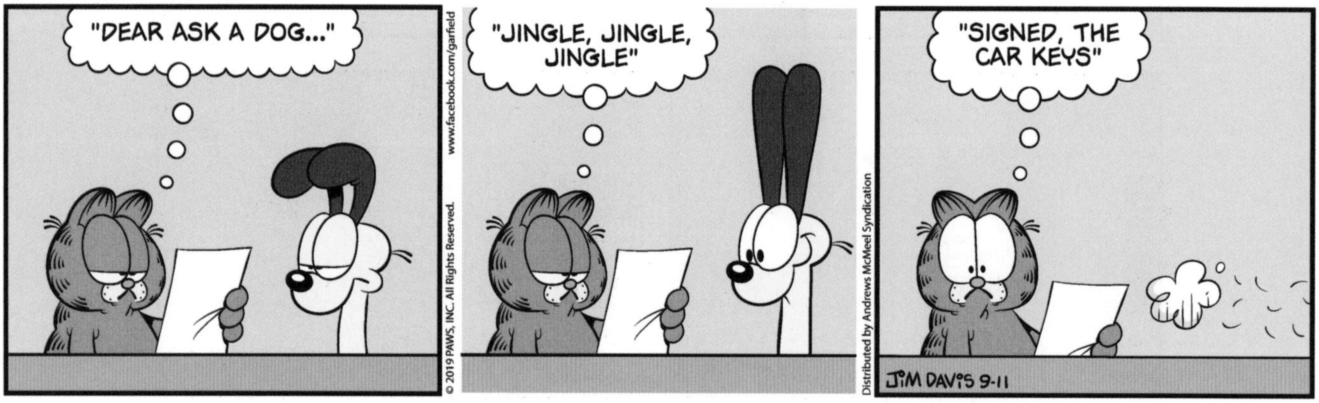
"DEAR ASK A DOG..."
"JINGLE, JINGLE, JINGLE"
"SIGNED, THE CAR KEYS"
JIM DAVIS 9-11
© 2019 PAWS, INC. All Rights Reserved.
www.facebook.com/garfield
Distributed by Andrews McMeel Syndication

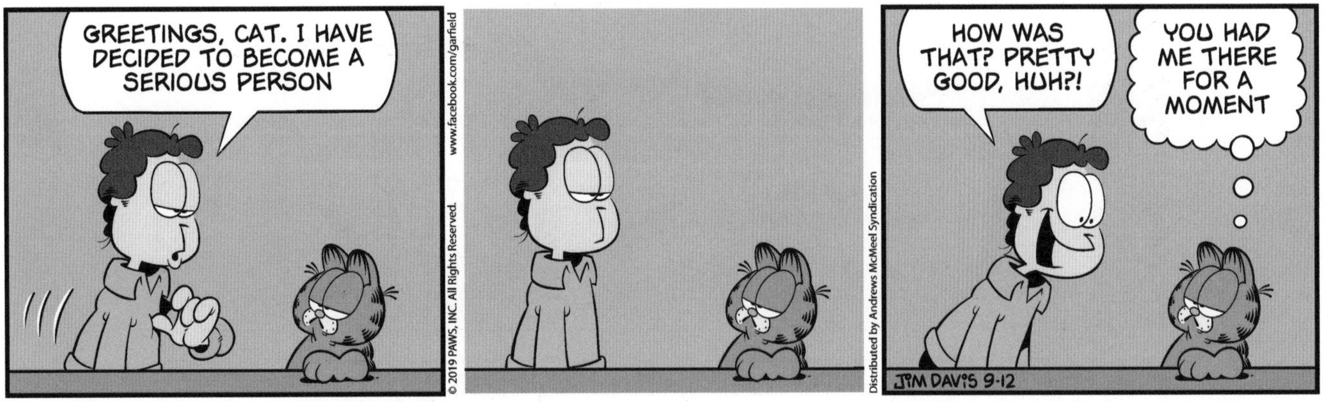
GREETINGS, CAT. I HAVE DECIDED TO BECOME A SERIOUS PERSON
© 2019 PAWS, INC. All Rights Reserved. www.facebook.com/garfield
HOW WAS THAT? PRETTY GOOD, HUH?!
YOU HAD ME THERE FOR A MOMENT
Distributed by Andrews McMeel Syndication
JIM DAVIS 9-12

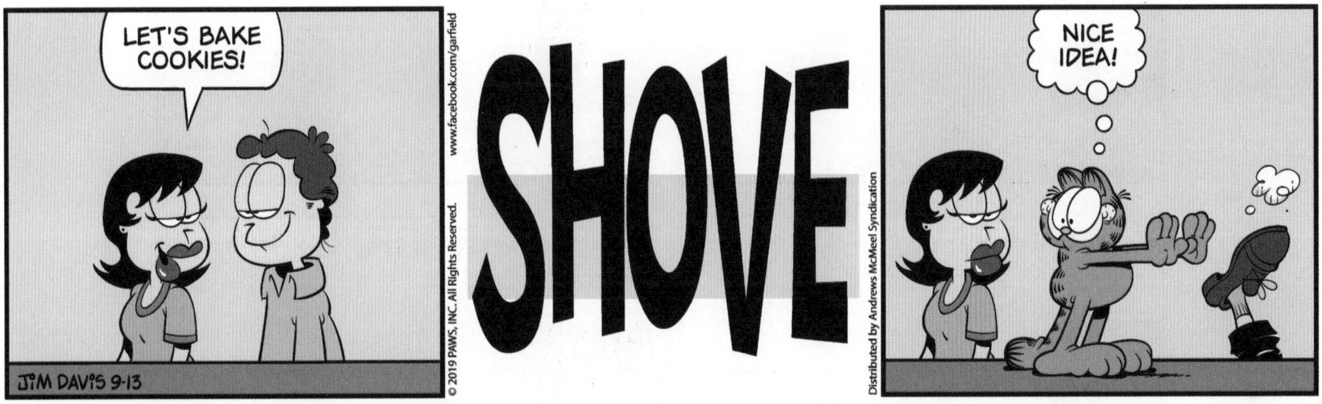
LET'S BAKE COOKIES!
JIM DAVIS 9-13
© 2019 PAWS, INC. All Rights Reserved. www.facebook.com/garfield
SHOVE
Distributed by Andrews McMeel Syndication
NICE IDEA!

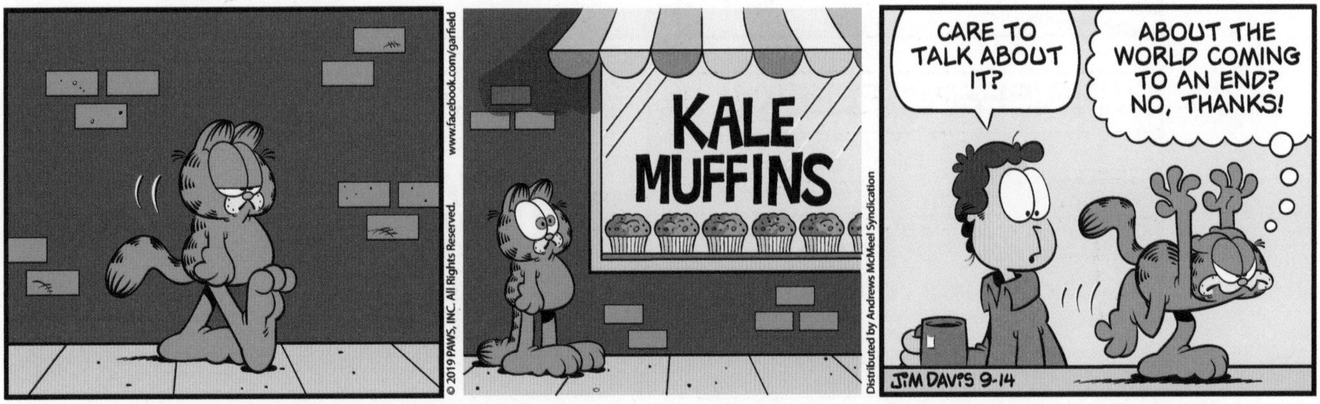
© 2019 PAWS, INC. All Rights Reserved. www.facebook.com/garfield
KALE MUFFINS
Distributed by Andrews McMeel Syndication
CARE TO TALK ABOUT IT?
ABOUT THE WORLD COMING TO AN END? NO, THANKS!
JIM DAVIS 9-14

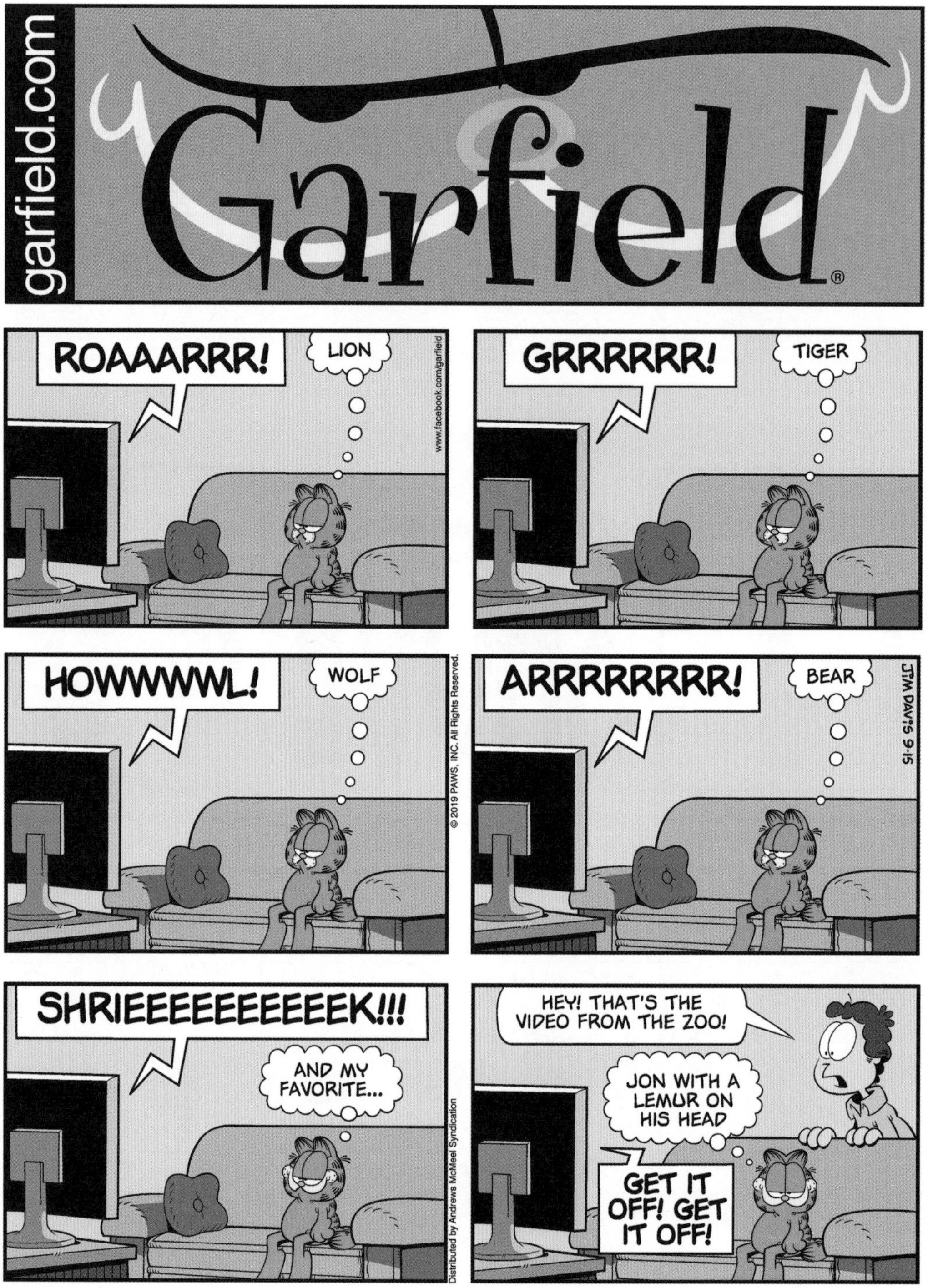

garfield.com
Garfield®
ROAAARRR!
LION
www.facebook.com/garfield
GRRRRRR!
TIGER
HOWWWWL!
WOLF
© 2019 PAWS, INC. All Rights Reserved.
ARRRRRRRR!
BEAR
JIM DAVIS 9-15
SHRIEEEEEEEEEEK!!!
AND MY FAVORITE...
Distributed by Andrews McMeel Syndication
HEY! THAT'S THE VIDEO FROM THE ZOO!
JON WITH A LEMUR ON HIS HEAD
GET IT OFF! GET IT OFF!

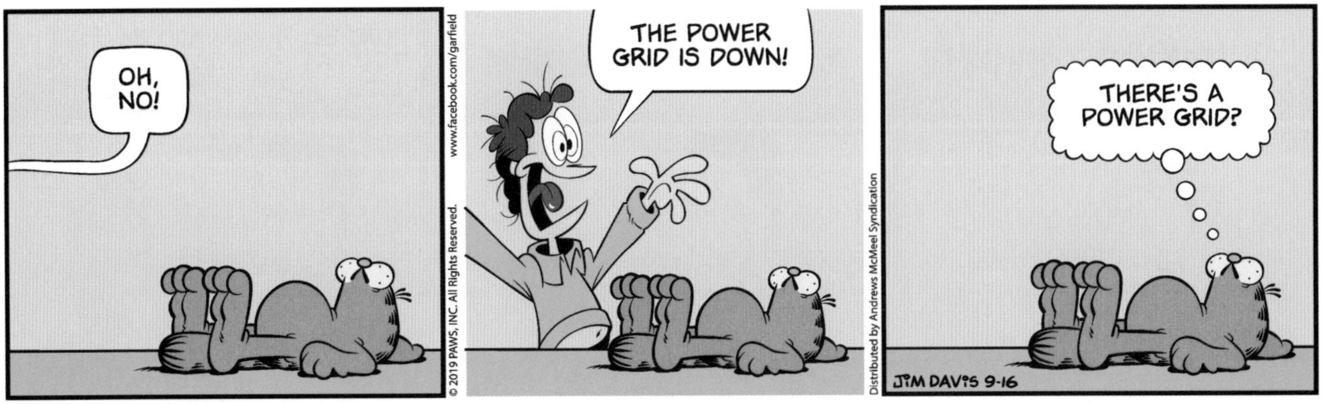
OH, NO!
THE POWER GRID IS DOWN!
THERE'S A POWER GRID?
JIM DAVIS 9-16
© 2019 PAWS, INC. All Rights Reserved.
www.facebook.com/garfield
Distributed by Andrews McMeel Syndication

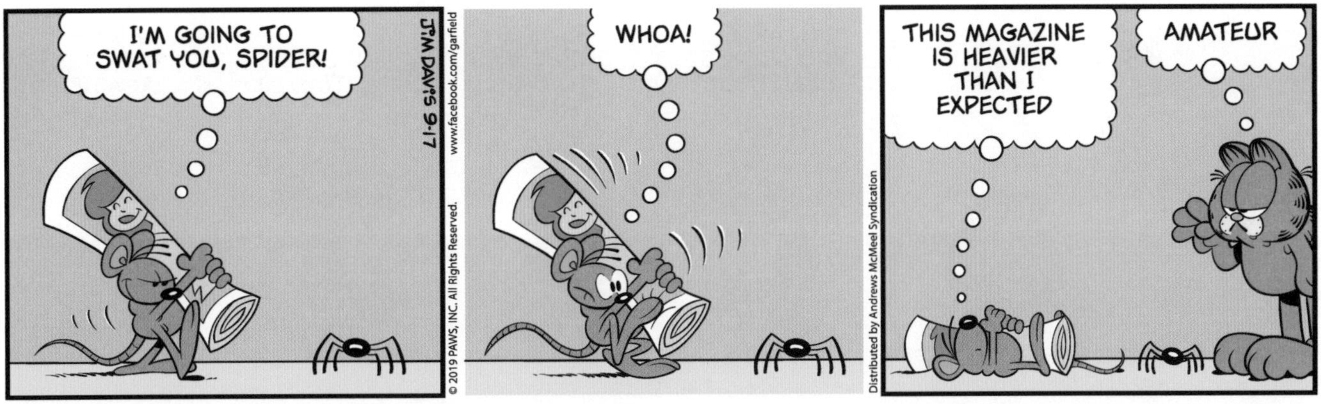
I'M GOING TO SWAT YOU, SPIDER!
JIM DAVIS 9-17
WHOA!
THIS MAGAZINE IS HEAVIER THAN I EXPECTED
AMATEUR
© 2019 PAWS, INC. All Rights Reserved.
www.facebook.com/garfield
Distributed by Andrews McMeel Syndication

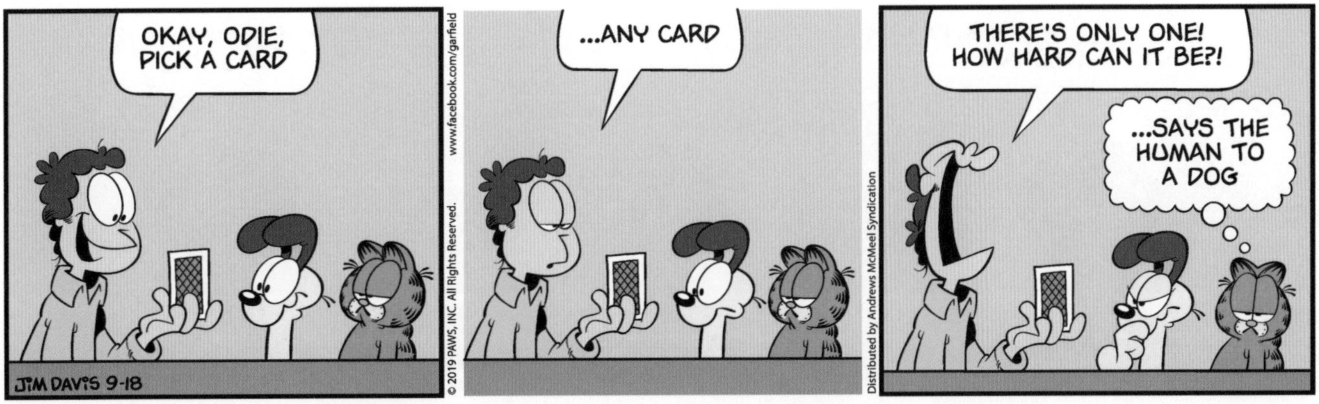
OKAY, ODIE, PICK A CARD
JIM DAVIS 9-18
...ANY CARD
THERE'S ONLY ONE! HOW HARD CAN IT BE?!
...SAYS THE HUMAN TO A DOG
© 2019 PAWS, INC. All Rights Reserved.
www.facebook.com/garfield
Distributed by Andrews McMeel Syndication

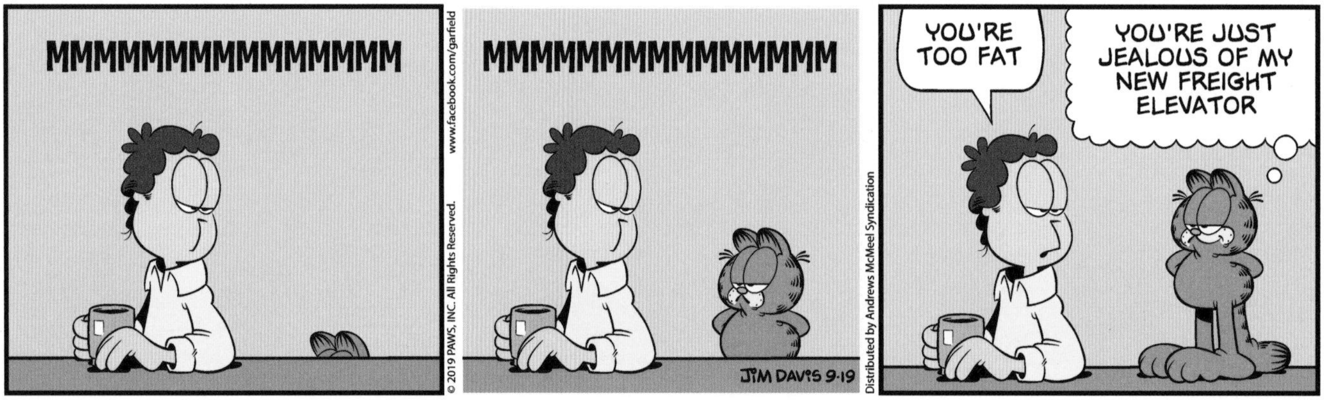
MMMMMMMMMMMMMMMM
MMMMMMMMMMMMMMMM
YOU'RE TOO FAT
YOU'RE JUST JEALOUS OF MY NEW FREIGHT ELEVATOR
JIM DAVIS 9-19
© 2019 PAWS, INC. All Rights Reserved. www.facebook.com/garfield
Distributed by Andrews McMeel Syndication

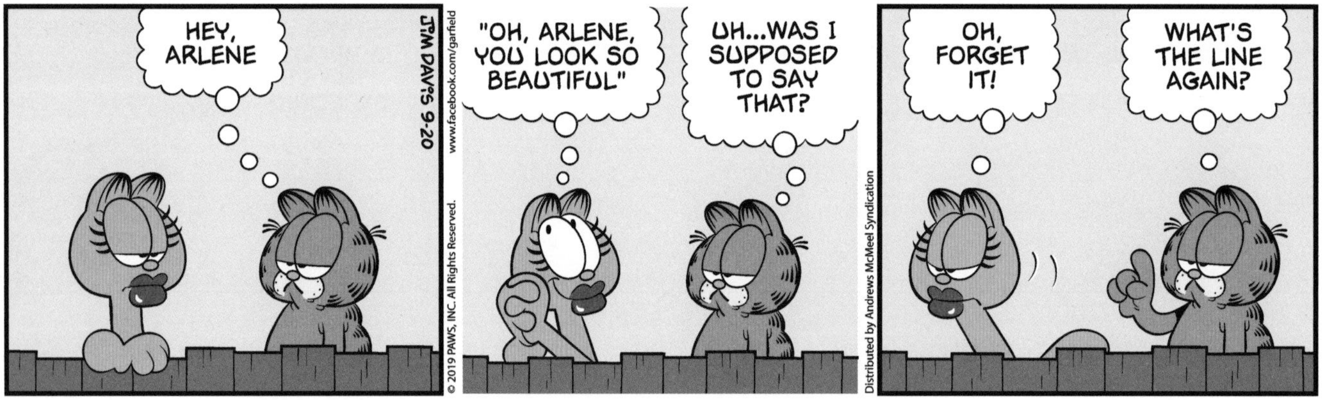
HEY, ARLENE
JIM DAVIS 9-20
"OH, ARLENE, YOU LOOK SO BEAUTIFUL"
UH...WAS I SUPPOSED TO SAY THAT?
OH, FORGET IT!
WHAT'S THE LINE AGAIN?
© 2019 PAWS, INC. All Rights Reserved. www.facebook.com/garfield
Distributed by Andrews McMeel Syndication

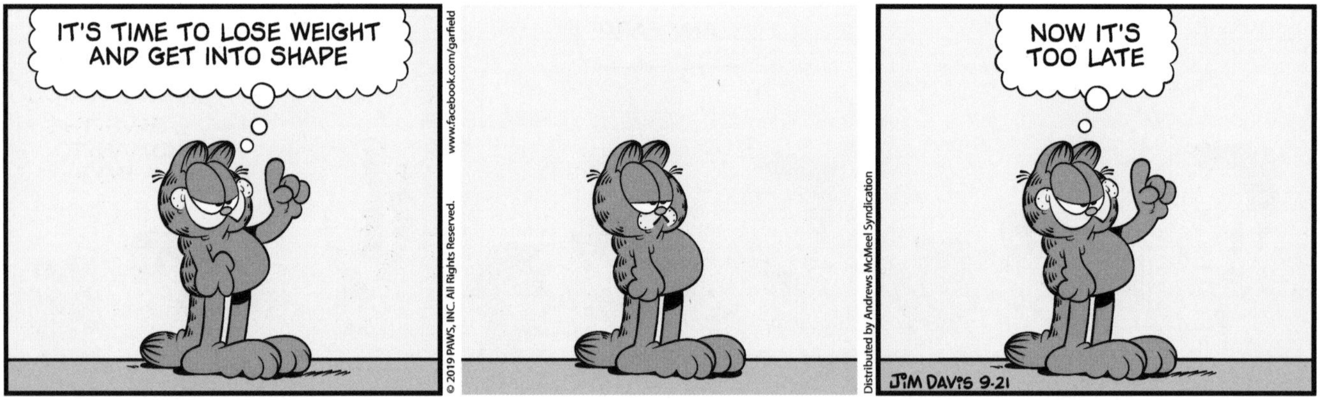
IT'S TIME TO LOSE WEIGHT AND GET INTO SHAPE
NOW IT'S TOO LATE
JIM DAVIS 9-21
© 2019 PAWS, INC. All Rights Reserved. www.facebook.com/garfield
Distributed by Andrews McMeel Syndication

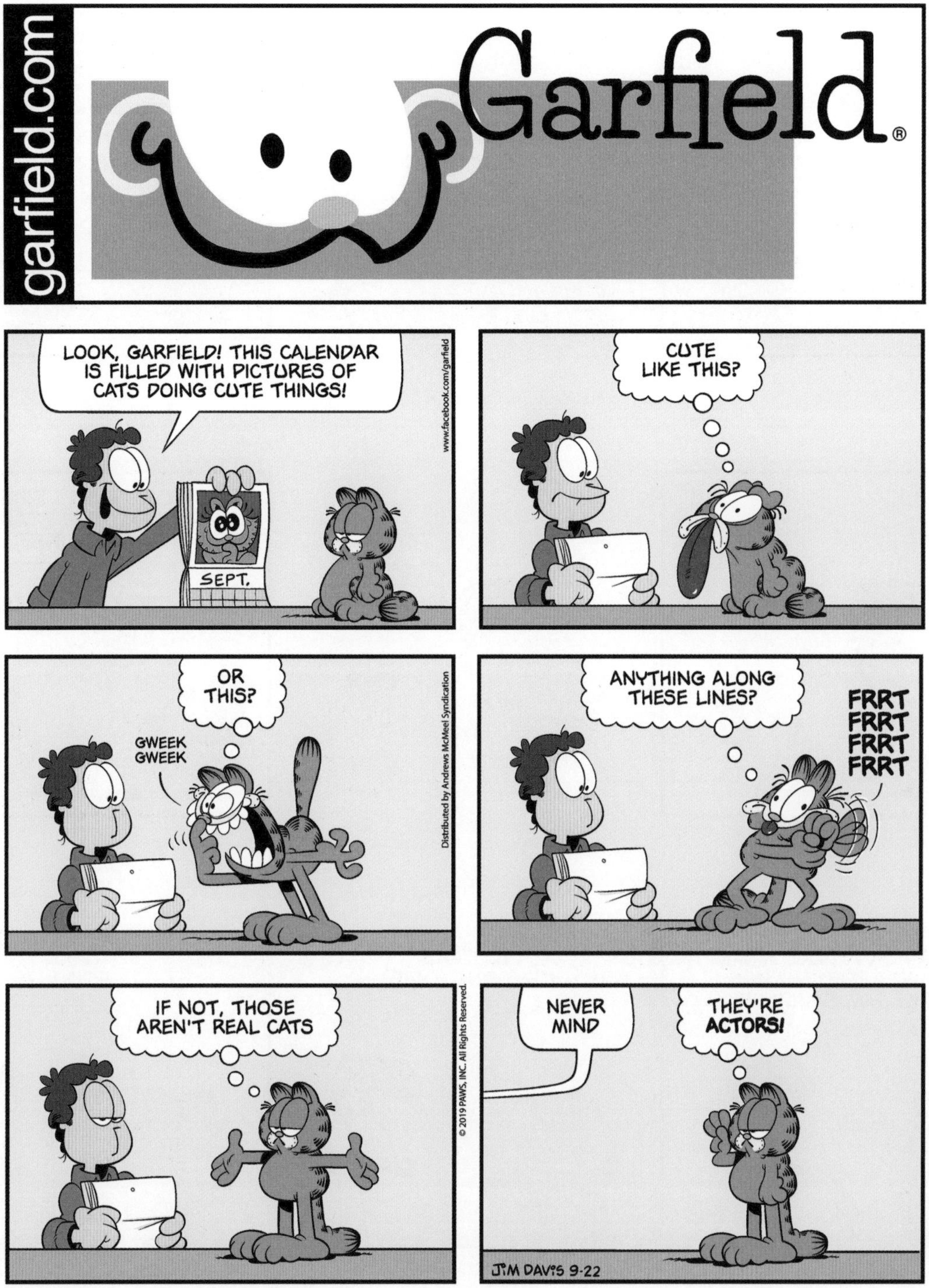
garfield.com
Garfield®
LOOK, GARFIELD! THIS CALENDAR IS FILLED WITH PICTURES OF CATS DOING CUTE THINGS!
SEPT.
www.facebook.com/garfield
CUTE LIKE THIS?
OR THIS?
GWEEK GWEEK
Distributed by Andrews McMeel Syndication
ANYTHING ALONG THESE LINES?
FRRT FRRT FRRT FRRT
IF NOT, THOSE AREN'T REAL CATS
© 2019 PAWS, INC. All Rights Reserved.
NEVER MIND
THEY'RE ACTORS!
JIM DAVIS 9-22

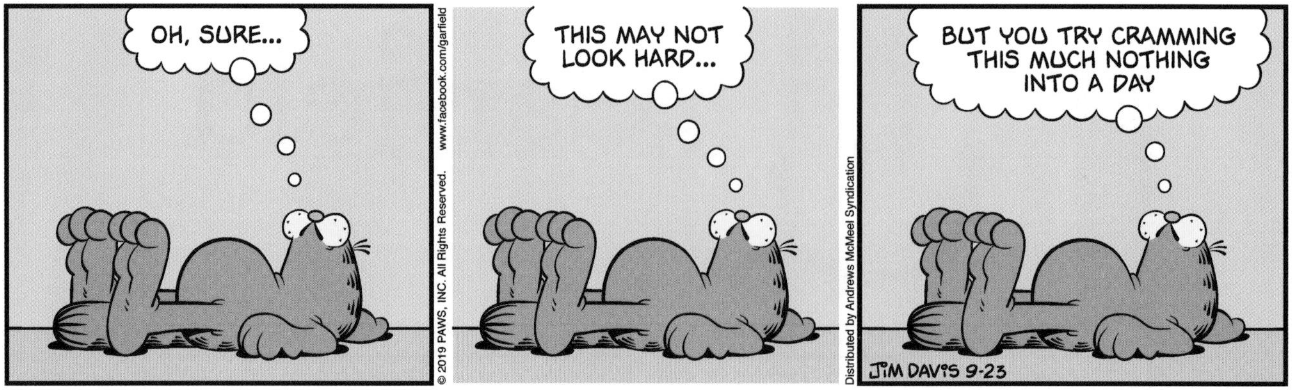
OH, SURE...
© 2019 PAWS, INC. All Rights Reserved. www.facebook.com/garfield
THIS MAY NOT LOOK HARD...
Distributed by Andrews McMeel Syndication
BUT YOU TRY CRAMMING THIS MUCH NOTHING INTO A DAY
JIM DAVIS 9-23

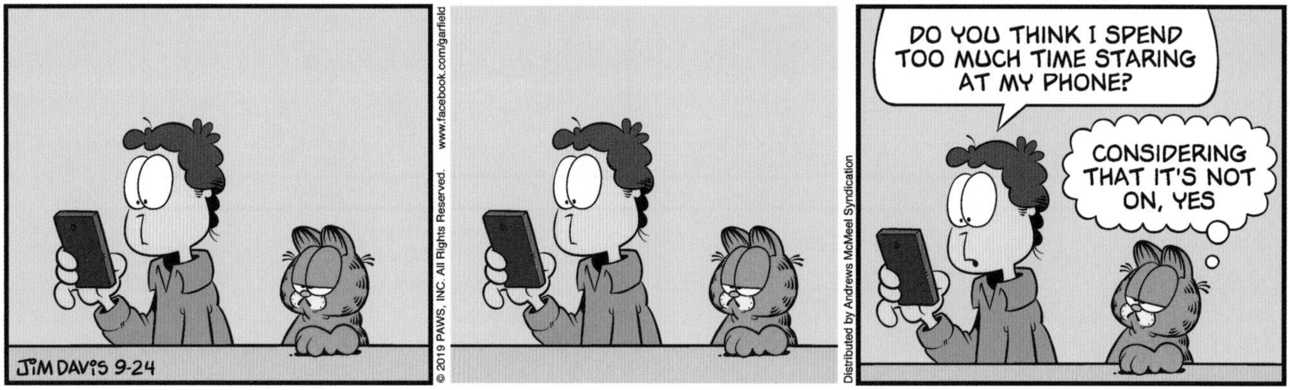
JIM DAVIS 9-24
© 2019 PAWS, INC. All Rights Reserved. www.facebook.com/garfield
Distributed by Andrews McMeel Syndication
DO YOU THINK I SPEND TOO MUCH TIME STARING AT MY PHONE?
CONSIDERING THAT IT'S NOT ON, YES

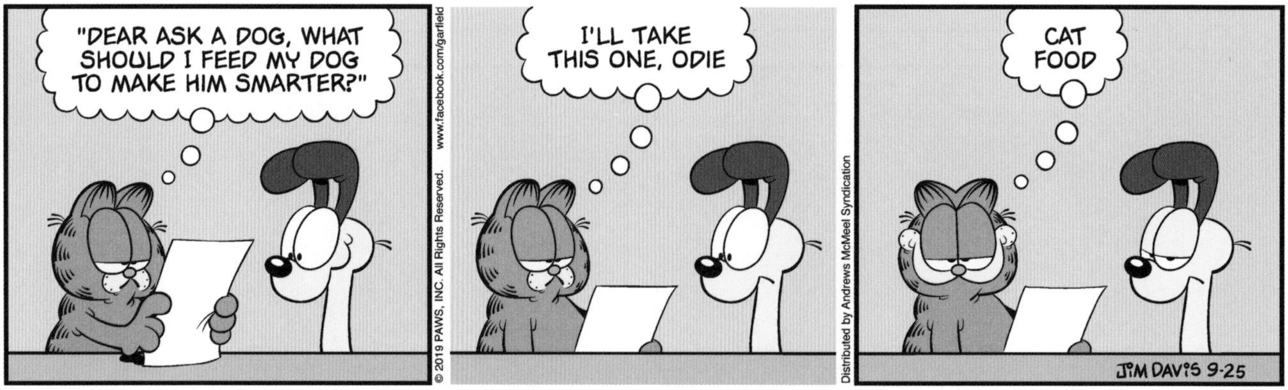
"DEAR ASK A DOG, WHAT SHOULD I FEED MY DOG TO MAKE HIM SMARTER?"
© 2019 PAWS, INC. All Rights Reserved. www.facebook.com/garfield
I'LL TAKE THIS ONE, ODIE
Distributed by Andrews McMeel Syndication
CAT FOOD
JIM DAVIS 9-25

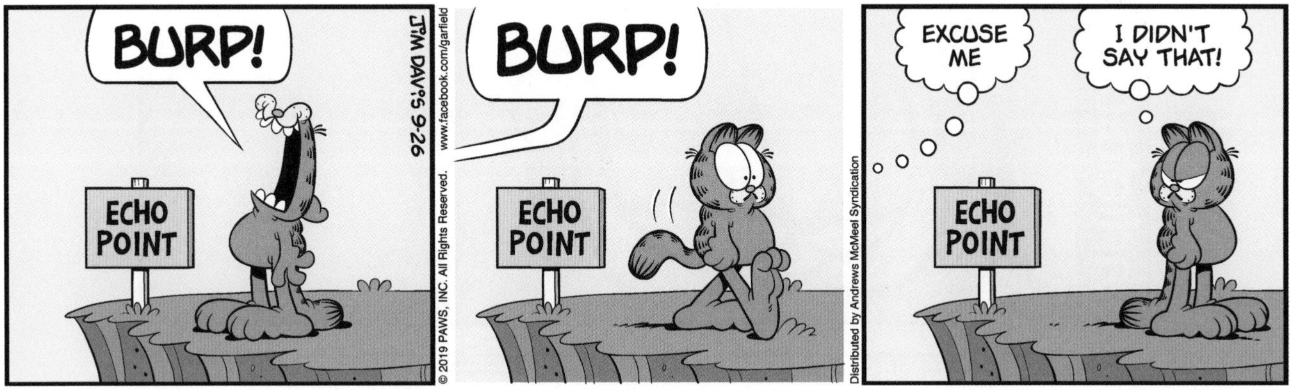
BURP!
JIM DAVIS 9-26
© 2019 PAWS, INC. All Rights Reserved. www.facebook.com/garfield
BURP!
ECHO POINT
Distributed by Andrews McMeel Syndication
EXCUSE ME
I DIDN'T SAY THAT!

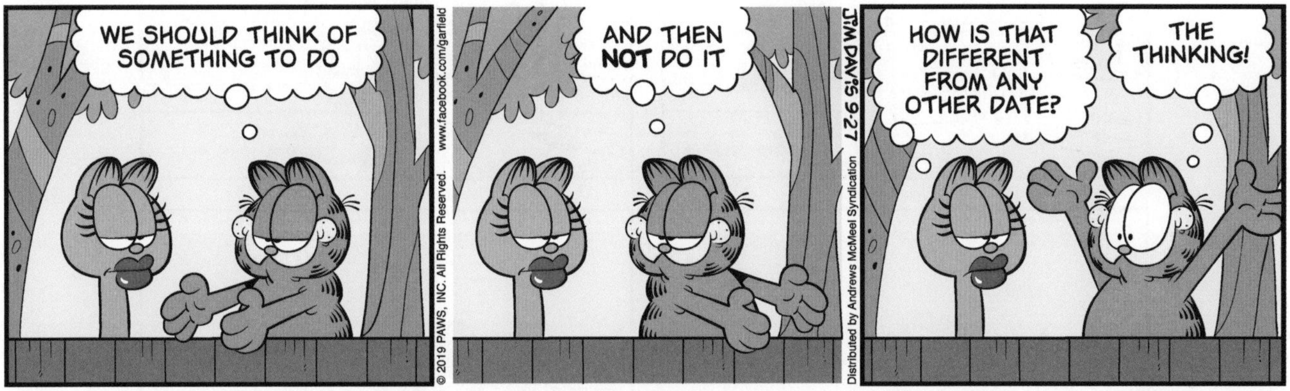
WE SHOULD THINK OF SOMETHING TO DO
© 2019 PAWS, INC. All Rights Reserved. www.facebook.com/garfield
AND THEN **NOT** DO IT
JIM DAVIS 9-27
Distributed by Andrews McMeel Syndication
HOW IS THAT DIFFERENT FROM ANY OTHER DATE?
THE THINKING!

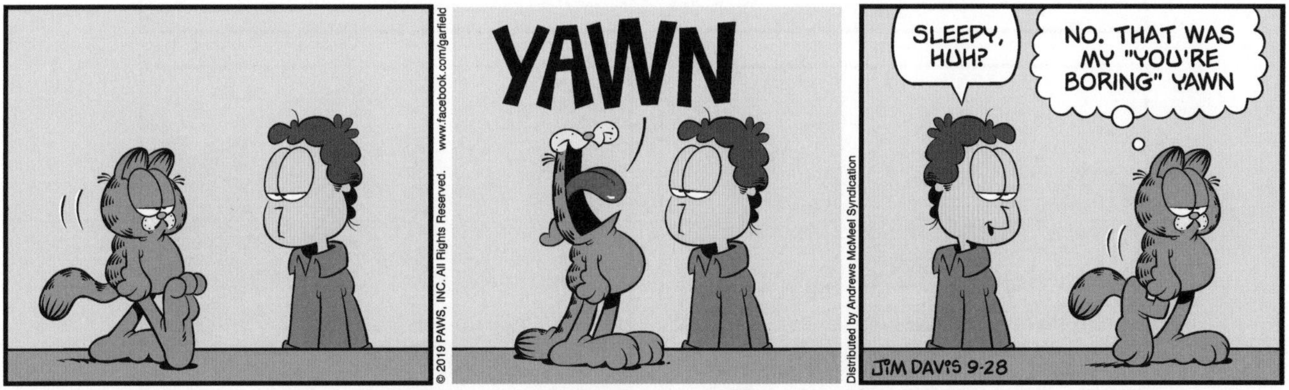
© 2019 PAWS, INC. All Rights Reserved. www.facebook.com/garfield
YAWN
Distributed by Andrews McMeel Syndication
SLEEPY, HUH?
NO. THAT WAS MY "YOU'RE BORING" YAWN
JIM DAVIS 9-28

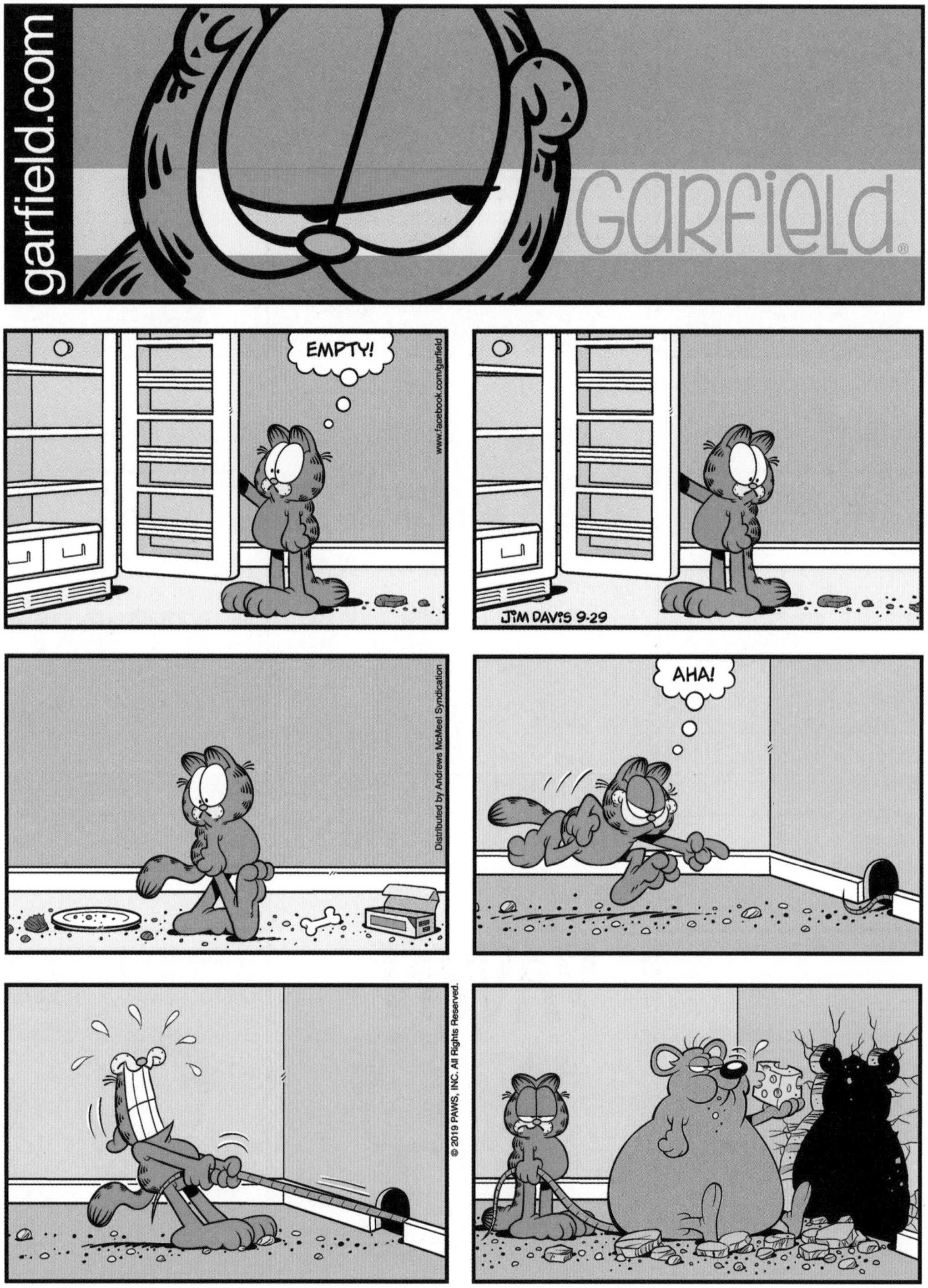
garfield.com
GARFIELD
EMPTY!
www.facebook.com/garfield
JIM DAVIS 9-29
Distributed by Andrews McMeel Syndication
AHA!
© 2019 PAWS, INC. All Rights Reserved.

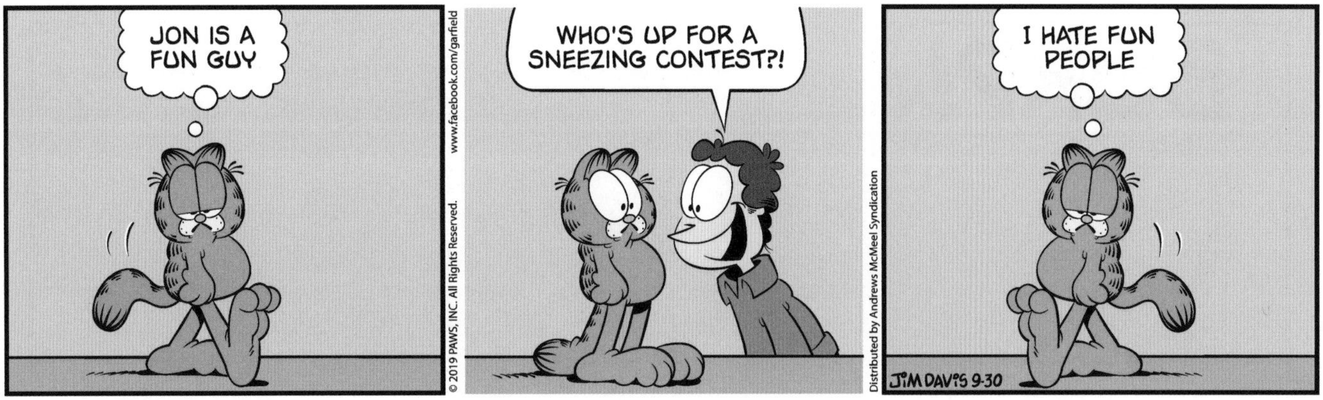
JON IS A FUN GUY
WHO'S UP FOR A SNEEZING CONTEST?!
I HATE FUN PEOPLE
© 2019 PAWS, INC. All Rights Reserved.
www.facebook.com/garfield
Distributed by Andrews McMeel Syndication
JIM DAVIS 9-30

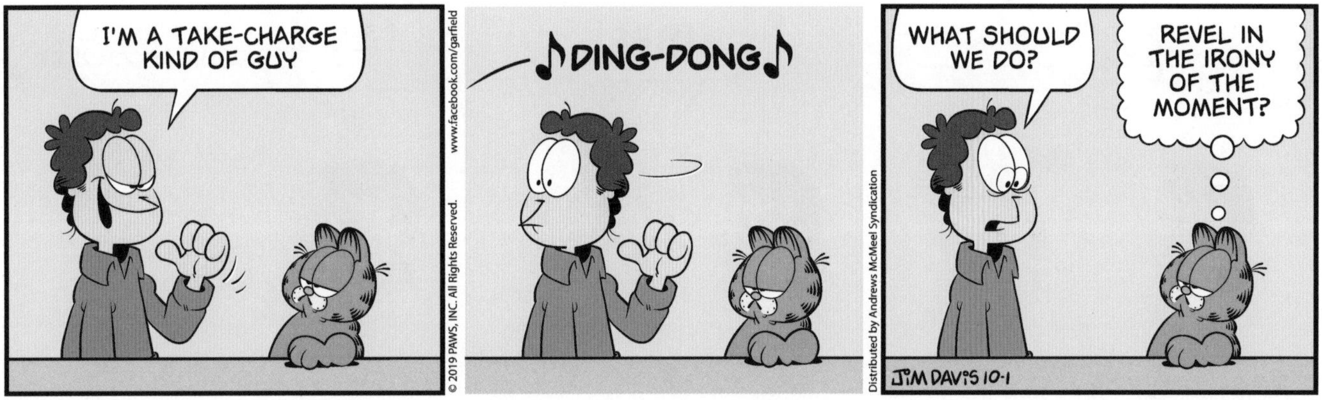
I'M A TAKE-CHARGE KIND OF GUY
♪DING-DONG♪
WHAT SHOULD WE DO?
REVEL IN THE IRONY OF THE MOMENT?
© 2019 PAWS, INC. All Rights Reserved.
www.facebook.com/garfield
Distributed by Andrews McMeel Syndication
JIM DAVIS 10-1

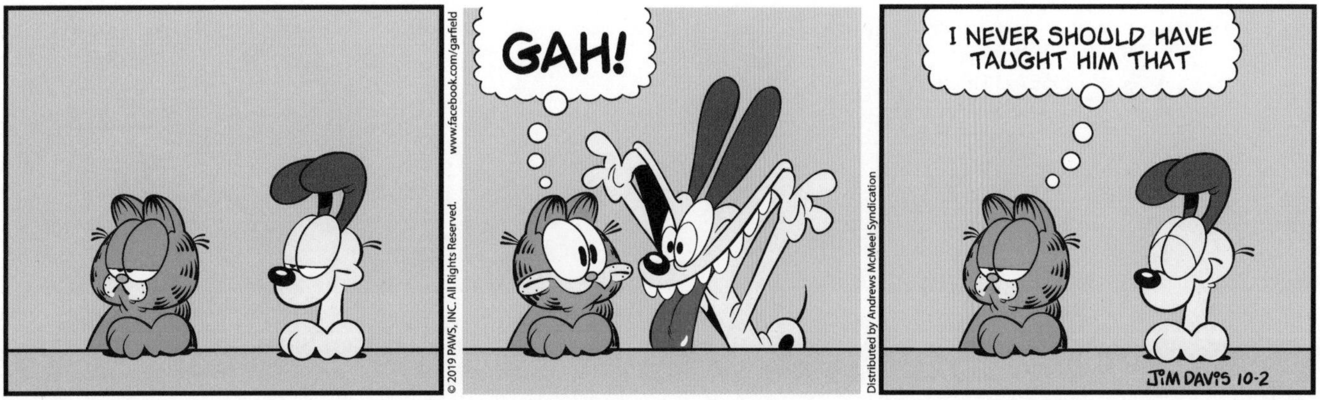
GAH!
I NEVER SHOULD HAVE TAUGHT HIM THAT
© 2019 PAWS, INC. All Rights Reserved.
www.facebook.com/garfield
Distributed by Andrews McMeel Syndication
JIM DAVIS 10-2

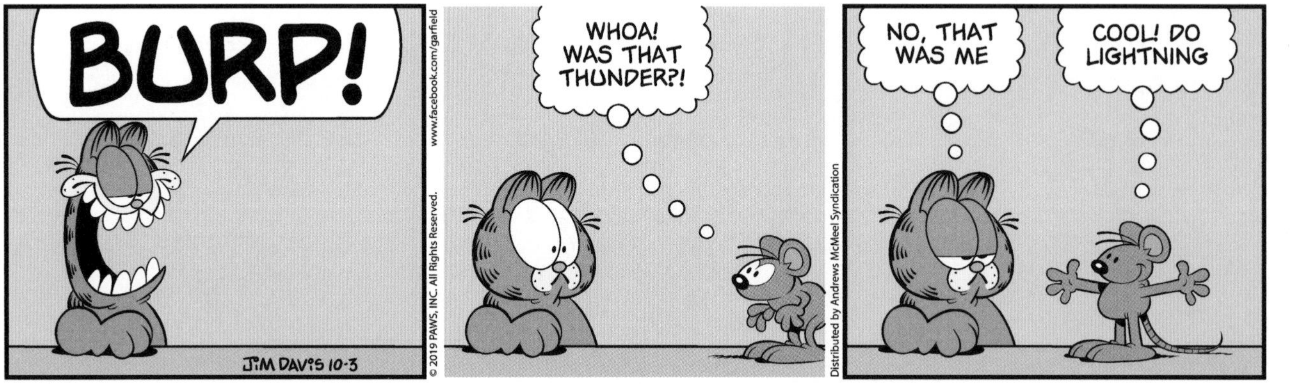
BURP!
JIM DAVIS 10-3
© 2019 PAWS, INC. All Rights Reserved. www.facebook.com/garfield
WHOA! WAS THAT THUNDER?!
Distributed by Andrews McMeel Syndication
NO, THAT WAS ME
COOL! DO LIGHTNING

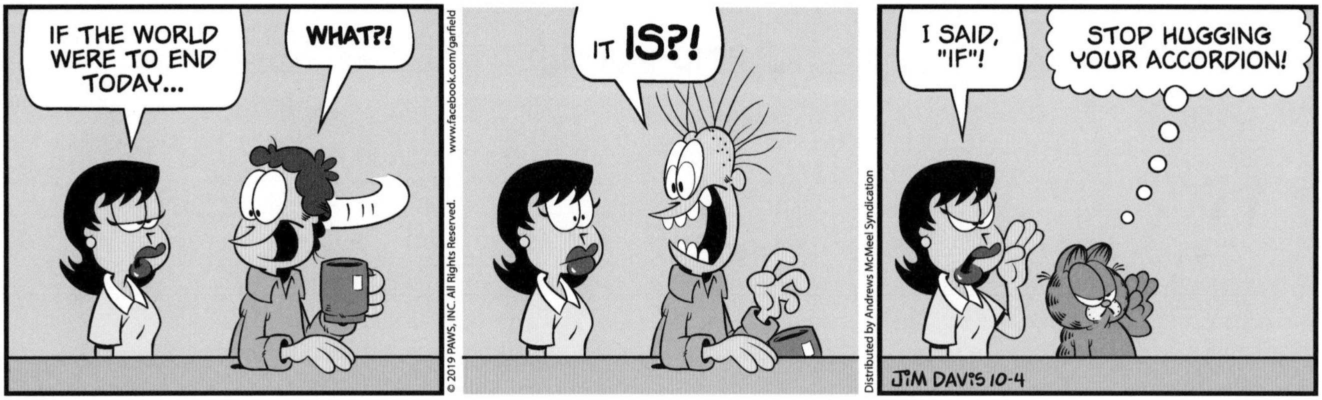
IF THE WORLD WERE TO END TODAY...
WHAT?!
© 2019 PAWS, INC. All Rights Reserved. www.facebook.com/garfield
IT IS?!
Distributed by Andrews McMeel Syndication
I SAID, "IF"!
STOP HUGGING YOUR ACCORDION!
JIM DAVIS 10-4

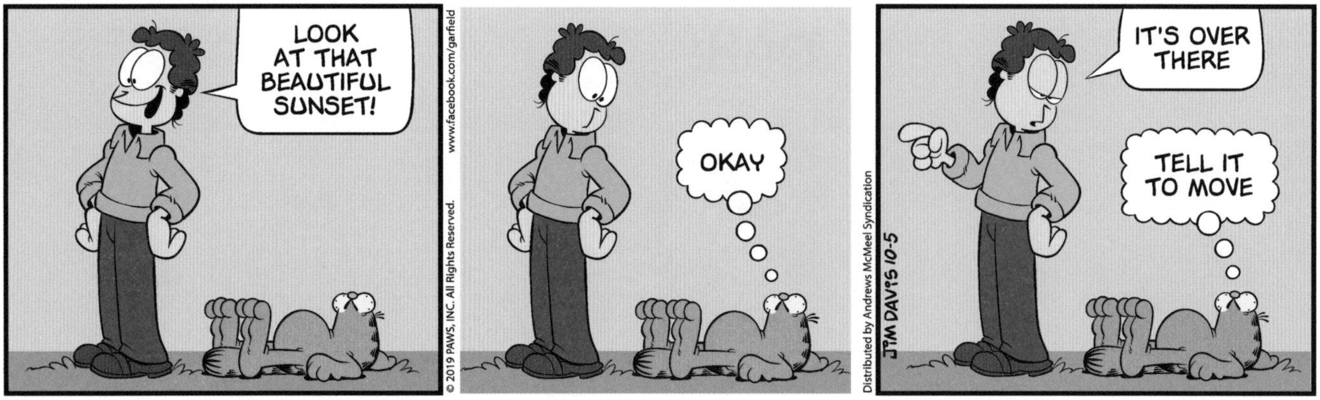
LOOK AT THAT BEAUTIFUL SUNSET!
© 2019 PAWS, INC. All Rights Reserved. www.facebook.com/garfield
OKAY
Distributed by Andrews McMeel Syndication
JIM DAVIS 10-5
IT'S OVER THERE
TELL IT TO MOVE

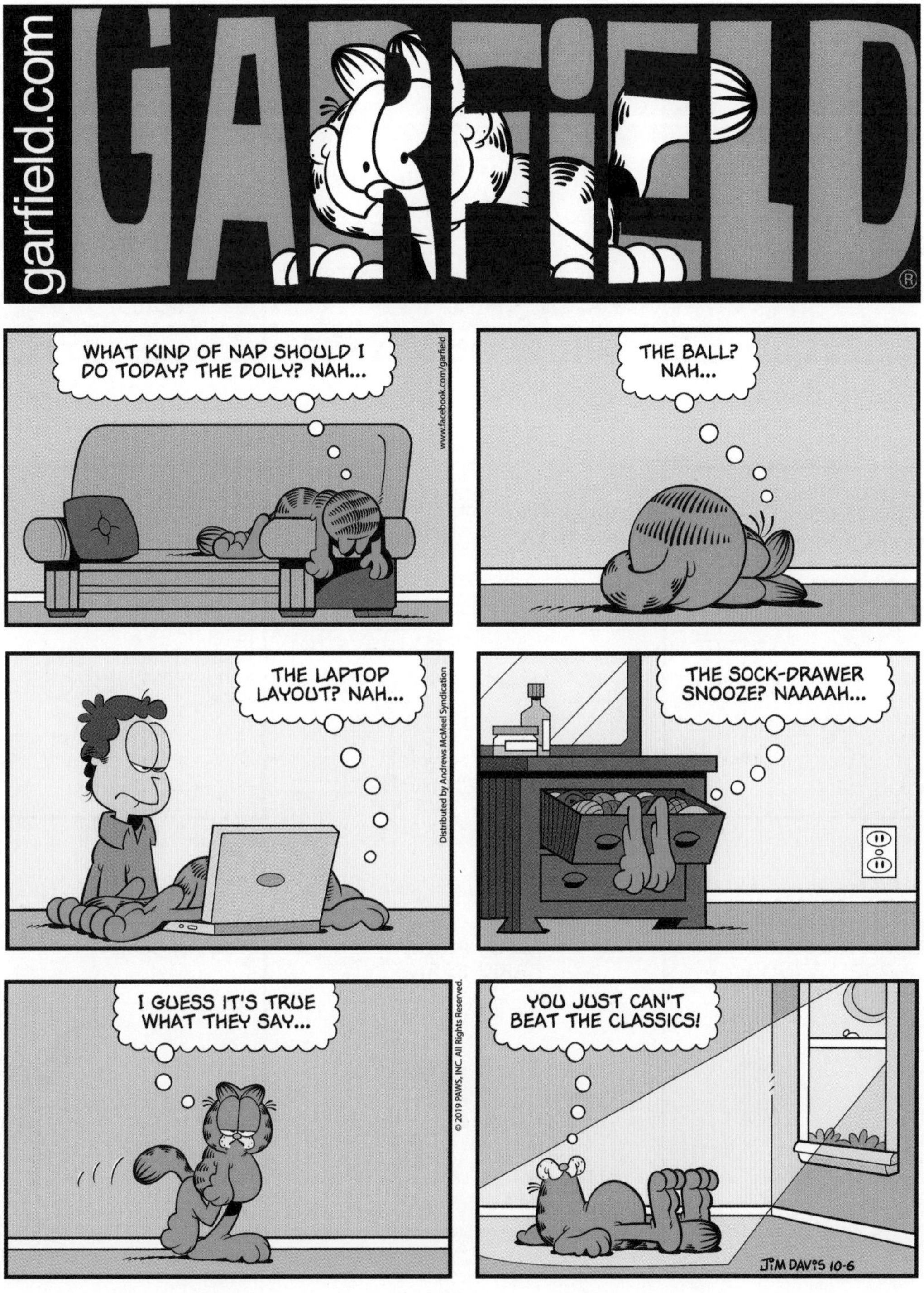
garfield.com
GARFIELD
WHAT KIND OF NAP SHOULD I DO TODAY? THE DOILY? NAH...
www.facebook.com/garfield
THE BALL? NAH...
THE LAPTOP LAYOUT? NAH...
Distributed by Andrews McMeel Syndication
THE SOCK-DRAWER SNOOZE? NAAAAH...
I GUESS IT'S TRUE WHAT THEY SAY...
© 2019 PAWS, INC. All Rights Reserved.
YOU JUST CAN'T BEAT THE CLASSICS!
JIM DAVIS 10-6

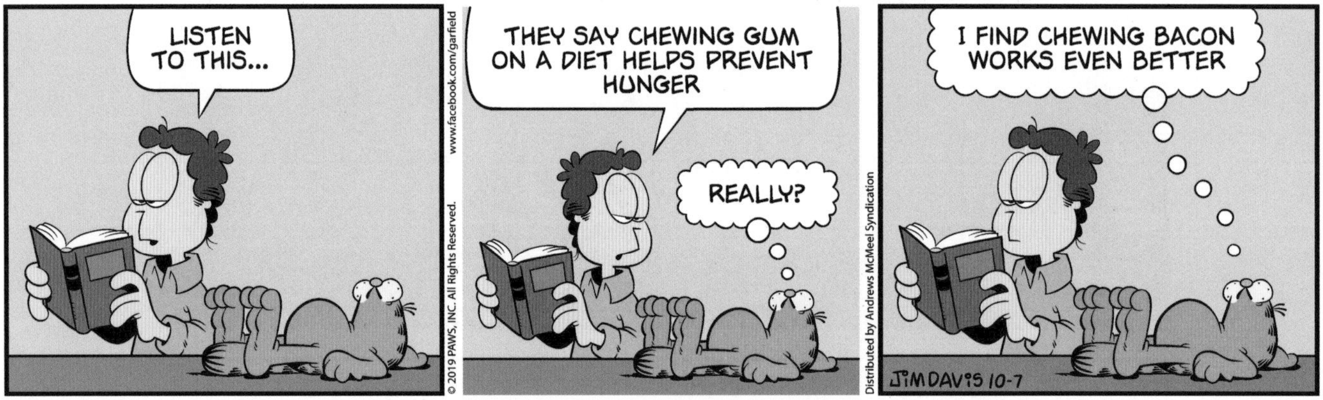

LISTEN TO THIS...
THEY SAY CHEWING GUM ON A DIET HELPS PREVENT HUNGER
REALLY?
I FIND CHEWING BACON WORKS EVEN BETTER
JIM DAVIS 10-7
© 2019 PAWS, INC. All Rights Reserved. www.facebook.com/garfield
Distributed by Andrews McMeel Syndication

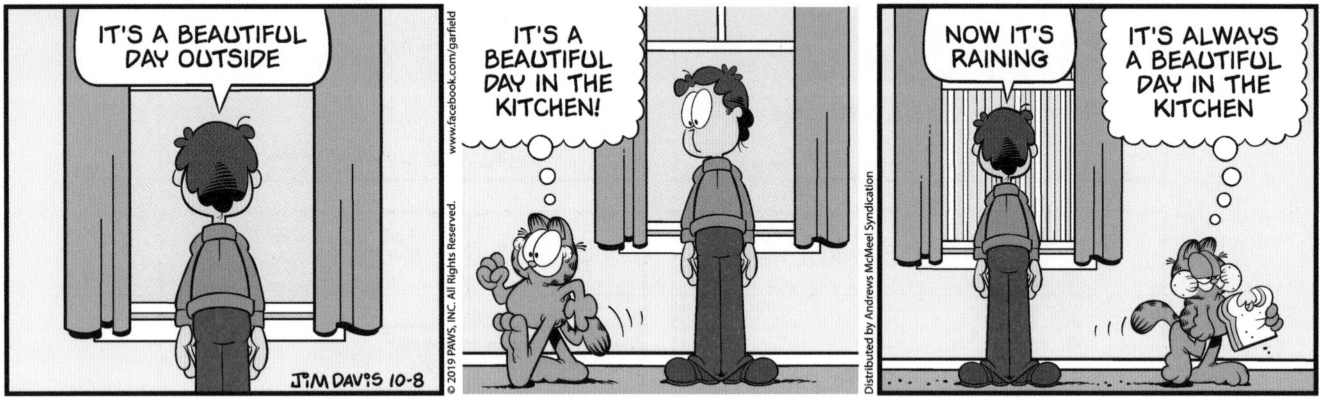

IT'S A BEAUTIFUL DAY OUTSIDE
IT'S A BEAUTIFUL DAY IN THE KITCHEN!
NOW IT'S RAINING
IT'S ALWAYS A BEAUTIFUL DAY IN THE KITCHEN
JIM DAVIS 10-8
© 2019 PAWS, INC. All Rights Reserved. www.facebook.com/garfield
Distributed by Andrews McMeel Syndication

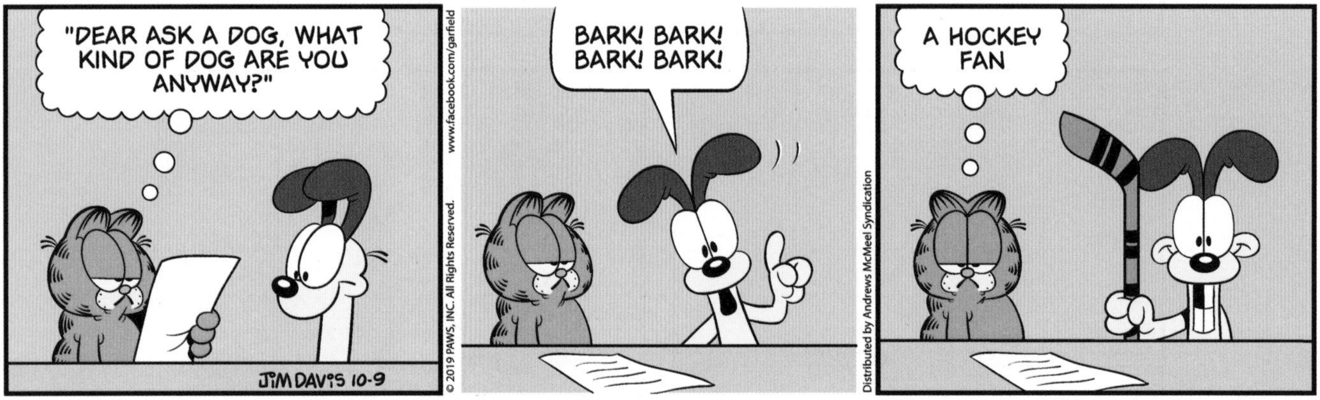

"DEAR ASK A DOG, WHAT KIND OF DOG ARE YOU ANYWAY?"
BARK! BARK! BARK! BARK!
A HOCKEY FAN
JIM DAVIS 10-9
© 2019 PAWS, INC. All Rights Reserved. www.facebook.com/garfield
Distributed by Andrews McMeel Syndication

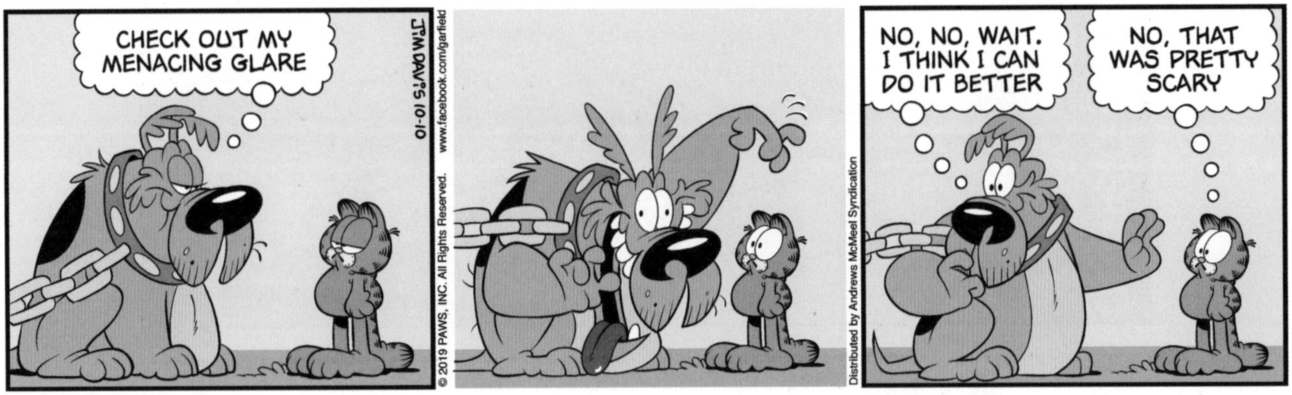
CHECK OUT MY MENACING GLARE
JIM DAVIS 10-10
© 2019 PAWS, INC. All Rights Reserved. www.facebook.com/garfield
NO, NO, WAIT. I THINK I CAN DO IT BETTER
NO, THAT WAS PRETTY SCARY
Distributed by Andrews McMeel Syndication

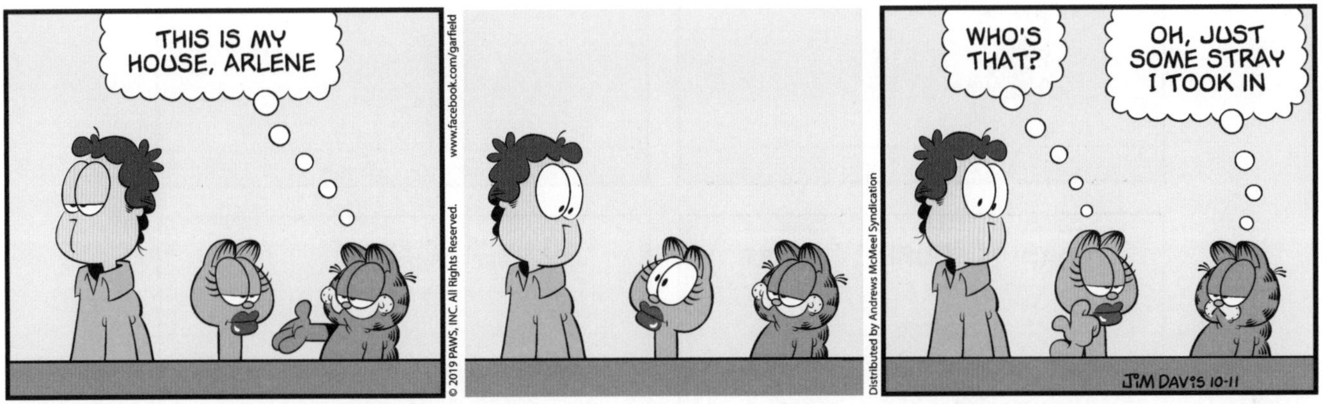
THIS IS MY HOUSE, ARLENE
© 2019 PAWS, INC. All Rights Reserved. www.facebook.com/garfield
WHO'S THAT?
OH, JUST SOME STRAY I TOOK IN
Distributed by Andrews McMeel Syndication
JIM DAVIS 10-11

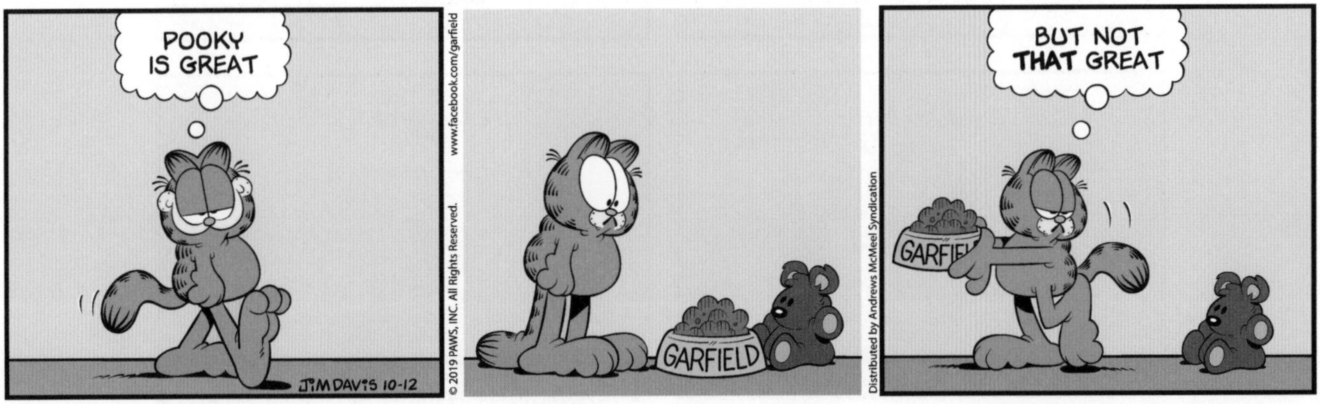
POOKY IS GREAT
JIM DAVIS 10-12
© 2019 PAWS, INC. All Rights Reserved. www.facebook.com/garfield
GARFIELD
BUT NOT **THAT** GREAT
GARFI
Distributed by Andrews McMeel Syndication

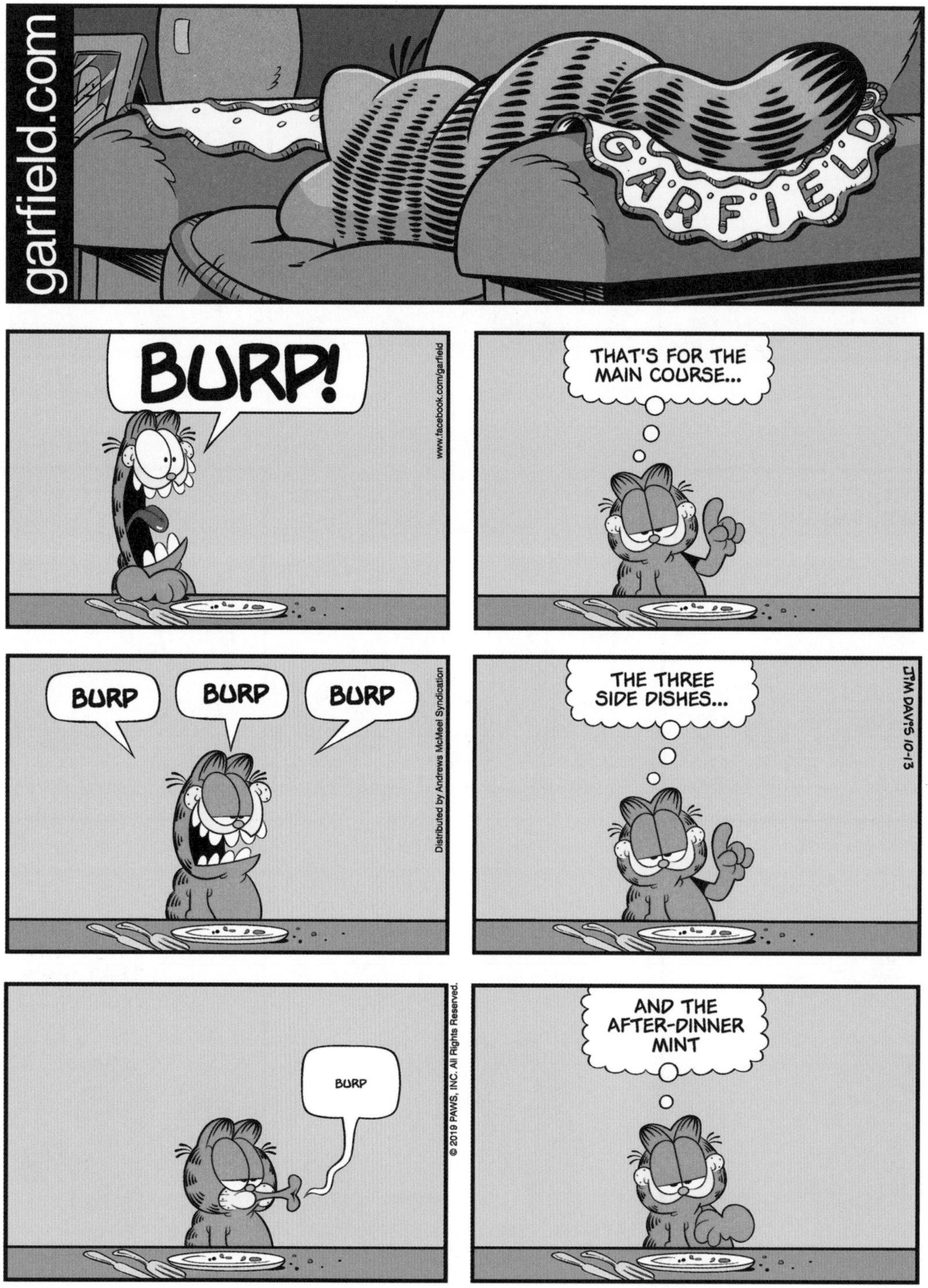
garfield.com
GARFIELD
BURP!
www.facebook.com/garfield
THAT'S FOR THE MAIN COURSE...
BURP
BURP
BURP
Distributed by Andrews McMeel Syndication
THE THREE SIDE DISHES...
JIM DAVIS 10-13
© 2019 PAWS, INC. All Rights Reserved.
BURP
AND THE AFTER-DINNER MINT

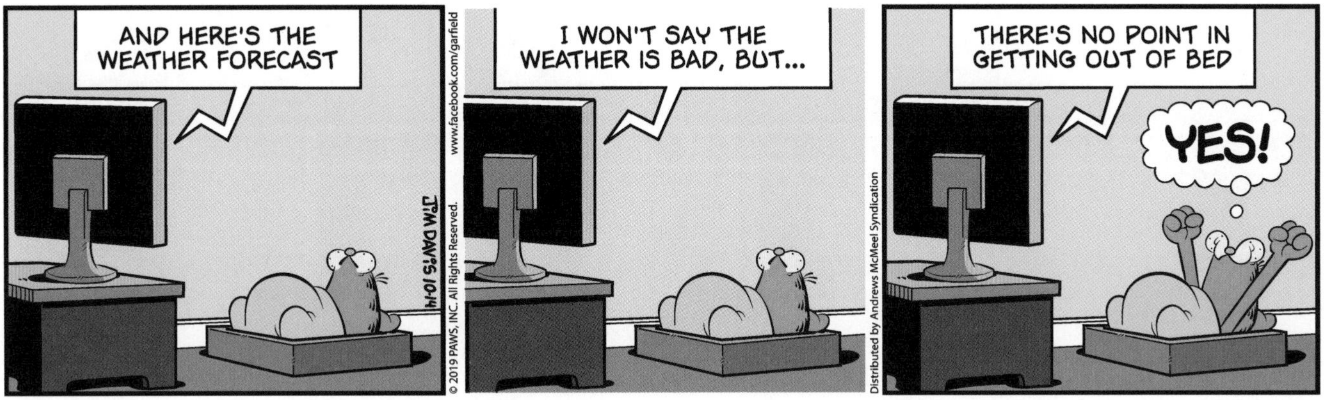
AND HERE'S THE WEATHER FORECAST
JIM DAVIS 10-14
© 2019 PAWS, INC. All Rights Reserved. www.facebook.com/garfield
I WON'T SAY THE WEATHER IS BAD, BUT...
Distributed by Andrews McMeel Syndication
THERE'S NO POINT IN GETTING OUT OF BED
YES!

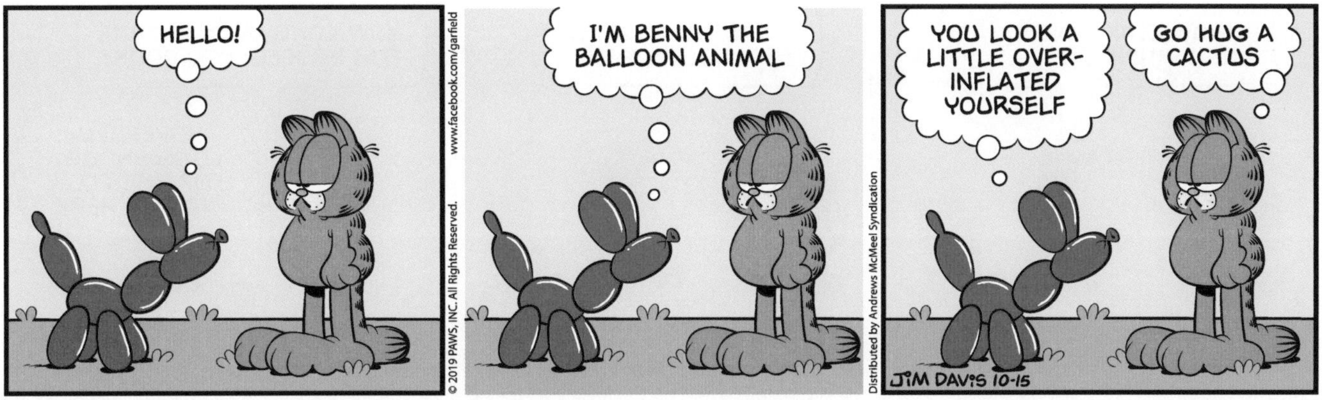
HELLO!
© 2019 PAWS, INC. All Rights Reserved. www.facebook.com/garfield
I'M BENNY THE BALLOON ANIMAL
Distributed by Andrews McMeel Syndication
YOU LOOK A LITTLE OVER-INFLATED YOURSELF
GO HUG A CACTUS
JIM DAVIS 10-15

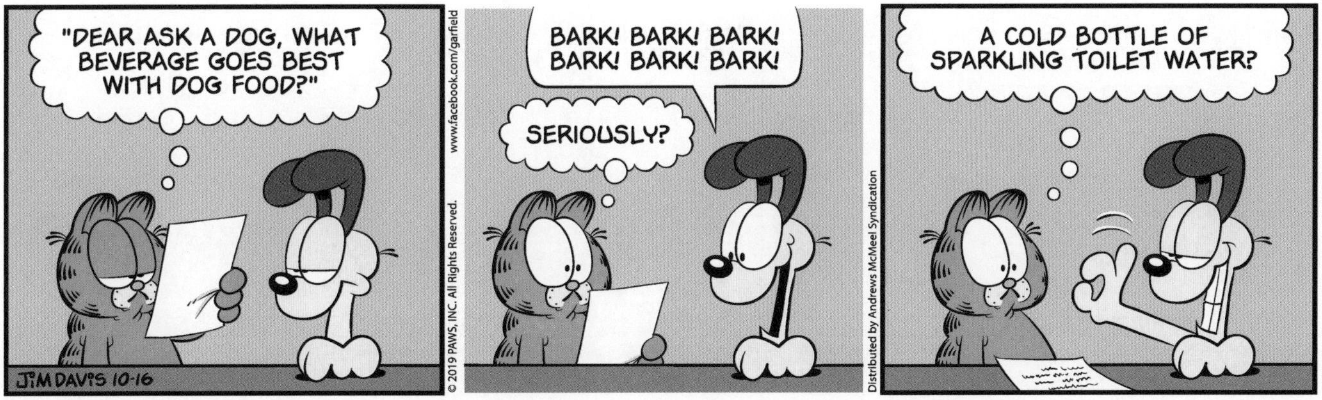
"DEAR ASK A DOG, WHAT BEVERAGE GOES BEST WITH DOG FOOD?"
JIM DAVIS 10-16
© 2019 PAWS, INC. All Rights Reserved. www.facebook.com/garfield
BARK! BARK! BARK! BARK! BARK! BARK!
SERIOUSLY?
Distributed by Andrews McMeel Syndication
A COLD BOTTLE OF SPARKLING TOILET WATER?

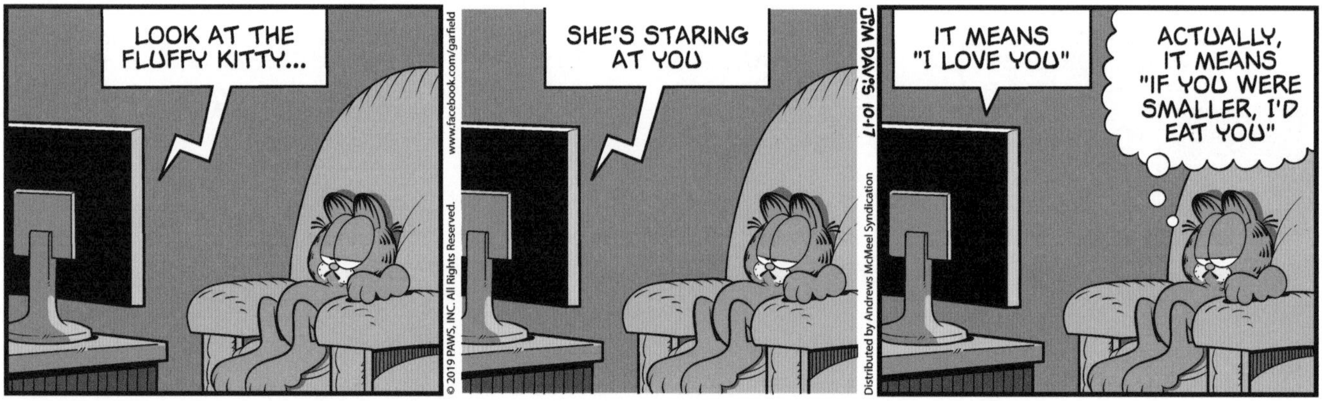
LOOK AT THE FLUFFY KITTY...
SHE'S STARING AT YOU
IT MEANS "I LOVE YOU"
ACTUALLY, IT MEANS "IF YOU WERE SMALLER, I'D EAT YOU"
JIM DAVIS 10-17
© 2019 PAWS, INC. All Rights Reserved. www.facebook.com/garfield
Distributed by Andrews McMeel Syndication

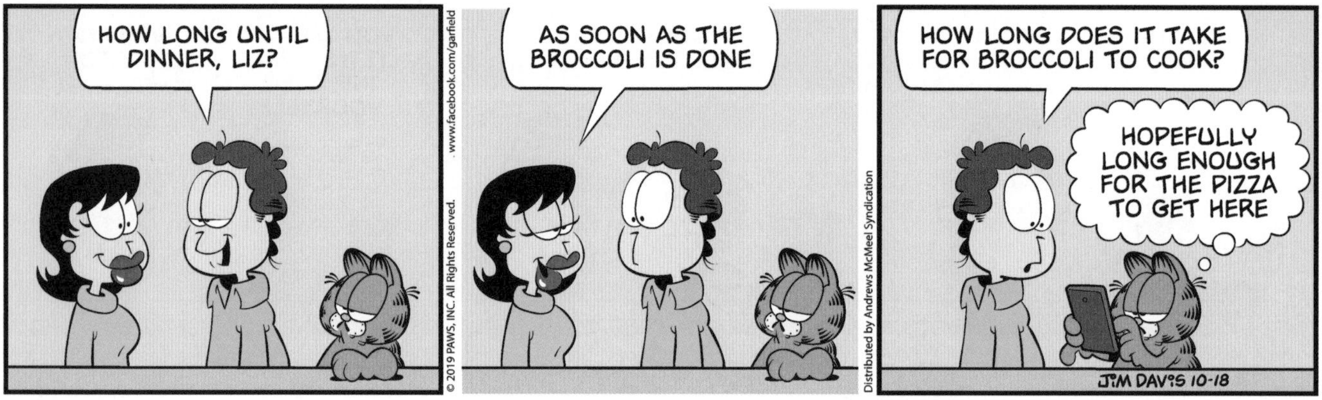
HOW LONG UNTIL DINNER, LIZ?
AS SOON AS THE BROCCOLI IS DONE
HOW LONG DOES IT TAKE FOR BROCCOLI TO COOK?
HOPEFULLY LONG ENOUGH FOR THE PIZZA TO GET HERE
JIM DAVIS 10-18
© 2019 PAWS, INC. All Rights Reserved. www.facebook.com/garfield
Distributed by Andrews McMeel Syndication

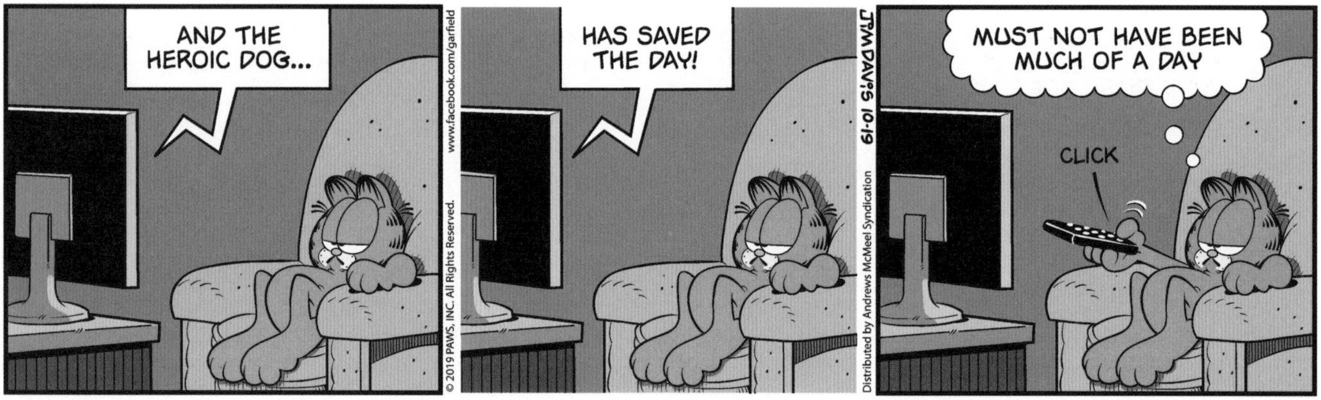
AND THE HEROIC DOG...
HAS SAVED THE DAY!
MUST NOT HAVE BEEN MUCH OF A DAY
CLICK
JIM DAVIS 10-19
© 2019 PAWS, INC. All Rights Reserved. www.facebook.com/garfield
Distributed by Andrews McMeel Syndication

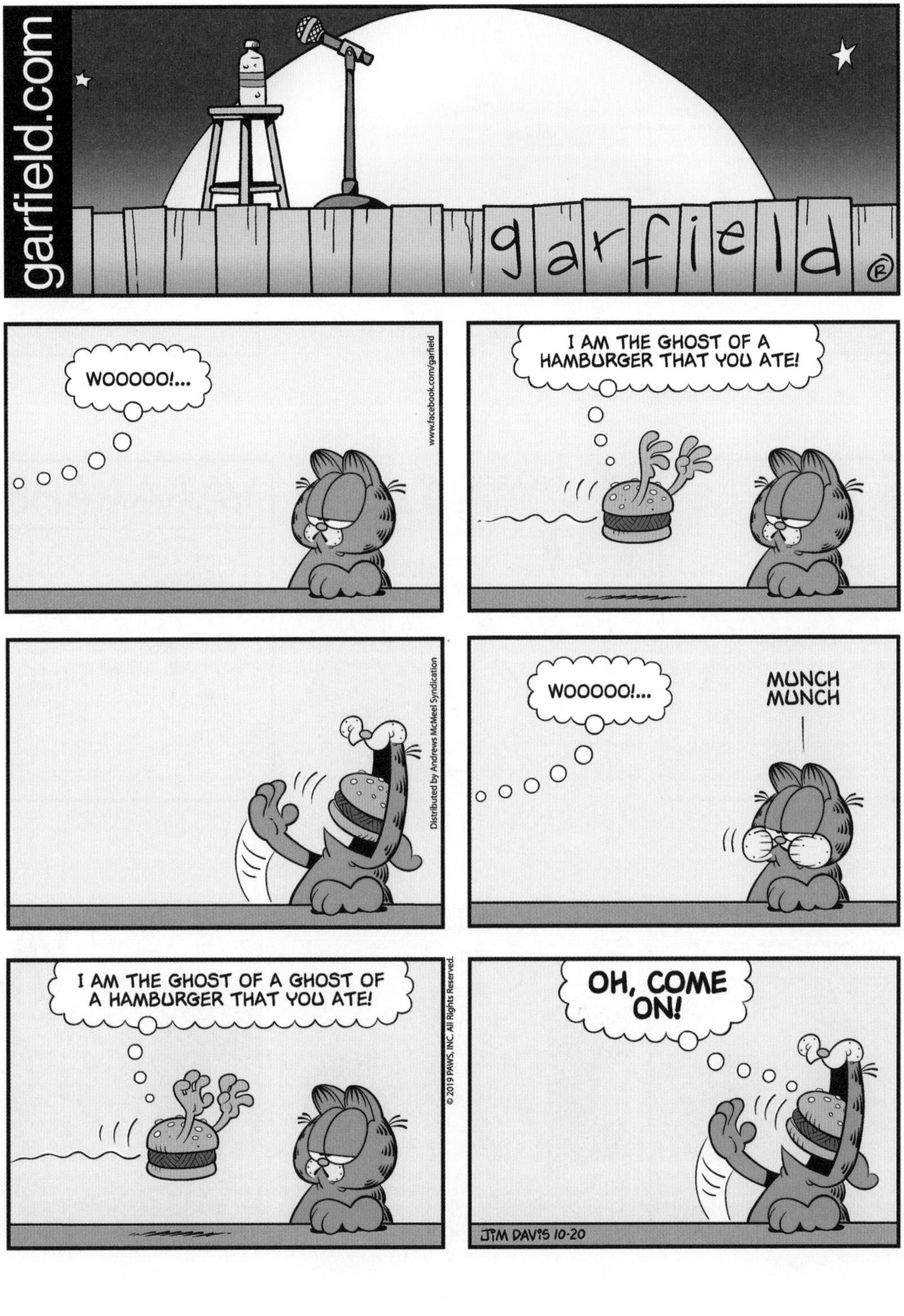
garfield.com
garfield
WOOOOO!...
www.facebook.com/garfield
I AM THE GHOST OF A HAMBURGER THAT YOU ATE!
Distributed by Andrews McMeel Syndication
WOOOOO!...
MUNCH MUNCH
I AM THE GHOST OF A GHOST OF A HAMBURGER THAT YOU ATE!
© 2019 PAWS, INC. All Rights Reserved.
OH, COME ON!
JIM DAVIS 10-20

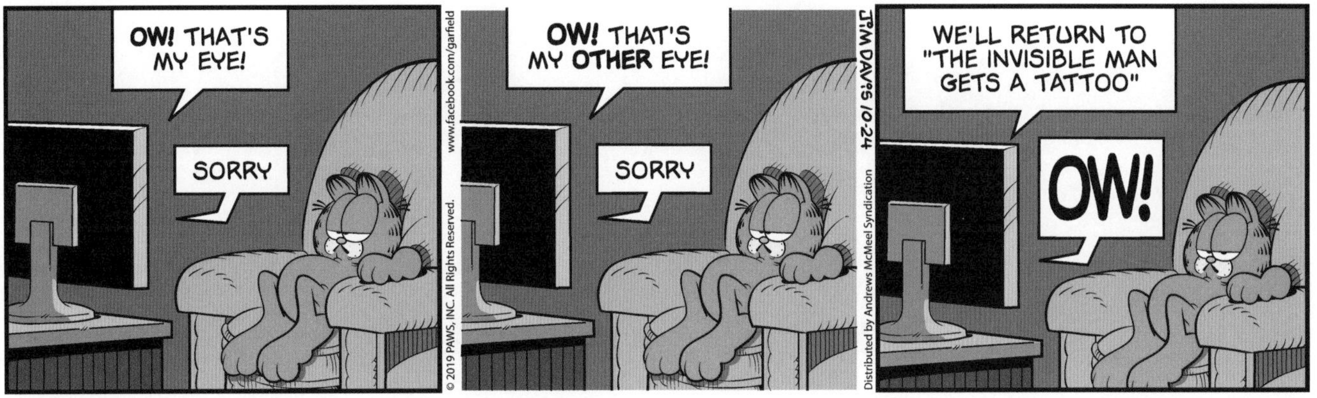
OW! THAT'S MY EYE!
SORRY
OW! THAT'S MY OTHER EYE!
SORRY
WE'LL RETURN TO "THE INVISIBLE MAN GETS A TATTOO"
OW!
JIM DAVIS 10-24
© 2019 PAWS, INC. All Rights Reserved. www.facebook.com/garfield
Distributed by Andrews McMeel Syndication

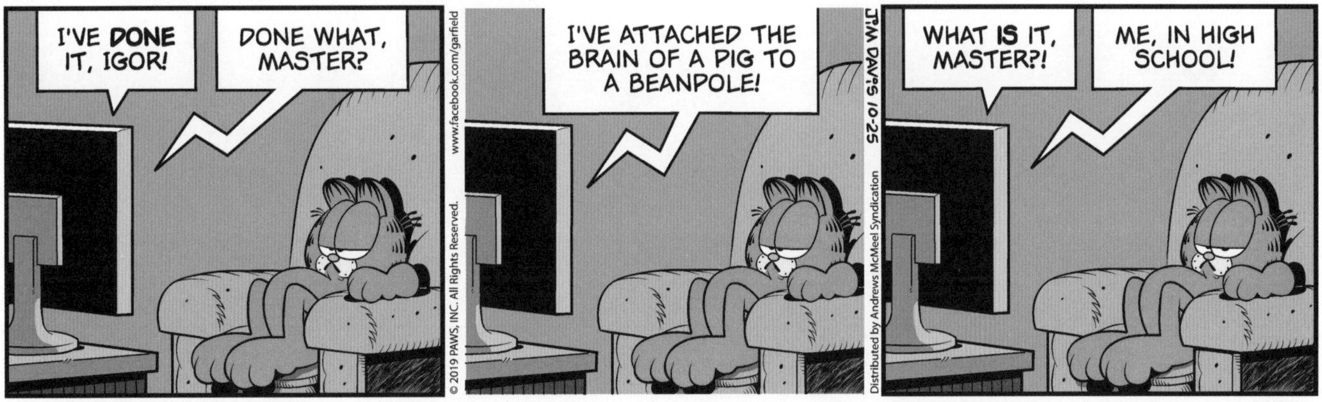
I'VE DONE IT, IGOR!
DONE WHAT, MASTER?
I'VE ATTACHED THE BRAIN OF A PIG TO A BEANPOLE!
WHAT IS IT, MASTER?!
ME, IN HIGH SCHOOL!
JIM DAVIS 10-25
© 2019 PAWS, INC. All Rights Reserved. www.facebook.com/garfield
Distributed by Andrews McMeel Syndication

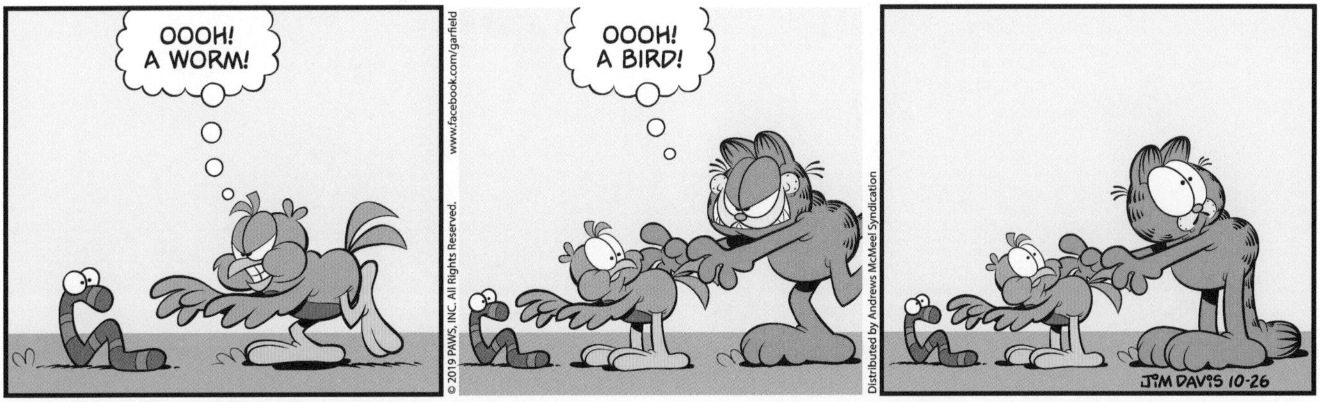
OOOH! A WORM!
OOOH! A BIRD!
JIM DAVIS 10-26
© 2019 PAWS, INC. All Rights Reserved. www.facebook.com/garfield
Distributed by Andrews McMeel Syndication

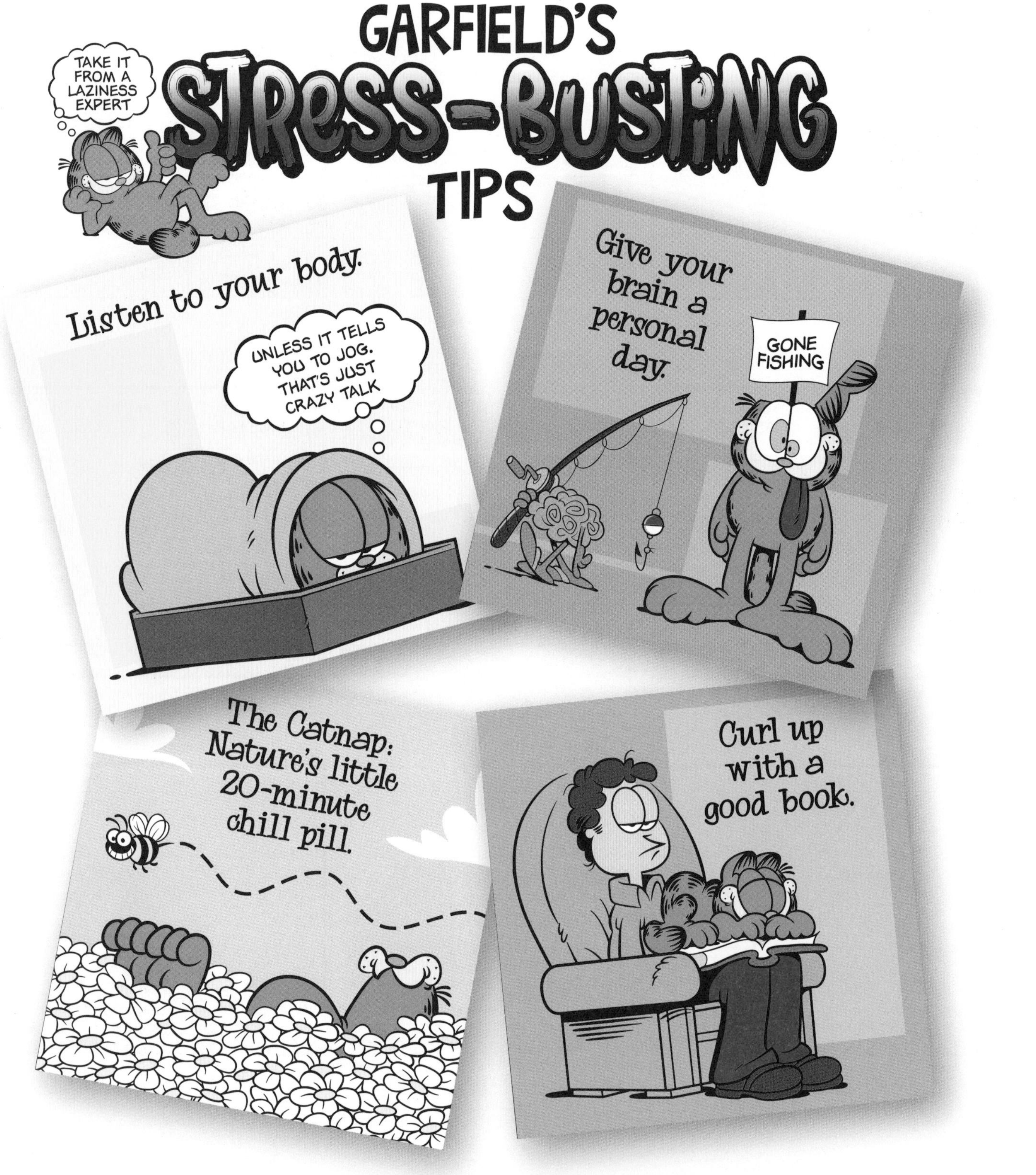
GARFIELD'S
STRESS-BUSTING
TIPS
TAKE IT FROM A LAZINESS EXPERT
Listen to your body.
UNLESS IT TELLS YOU TO JOG. THAT'S JUST CRAZY TALK
Give your brain a personal day.
GONE FISHING
The Catnap: Nature's little 20-minute chill pill.
Curl up with a good book.

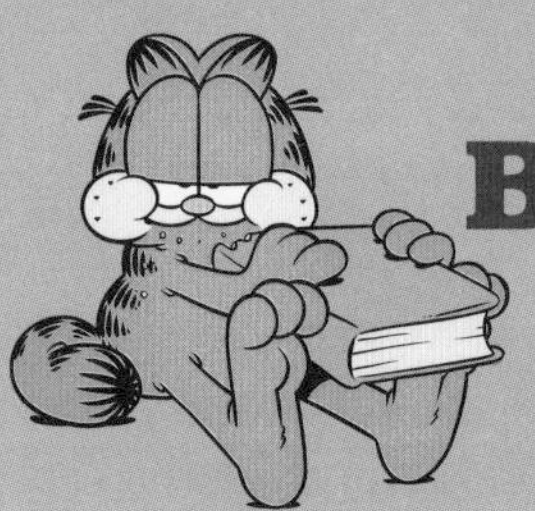

STRIPS, SPECIALS OR BESTSELLING BOOKS . . .

GARFIELD'S ON EVERYONE'S MENU.

Don't miss even one episode in the Tubby Tabby's hilarious series!

GARFIELD AT LARGE (#1) 978-0-345-44382-3
GARFIELD GAINS WEIGHT (#2) 978-0-345-44975-7
GARFIELD BIGGER THAN LIFE (#3) 978-0-345-45027-2
GARFIELD WEIGHS IN (#4) 978-0-345-45205-4
GARFIELD TAKES THE CAKE (#5) 978-0-345-44978-8
GARFIELD EATS HIS HEART OUT (#6) 978-0-345-46459-0
GARFIELD SITS AROUND THE HOUSE (#7) 978-0-345-46463-7
GARFIELD TIPS THE SCALES (#8) 978-0-345-46909-0
GARFIELD LOSES HIS FEET (#9) 978-0-345-46467-5
GARFIELD MAKES IT BIG (#10) 978-0-345-46468-2
GARFIELD ROLLS ON (#11) 978-0-345-47561-9
GARFIELD OUT TO LUNCH (#12) 978-0-345-47562-6
GARFIELD FOOD FOR THOUGHT (#13) 978-0-345-47563-3
GARFIELD SWALLOWS HIS PRIDE (#14) 978-0-345-91386-9
GARFIELD WORLDWIDE (#15) 978-0-345-91754-6
GARFIELD ROUNDS OUT (#16) 978-0-345-49169-5
GARFIELD CHEWS THE FAT (#17) 978-0-345-49170-1
GARFIELD GOES TO WAIST (#18) 978-0-345-49173-2
GARFIELD HANGS OUT (#19) 978-0-345-49174-9
GARFIELD TAKES UP SPACE (#20) 978-0-345-49178-7
GARFIELD SAYS A MOUTHFUL (#21) 978-0-345-49179-4
GARFIELD BY THE POUND (#22) 978-0-345-52558-1
GARFIELD KEEPS HIS CHINS UP (#23) 978-0-345-52559-8
GARFIELD TAKES HIS LICKS (#24) 978-0-345-52587-1
GARFIELD HITS THE BIG TIME (#25) 978-0-345-52589-5
GARFIELD PULLS HIS WEIGHT (#26) 978-0-345-52594-9
GARFIELD DISHES IT OUT (#27) 978-0-345-52595-6
GARFIELD LIFE IN THE FAT LANE (#28) 978-0-345-52600-7
GARFIELD TONS OF FUN (#29) 978-0-345-52601-4
GARFIELD BIGGER AND BETTER (#30) 978-0-345-52605-2
GARFIELD HAMS IT UP (#31) 978-0-345-52606-9
GARFIELD THINKS BIG (#32) 978-0-425-28516-9
GARFIELD THROWS HIS WEIGHT AROUND (#33) 978-0-425-28559-6
GARFIELD LIFE TO THE FULLEST (#34) 978-0-425-28564-0
GARFIELD FEEDS THE KITTY (#35) 978-0-425-28569-5
GARFIELD HOGS THE SPOTLIGHT (#36) 978-0-425-28574-9
GARFIELD BEEFS UP (#37) 978-0-345-44109-6
GARFIELD GETS COOKIN' (#38) 978-0-345-44582-7
GARFIELD EATS CROW (#39) 978-0-345-45201-6
GARFIELD SURVIVAL OF THE FATTEST (#40) 978-0-345-46458-3
GARFIELD OLDER AND WIDER (#41) 978-0-345-46462-0
GARFIELD PIGS OUT (#42) 978-0-345-46466-8
GARFIELD BLOTS OUT THE SUN (#43) 978-0-345-46615-0
GARFIELD GOES BANANAS (#44) 978-0-345-91346-3
GARFIELD LARGE & IN CHARGE (#45) 978-0-345-49172-5
GARFIELD SPILLS THE BEANS (#46) 978-0-345-49177-0
GARFIELD GETS HIS JUST DESSERTS (#47) 978-0-345-91387-6
GARFIELD WILL EAT FOR FOOD (#48) 978-0-345-49176-3
GARFIELD WEIGHS HIS OPTIONS (#49) 978-0-345-49181-7
GARFIELD POTBELLY OF GOLD (#50) 978-0-345-52244-3
GARFIELD SHOVELS IT IN (#51) 978-0-345-52419-5
GARFIELD LARD OF THE JUNGLE (#52) 978-0-345-52584-0
GARFIELD BRINGS HOME THE BACON (#53) 978-0-345-52586-4
GARFIELD GETS IN A PICKLE (#54) 978-0-345-52590-1
GARFIELD SINGS FOR HIS SUPPER (#55) 978-0-345-52593-2
GARFIELD CAUTION: WIDE LOAD (#56) 978-0-345-52596-3
GARFIELD SOUPED UP (#57) 978-0-345-52598-7

New larger, full-color format!

GARFIELD GOES TO HIS HAPPY PLACE (#58) 978-0-345-52602-1
GARFIELD THE BIG CHEESE (#59) 978-0-345-52604-5
GARFIELD CLEANS HIS PLATE (#60) 978-0-345-52608-3
GARFIELD CHICKENS OUT (#61) 978-0-425-28515-2
GARFIELD LISTENS TO HIS GUT (#62) 978-0-425-28557-2
GARFIELD COOKS UP TROUBLE (#63) 978-0-425-28562-6
GARFIELD FEEDS HIS FACE (#64) 978-0-425-28567-1
GARFIELD EATS AND RUNS (#65) 978-0-425-28572-5
GARFIELD NUTTY AS A FRUITCAKE (#66) 978-0-425-28576-3
GARFIELD SLURPS AND BURPS (#67) 978-1-9848-1773-0
GARFIELD BELLY LAUGHS (#68) 978-1-9848-1777-8
GARFIELD EASY AS PIE (#69) 978-0-593-15640-7
GARFIELD GOES HOG WILD (#70) 978-0-593-15642-1

DVD TIE-INS

GARFIELD AS HIMSELF 978-0-345-47805-4
GARFIELD HOLIDAY CELEBRATIONS 978-0-345-47930-3
GARFIELD TRAVEL ADVENTURES 978-0-345-48087-3

AND DON'T MISS . . .

GARFIELD AT 25: IN DOG YEARS I'D BE DEAD 978-0-345-45204-7
GARFIELD'S JOKE ZONE/INSULTS 978-0-345-46263-3
GARFIELD FAT CAT 3-PACK/ VOL. 1 978-0-345-46455-2
GARFIELD FAT CAT 3-PACK/ VOL. 2 978-0-345-46465-1
GARFIELD FAT CAT 3-PACK/ VOL. 3 978-0-345-48088-0
GARFIELD FAT CAT 3-PACK/ VOL. 4 978-0-345-49171-8
GARFIELD FAT CAT 3-PACK/ VOL. 5 978-0-345-49180-8
GARFIELD FAT CAT 3-PACK/ VOL. 6 978-0-345-52420-1
GARFIELD FAT CAT 3-PACK/ VOL. 7 978-0-345-52588-8
GARFIELD FAT CAT 3-PACK/ VOL. 8 978-0-345-52599-4
GARFIELD FAT CAT 3-PACK/ VOL. 9 978-0-345-52607-6
GARFIELD FAT CAT 3-PACK/ VOL. 10 978-0-425-28558-9
GARFIELD FAT CAT 3-PACK/ VOL. 11 978-0-425-28566-4
GARFIELD FAT CAT 3-PACK/ VOL. 12 978-0-425-28578-7
GARFIELD FAT CAT 3-PACK/ VOL. 13 978-0-345-46460-6
GARFIELD FAT CAT 3-PACK/ VOL. 14 978-0-345-49175-6
GARFIELD FAT CAT 3-PACK/ VOL. 15 978-0-345-52585-7
GARFIELD FAT CAT 3-PACK/ VOL. 16 978-0-345-52592-5
GARFIELD FAT CAT 3-PACK/ VOL. 17 978-0-345-52603-8
GARFIELD FAT CAT 3-PACK/ VOL. 18 978-0-399-59440-3
GARFIELD FAT CAT 3-PACK/ VOL. 19 978-0-425-28561-9
GARFIELD FAT CAT 3-PACK/ VOL. 20 978-0-425-28571-8
GARFIELD FAT CAT 3-PACK/ VOL. 21 978-1-9848-1775-4
GARFIELD FAT CAT 3-PACK/ VOL. 22 978-0-593-15638-4
GARFIELD'S 20TH ANNIVERSARY COLLECTION 978-0-345-42126-5
SEASON'S EATINGS: A VERY MERRY GARFIELD CHRISTMAS 978-0-345-47560-2
GARFIELD'S GUIDE TO EVERYTHING 978-0-345-46461-3
ODIE UNLEASHED! 978-0-345-46464-4
GARFIELD'S BOOK OF CAT NAMES 978-0-345-48516-8
THE GARFIELD JOURNAL 978-0-345-46469-9
LIGHTS, CAMERA, HAIRBALLS!: GARFIELD AT THE MOVIES 978-0-345-49134-3
30 YEARS OF LAUGHS AND LASAGNA 978-0-345-50379-4
GARFIELD MINUS GARFIELD 978-0-345-51387-8
GARFIELD FROM THE TRASH BIN 978-0-345-51881-1
GARFIELD LEFT SPEECHLESS 978-0-345-53058-5
MY LAUGHABLE LIFE WITH GARFIELD 978-0-345-52591-8
GARFIELD'S SUNDAY FINEST 978-0-345-52597-0
AGE HAPPENS: GARFIELD HITS THE BIG 4-0 978-0-345-52609-0
GARFIELD COMPLETE WORKS: VOLUME ONE: 1978 & 1979 978-0-425-28712-5
GARFIELD COMPLETE WORKS: VOLUME TWO: 1980 & 1981 978-0-425-28713-2

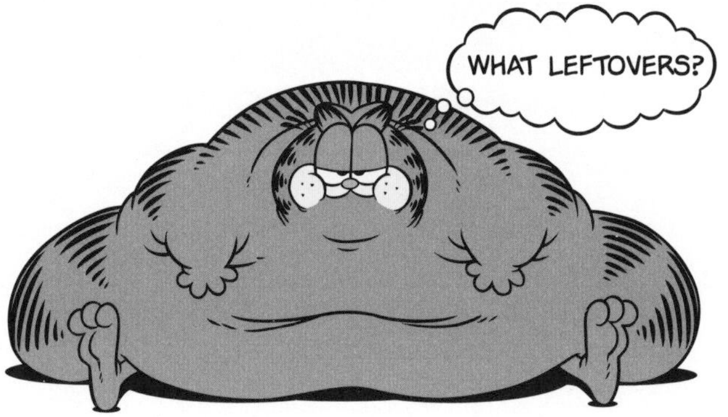
WHAT LEFTOVERS?